Security Controls
for Sarbanes-Oxley Section 404
IT Compliance: Authorization,
Authentication, and Access

Security Controls for Sarbanes-Oxley Section 404 IT Compliance: Authorization, Authentication, and Access

Dennis C. Brewer

WILEY

Wiley Publishing, Inc.

Security Controls for Sarbanes-Oxley Section 404 IT Compliance: Authorization, Authentication, and Access

Published by
Wiley Publishing, Inc.
10475 Crosspoint Boulevard
Indianapolis, IN 46256
www.wiley.com

Published simultaneously in Canada

ISBN-13: 978-0-7645-9838-8
ISBN-10: 0-7645-9838-4

Manufactured in the United States of America

10 9 8 7 6 5 4 3 2 1

1MA/QU/RQ/QV/IN

Limit of Liability/Disclaimer of Warranty: The publisher and the author make no representations or warranties with respect to the accuracy or completeness of the contents of this work and specifically disclaim all warranties, including without limitation warranties of fitness for a particular purpose. No warranty may be created or extended by sales or promotional materials. The advice and strategies contained herein may not be suitable for every situation. This work is sold with the understanding that the publisher is not engaged in rendering legal, accounting, or other professional services. If professional assistance is required, the services of a competent professional person should be sought. Neither the publisher nor the author shall be liable for damages arising herefrom. The fact that an organization or Website is referred to in this work as a citation and/or a potential source of further information does not mean that the author or the Publisher endorses the information the organization or Website may provide or recommendations it may make. Further, readers should be aware that Internet Websites listed in this work may have changed or disappeared between when this work was written and when it is read.

For general information on our other products and services or to obtain technical support, please contact our Customer Care Department within the U.S. at (800) 762-2974, outside the U.S. at (317) 572-3993 or fax (317) 572-4002.

Wiley also publishes its books in a variety of electronic formats. Some content that appears in print may not be available in electronic books.

Library of Congress Cataloging-in-Publication Data

Brewer, Dennis C., 1949-
 Security controls for Sarbanes-Oxley section 404 IT compliance : authorization, authentication, and access / Dennis C. Brewer.
    p. cm.
 Includes index.
 ISBN-13: 978-0-7645-9838-8 (pbk.)
 ISBN-10: 0-7645-9838-4 (pbk.)
1. Computer security. 2. Data protection. 3. Computers--Access control. 4. Computer architecture. I. Title.
 QA76.9.A25B7597 2005
 005.8--dc22

                                    2005023678

Trademarks: Wiley and related trade dress are registered trademarks of Wiley Publishing, Inc., in the United States and other countries, and may not be used without written permission. All other trademarks are the property of their respective owners. Wiley Publishing, Inc., is not associated with any product or vendor mentioned in this book.

This book is dedicated to all the people who played a role in my education, both the book learning and the harder-to-learn life lessons.

About the Author

Dennis C. Brewer holds a Bachelor of Science degree in Business Administration from Michigan Technological University in Houghton, Michigan. He is a network engineer and information technology solutions specialist for the State of Michigan with more than 12 years of experience in the computer technology field. His most recent experience includes a portfolio of computer security responsibilities, including identity management, identity provisioning, and privacy protection initiatives for state government. Over the last 10 years, Dennis has worked on networking and computer technology from the level of hands-on personal computer repair all the way to up to setting policy and charting future direction. During his career with the State of Michigan, he supported end users, networks, and computer systems at the Department of Military Affairs, led a technology team at the state's Consolidated Network Operations Center, and provided technology research for the Office of Information Technology Solutions at the Department of Management and Budget. He has authored numerous enterprise-level information technology and telecommunications policies, procedures, and standards currently in use by the State of Michigan, and was a technology consultant to the team that created the award-winning e-Michigan consolidated Web presence.

When not involved with computer technology, Dennis enjoys camping in Michigan's numerous state parks, bicycling, and taking writing courses. He is planning on returning soon to his hometown of Calumet in Michigan's Upper Peninsula, which he says "... is a great sanctuary for anyone wanting to write more books!"

Credits

Acquisitions Editor
Carol Long

Development Editor
Maryann Steinhart

Production Editor
Pamela Hanley

Copy Editor
Joanne Slike

Editorial Manager
Mary Beth Wakefield

Vice President & Executive Group Publisher
Richard Swadley

Vice President and Publisher
Joseph B. Wikert

Project Coordinators
Erin Smith
Michael Kruzil

Graphic and Layout Technicians
Carrie A. Foster
Stephanie D. Jumper
Alicia South

Quality Control Technicians
David Faust
Jessica Kramer
Carl William Pierce

Proofreading and Indexing
David Faust
TECHBOOKS Production Services

Contents

Acknowledgments

Thanks to my fiancé, Penny, for her constant encouragement; my friend Peggy for her sage advice and compliments; my older son, Jason, for setting the standard to reach for in technical writing; and my younger son, Justin, for reminding me that nearly everything worthwhile, writing included, is at least part art and not all science. Many thanks to my mother, Verna, who convinced me at an early age that you could accomplish most things you are willing to work at with some tenacity.

Thanks to my literary agent, Carole McClendon at Waterside Productions, for believing I had something to offer as a technical author; Carol Long, Acquisitions Editor at Wiley Publishing, for taking a chance on a new writer; and Maryann Steinhart, the Development Editor, for making this book turn out far better than it began. Thanks to everyone else at Wiley for their excellent work and for always being so pleasant to work with. Thank you all!

Introduction

Identity theft and fraudulent access is a huge global problem. IT systems managers are charged with protecting privacy and personally identifying financial information, and are responsible for building access controls capable of protecting the integrity of financial statements and safeguarding intellectual property in a strong and growing regulatory environment against a worldwide threat force that never sleeps. Systems designers are challenged to create authentication strategies and access controls that work, and after end users are authenticated, to provide discerning authorizations to system resources. These are the critical elements in creating quality systems designs.

This book was written to move the discussion of authentication, authorization, and access controls in a direction intended to meet current and expected regulatory requirements, and is intended for IT systems architects, directory engineers, technology consultants, systems analysts and designers, applications developers, and systems integrators. It also will benefit IT systems managers and decision makers in government and the private sector, including chief information officers, chief security officers, project managers, and anyone in the public or private sector who may be held accountable in any way for making sure systems designs protect personally identifying, medical, and financial information or protect the systems that house that information to meet external regulatory requirements. Others who would gain from reading this book include college-level course instructors and students; policy makers on the federal, state, and local levels; IT system auditors; inspectors general; and accountants.

Anyone wanting to know enough to hold the trustees of his or her personally identifying, medical, and financial information accountable for providing adequate protections could also learn something by reading this book, as would principals in publicly traded companies who attest to the adequacy of or rely on IT controls. IT consultants who have products and services to offer will gain valuable insights into their customers' needs from this book.

Offering a Strategy

This book presents a strategy for developing architecture that private-sector and government systems designers can use for identity controls where privacy or protected information is shared and used online.

Consumers of information technology services and systems designers and implementers will be exposed to a design concept for appropriately dealing with end-user identities, authentication, and access controls that are intended to meet the regulatory requirements of Sarbanes-Oxley Section 404 criteria for adequate controls. This book explains how to leverage existing technologies through proper design combinations and discusses the elements of architecture documentation needed to realize implementation. It presents the critical concepts necessary to design and create a system that integrates the elements of the controls architecture for the following:

- Identity management (dealing with identity in the modern enterprise)
- Meta-directories (leveraging to reduce administration and improve access controls)
- Identity provisioning (value provided, accuracy gained)
- Authentication (options and limits)
- Access controls (fine-grained controls necessary to protect data and privacy)

Readers will learn what it takes to design an information technology infrastructure capable of protecting the privacy and access integrity of computer data, particularly in the Web applications environment.

How This Book Is Organized

The book is set up in such a way that each chapter's information provides the necessary background information for ideas that are discussed further or used in subsequent chapters. Skipping chapters or reading them out of order isn't advised unless you are already familiar with the earlier chapters' content.

Chapter 1 begins with a discussion of what IT architecture is and is not, and Chapter 2 introduces the eight concepts that constitute privacy of information and examines the protection of the data housed in your computer systems.

Chapter 3 starts describing how a discipline of architecture practice manifests itself in the enterprise infrastructure to achieve system objectives. It includes a discussion of the documentation that both defines and enforces systems architecture in the enterprise. Chapter 4 introduces the "big blocks"—external forces, internal influences, and IT assets—that drive systems designs, and the role they play.

Chapter 5 begins to frame the security discussion in a uniform way by setting the definitions for the essential ingredients of security. It discusses the limits of today's technology for providing nonrepudiation from authentication methods and explores these security basics:

- Identification
- Authentication
- Authorization
- Access control
- Administration
- Assessment
- Auditing

Chapter 6 takes a look at how the features present in directory technology, directory schema, and meta-synchronization can be leveraged in a complementary way to improve systems' security profiles. Chapter 7 covers the logic, core critical elements, and the relationships that must be used to successfully achieve identity management and identity provisioning in the Web applications environment. It also examines how these elements are leveraged within IT and business processes alike to achieve granular control over data and information.

Chapter 8 puts together the information from the previous chapters and discusses ways to build support and integrate the architecture into legacy, current, and future applications in business and government organizations. Chapter 9 discusses the protection target—data information—and how it will and must be related and linked to the identities of the people and systems that will be allowed access.

Chapter 10 brings it all together in the Web applications environment. Chapter 11 discusses the shortcomings of federated identity schemes and the risks of relying on outside sources for permitting access.

The final chapter, 12, explores a future where every access control system across the Web is tied to AAA (authentication, authorization, and accounting) servers for access to sensitive systems and data—a future in which privacy boundaries are respected, systems are capable of enforcing them, and digital credentials can be trusted.

Several appendixes provide resources, examples, and other information that can help you in meeting the newest regulations IT faces.

The information in this book is valuable because it explains why it is necessary to link populations to independent service directories and the best ways to use identity vaults and service directories in the overall systems design to achieve business goals for access while protecting privacy and financial data in all application development. It outlines a process for creating security domain definitions that are designed to stop data predators at the front door. A paradigm shift is outlined to recognize the need for population-specific access control implementations. While others focus more on the nuts-and-bolts details, this book covers the high-level design and principles needed to understand the controls issue from a comprehensive identity life cycle viewpoint.

Security Controls for Sarbanes-Oxley Section 404 IT Compliance: Authorization, Authentication, and Access

The Role of Information Technology Architecture in Information Systems Design

How many laws and regulations affect your business? How many of them affect your organization's computer applications? Do your computer systems comply with all of them? All are good questions with transitive answers. Sarbanes-Oxley (SOX) is one of many new regulations making its mark on how business is conducted. There will more new ones not too far down the road.

By taking action now in conforming to the mandate for adequate controls on information technology systems and applications required by SOX, you also position your organization to meet privacy protection mandates, disclosure requirements, and what may be needed for the next round of regulation that could affect your data systems.

Meeting the SOX Challenge

The Sarbanes-Oxley Section 404 requirements to maintain adequate security controls over information technology systems forge a challenging and perhaps somewhat intimidating task. Add to them a multitude of regulatory agencies at all levels of government that are endlessly generating requirements (federal HIPAA statutes and California's privacy protection initiative that requires firms to make individual disclosures of known compromises to anyone's private information that might result in identity theft, for example) that your information technology security and privacy protection controls also must meet, and the whole undertaking could seem overwhelming.

With all of the sometimes confusing and often conflicting requirements placed on an organization's IT (information technology) practitioners today, charting a practical course for compliance with Sarbanes-Oxley seems very hard to achieve. IT managers face the ever-present need to provide easy-to-use applications on systems that directly support the business processes to efficiently get the work done. They also are now required to place on the end users and systems a set of controls that support and meet the requirements of the regulatory agencies. SOX brings all of the historical requirements of cash controls, accounting standards, and audit oversight and reporting to the micro bits and bytes information technology realm often ruled by a more laissez-faire approach to getting things done "yesterday if possible."

Understanding the New Definition of Adequate

The big story in Sarbanes-Oxley for the IT professional is that earlier approaches to quickly getting applications built and in place to support the business (punch a few holes in the firewall and worry about security later) will no longer pass the inevitable audit. Access controls that give everyone in the same OU (organizational unit container) the same access rights are no longer considered "adequate" security controls. Meeting the test of maintaining effective internal control structure and processes supporting accurate financial reporting requires treating SOX 404 compliance with a focus and discipline not always evident in existing information systems designs.

The annual audit findings that report substantial weaknesses in controls will attest to these shortcomings in existing IT designs in small and large companies alike. Looking forward, there's just no point to building tomorrow's audit failures today. Legacy systems and existing applications must be brought into compliance. Failure to do so has the potential of a big negative impact on the value of the public companies that do not meet the compliance tests during audits. Public audit of internal controls linked to Section 404(b) requires auditors to assess whether the internal control structure and procedures contain any substantial weaknesses of any kind. The audit reports are expected to attest to the success of the company's internal control structure and procedures for financial reporting purposes.

Any flaw in an organization's control relationship between identity, authentication, access control measures, and the links made to financial or privacy data are subject to audit and adverse reporting. As the rules are refined and auditors become more knowledgeable about the technologies involved, any imperfections in the controls will likely be discovered over time.

High Stakes for Compliance Failures

One could easily imagine a corporation that doesn't look too bad on its first audit, but some material findings emerge related to SOX 404 issues. The company fixes some things and then gets audited by a different team capable of a more detailed technology audit, leading to more negative findings in audit year two. The company fixes the year-two findings only to be audited in year three by yet another more sophisticated team, and behold, more negative audit findings related to the quality of controls. After a scenario like that, Wall Street analysts may feel compelled to point out to the stock-buying public that company X seems to be having difficulty correcting its compliance issues, and they may downgrade the outlook for the company because it just can't seem to get a grip on instituting the necessary controls.

The control issues surrounding compliance with SOX-like mandates do not apply only to public companies. Governments at all levels, the nonprofit sector, and closely held companies all face the need to satisfactorily protect the integrity of their confidential information and provide adequate controls on access to data stores and to counter the liability of losses of clients and members personally identifying information. For some nonprofit organizations, the financial risk of litigation resulting from inadequate controls may be far greater than any harm from adverse audit findings.

This book is intended to help those responsible for establishing and maintaining adequate information technology security controls. The information applies regardless of the kind of business. As the oversight and regulation environment is perfected, it will inevitably require organizations of all types to put in place controls that will be deemed adequate for compliance with SOX, HIPAA, or other oversight entity's rules. Even if the controls are not required by laws or regulations, it simply makes sense to implement and maintain sufficient controls for just generally protecting privacy information or access to confidential or valuable information.

Examining the Role of Architecture

Using ITA (information technology architecture) design concepts and the documentation used to express IT design is the only approach to successfully bring existing or new applications, systems, or networks into the condition of having an "adequate internal control structure," quoting the phrase used by SOX in section 404.

Regardless of the source of the control criteria, be it internally or externally imposed, there is value in using a systematic approach to the overall design of the security controls. ITA is a disciplined process that provides the method and defines the documentation necessary for successful technology designs. All of the other architectures — data, technology, systems, or network — become subcomponents of the whole ITA approach. Sometimes the term *enterprise architecture* is used to define the "go to" or goal architecture. In reality, each of these subsets in an existing organization could have three architecture stages: the existing, transition, and target architectures.

The most important message is how to use the discipline of architecture as described in this book to organize and manage the design process whether you're designing from a blank slate or trying to fix a complex existing system. The process fits each of the architecture work areas from network design to data structures with only minor modification involving the required documentation.

Looking Forward

Later in this book, the seven essential elements of the security matrix are defined as the framework encompassing security controls. This framework is important because it helps define the outside limits for the security controls design work. You'll explore some of the limitations inherent within each area of concern.

Several chapters center on using the architectural process to focus on all of the principles and design tasks necessary to deal effectively with identity, authentication, and access controls relating to protecting any categories of applications, information, or data. The role of directory services and meta-functionality is examined, and you'll see how they can be designed to work together to provide the basis for links between identity and access control.

Toward the end of the book, you'll look at the value present in federated identity schemes and how they might be treated, as well as potential risks in going too far with federated identity in light of SOX oversight. The end describes a vision of the future perfect world in which privacy and confidentiality boundaries are respected and enforced by design and digital credentials can be trusted.

Several appendixes provide useful information and guidance for the process.

Blending Science and Art

At a very fundamental level, Sarbanes-Oxley is calling for the genteel merging of the science of accounting and auditing with the science and art of information systems design. If there were no computers or calculation machines of any type, all of the SOX controls would be relegated to the physical world of locks and keys, combinations, paper trails, and security guards. Because computers and applications and Internet access are integrated into so much of what is done today in business and private lives, stepping up of the controls in the digital world is long past needed. It is easy to predict that SOX over time will prove to be just another in a long line of access control quality issues facing organizations. The time to meet the security controls challenge and lay the new digital control foundation is now.

That bridge to the design of desired state of access controls is what this book is about. The science and art of applying architecture principles will get you there.

Seeing the Whole Picture

Security controls must be dealt with in a complete context. You can't just check a box because you are using SSL to secure the data transmission and are requiring a user ID and password. Yes, those steps are necessary, but they're only two of many layers and dimensions that must be considered individually and collectively to achieve adequate control mechanisms over access and data. Applying a systematic method of ITA design principles and enforcement documentation is the way to succeed. The documents resulting from the ITA effort capture the requirements for the controls, provide the basis for implementation, facilitate operations and ongoing management, become input into any needed analysis or change process, and provide proof of due diligence during audits. When the ITA process relating to security controls is ongoing, it shows an expected level of due care.

Reaching a fundamental understanding of what ITA is and how to recognize it is necessary. Technology terms are often used inappropriately, creating confusion. This is often true of the use of the word *architecture* when applied in the context of IT. Some in the IT field, in sales pitches or design discussions, present something way less than architecture and call it architecture anyway. Others with a business operations focus or in management roles think they know what IT architecture is, although they cannot explain to you what it means to them or, more importantly, what benefits it can bring to their IT operations or in meeting the organization's business goals and objectives. What's often being passed off as architecture is more like IT confusion or a game of "my picture is better than your picture."

This book provides you with some valuable insights into what constitutes ITA. More important, it will help you learn how to systematize your thinking on the subject and become better able to properly document your organization's technology plans and designs. Using the process of ITA design for security controls will, within a short time period, help you and your organization achieve a bold and understandable architectural model for successfully designing for the currently critical security areas of identity management, access control, and authentication. The process provides a basis for creating adequate protection of private or protected information and data in your information systems designs and projects.

My own transition from a facilities management specialist working with hundreds of building architects and civil, mechanical, and electrical engineers on scores of construction projects over a 10-year period to an IT specialist made the concept of IT architecture easy to grasp but the details equally elusive. The effort and person-hours necessary to design and fully document an IT architecture supporting a complex heterogeneous enterprise scattered over a large geographical area with diverse lines of business and operational requirements is a daunting task. When it is divided into smaller building blocks or subcomponents, the job is much easier to envision and actually complete and implement during the build phase.

Document, Document, Document

Soon you'll see the documentation components required for successful ITA implementation of security controls in modern enterprises of all kinds that utilize computer information systems, networks, and data applications that do financial processing or house confidential information.

The order of doing the ITA design work is important. Just as buildings are rarely constructed from the roof down, when certain computer technology components are chosen that become foundations for follow-on components, the rest of the effort necessary for the design, documentation, and implementation all become easier to achieve within the overall systems environment one layer at a time. The foundation-first principle is truer in the technology field. There is a succession of thought that must follow a line of natural progression to develop the architecture from nothing for a new organization or from an "as-is" condition for one already invested with computer systems and applications to a new or desired vision state. The vision state or "to be" may also be called the target state or desired target or even target condition. You will see one path of this progression in Chapter 3 where the documentation process begins with business objectives and builds from there to successively include more detailed and often more complex documentation, each building on the documents that preceded its own development.

Seeing Caution Flags

All too often a CEO or CIO allows a single contractor or a mix of vendors to quickly decide what is in the best interest of the project or what best meets the company's needs in a given area of technology. This is as understandable as it is pitiful. The principal cause for this situation is the time pressure to get it done right now, which frequently gets in the way of getting it done right. Unfortunately, vendors rarely have time to sufficiently understand a client's business needs and are also reluctant to suggest a competing product as the best fit to solve a problem.

Companies on both sides of the contractor/contracting relationship rarely have sufficient time or all the in-house talent necessary to get every piece of the technology puzzle 100 percent correct in the specification or within the implementation process. "Correct" in this instance means performing to a standard as good as it can be, given the current technology available.

Shortcomings always exist in request-for-proposal specifications or in a project's management or within the implementation and delivery, hence the incredible forced popularity of the usually undesirable and expensive change-order process. Failure to apply a methodical design process is manifested in the worst situations where a technology consulting contract takes shape in only days or weeks and is given an expected delivery duration of 9 to 12 months, and after 3 years, the consultant still occupies a corner office. The company's comptroller is still writing or approving checks for cashing in a far-away bank. To add insult to injury, the original project scope is not finished yet and few if any of the original project deliverables perform as envisioned by the management group that first approved the project.

You can prevent this kind of scenario by having appropriate information technology architecture and an established process for information technology architecture design, changes, and redesign, and the necessary documentation. A repeatable ITA process is fundamental to preventing costly, even disastrous projects from wasting resources.

Increased Technical Complexity

Historical architecture models or starting frameworks such as those originally presented by J. A. Zachman in the *IBM Systems Journal* (Vol. 26, No. 3, 1987) are great at organizing both the questions that need answering and the array of perspectives required in considering the design views. However, they rarely provide the means to achieve the levels of detail really needed in a successful architecture design project. From the perspective of the interfaces, the earlier approaches are a great starting point, but all too often, they do not capture the multidimensional nature of the many relationships and flow-of-data interfaces required to make current applications work within the systems environment or complex interconnected networks and N-tier systems commonly in use today.

You and your organization are on the way to being better prepared to answer the question: How do you handle the issues of identity, authentication, and access control in your information technology environment to meet access control objectives? With the added emphasis today on compliance with government regulatory agencies' requirements to first provide accurate data to the agencies and the public, and with the groundswell of cases of identity theft in the morning news, appropriate access control strategies become critical to every computer environment.

Architecture Basics

After you explore basic ITA concepts in a general way, you'll examine a method for achieving the inclusion of architectural principles and appropriate documentation in your systems' design process. This is a design process that is both logical in approach, workable, and sustainable moving forward. The added benefit of using this approach is in having developed sets of documentation that flow naturally to uses in the operations environment. Once developed, these documents also take great strides toward the standardizing of daily IT systems operations.

Stepping Back

To see the concepts behind information systems architecture, first take a quick look outside the area of IT and computers at an example that applies a well-established architectural discipline to the design process: land-use planning and building construction. The field of land-use, zoning, and city or area planning works with architectural models or patterns on huge maps outlining where the various residential and specific-use areas will be placed, along with the density of construction in each of the specific-use areas. The locations for streets and water, sewer, gas and electric lines are well described and sized by engineers. Shopping areas, industrial zones, and green spaces are all placed on the map to create useful relationships, traffic flows, and use patterns.

To satisfy the political interest and at the same time accomplish the developer's objectives, various standard land-use design patterns are applied. These are transferred first to the maps and then later to the land itself during construction. In good land-development projects, a measure of creativity is applied as well to make the area aesthetically appealing to a particular target demographic.

After the land-use planners leave their work and move on to the next project, other professional disciplines such as civil engineers, building architects, and electrical and mechanical engineers become more involved in the architectural design process. Each engineering specialty in turn adds significantly to the collection of documentation and mounting details that help further determine the shape and look of the construction of buildings, the environment in which they will rest, and the infrastructure that will make it all work together as a connected working community.

Then interior designers and landscape architects and gardeners apply the finishing touches and further add to the beauty, usefulness, and utility of the structures and surrounding areas. Complementary colors and textures and just the right furnishings are added to the indoor and outdoor living spaces. A garden here, a few trees there, a well-placed shrub, flowers, topiary, outdoor furniture, and some outdoor play equipment are fixed into the individual yards to further advance the vision of quality living space.

Finally the most adaptable element is added to the implementation: the residents — the people that live, interact, and work there, making the system complete.

When you drive through a new subdivision, the architectural choices and styles become overwhelmingly evident even if you are not particularly attuned to the topic of architecture. Observers tend to say things like "drive past all the tick-tack houses until you come to the wrought-iron fence, and turn in where all the Victorian houses are." Although houses in a subdivision are not exactly the same, you can usually recognize them for their similar architectural styles. Theoretically, five separate houses could be designed and constructed to meet the exact same specific owner needs and requirements; contain precisely the same number, function, and size of rooms, doors, and windows; and include the equivalently useful fixtures, appliances, and equally desirable finishing elements and yet appear to be totally different from any of the other houses. In historical building architectural terms, descriptive names and styles are ascribed to the range of different homes: Victorian, Arts and Crafts, Postmodern, and Early Modern, for example. Each of these homes could be equally useful to the prospective owner in every respect, yet they could be strikingly different from one another visually and in their respective relationship to the environment and still be recognizable as belonging to its type.

Stepping Forward

Just like neighborhoods, houses, or building interiors, your enterprise's computer information systems architecture will take shape either by chance or by choice. The decision is yours.

Every neighborhood has a house that was built haphazardly and incrementally over time where nothing matches or fits the rest exactly right. You may have been to or even inside of places that are a true hodgepodge of pieces hammered together over time where nothing seems to go with anything else in any perceivable way. If that is how an observer would describe your company's computer system environment, you are really in need of the discipline of information systems architecture.

Process and Result

Architecture applied to design is fundamentally two things. First, it is a regimented process used to design or create something of value. A car, a house, a garden, or a computer system may each use an architectural process in the planning and design and enforce a method of assembly or construction that adheres to the features and appearance of the designer's vision. Second, the use of architects or the architectural process implies that it is intended to lead to a qualitative result that can be readily recognized for what it is and as belonging to or as a recognizable member of its defined class by others knowledgeable enough to discern the difference. The resultant end product can be identified because it conforms to a defined pattern and set of standards.

When you think about applying a regimented process to information technology systems designs, the operative principle is control, actually a very high level of control derived from having a handle on a painstaking level of details. The complexity required to build a network and to place systems in it along with software and applications that function well for the end user works against achieving a high level of control in the early stages of the design process. That's mostly because getting to the level of detail needed is hard work — very hard work — and usually beyond the technical capability of any one person, even for a small-scale system. Recall that the building construction analogy alluded to the same issue. Building architects must work together with other engineering disciplines to work out all of the necessary details that are within the vision of the architect's objectives to create something new and distinctive but constrained by using currently available components and technology.

Applying Architecture to Legacy Systems

Information technology architecture improvement efforts and initiatives are frequently compounded, even confounded, by legacy systems. Legacy systems are the aged ones that are made up of older technology riding on sometimes clunky hardware that, unfortunately, end users and business processes use every day to keep the company running. Legacy systems and software impede progress because they are difficult to abandon and costly to replace. The organization that constantly postpones, delays, or ignores taking the steps to use and assigning the resources for an architectural team and process fails to achieve good design because they defer to tactical decision requirements over strategic planning. They often compound their own problems from having to deal with those costly and inefficient systems.

Legacy systems and existing applications are not exempt from regulatory oversight. The need to tighten security controls over existing systems and applications cannot be overlooked; otherwise, compliance audits will reveal the predicament.

Staffing the IT Architecture Design Team

ITA efforts require a high degree of commitment for success from the organization's top management. The right team of professionals must be assembled;

they have to understand the complexity of any legacy systems currently supporting the organization and the points where business processes and technology converge. Sponsors at the management level must be sure to appoint to the design team people who understand the target technologies and, most importantly, what is possible to achieve by using them.

The organization's business operations units will rely on the newly designed or reengineered systems to support their daily work. Representatives of those units must be included on the team to maintain the IT connection to the business. Their early participation makes the purposes for investing in and building the new or improved systems and application environment easier to attain.

Selecting the right reporting and accountability relationship for the information systems architecture team is perhaps the second most important executive decision. It is at least equal in magnitude to getting the right people on the team. If the objective is to make bold leaps into the latest technologies for reaching a goal of distinct and measurable competitive advantage in your organization's field of endeavor or your company's business against rivals, then having the team report to the chief information officer may not be the right choice. Most chief information officers and chief systems security officers today spend an inordinate amount of time reacting to issues brought about by daily operations and ever-increasing levels of security threats. All too often they are also required to meet these daily challenges with reduced staff rosters. Under these circumstances, a CIO could easily be both risk- and change-averse, and inclined to inappropriately tone down what a freethinking, empowered architecture team could propose.

Having the architecture team reporting to the highest level of management possible within the organization is perhaps the most desirable reporting structure. The chief executive officer who recognizes the potential competitive value of staying current with technology may well be the best guarantor of and accountability point for a truly empowered IT architecture team. Figure 1-1 illustrates a couple of the relationship choices you might make.

Today, in addition to the opportunity for the architecture team to improve systems for competitive advantage, there is the challenge of meeting regulatory compliance for security controls and system protective measures on state, national, and even international levels. The architecture process can also begin to design in security features to counter the liability risk facing every organization from system breaches leading to identity theft and compromises of privacy information.

So what should an information technology architecture team be charged with doing? What is their role? Why should any organization with significant capital outlay and operational expense for technology have such a team?

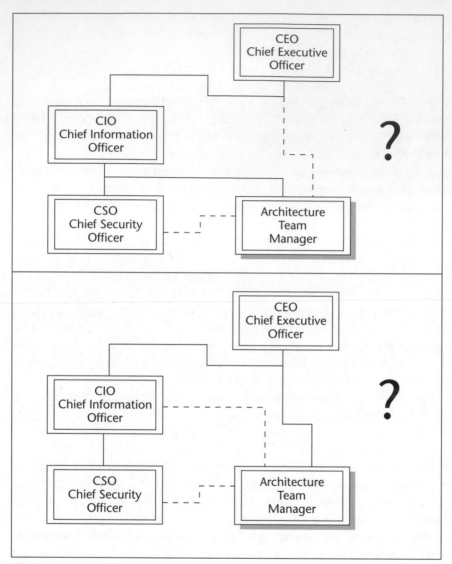

Figure 1-1   Carefully consider the reporting relationships for the architecture team manager.

Creating, Documenting, and Enforcing Architectural Design

There are five universal situations in which an information systems architecture team can greatly benefit an organization:

- A newly created organization that has no existing IT systems.

- A business where there is an investment in technology but management perceives that the technology is not serving its purpose very well, is not very efficient to use, and is too costly to operate, or the legacy systems are facing obsolescence.

- An organization in which internal parts are being fused to another part or when a whole company merges with another through consolidations or buyouts.

- An organization in which the existing investment in the IT systems is not providing the competitive advantage in the marketplace that could be gained from new systems or application improvements or replacement. (This is perhaps the highest strategic reason for using an information systems architecture team.)

- A business in which an objective evaluation of the existing systems clearly shows that the systems and applications as they exist do not provide for the levels of security controls necessary to meet compliance audits or an adequate defense against those who would do harm.

In all these cases, but possibly greatest in the last two examples, the team's goal is to apply their collective creativity and discipline to creating a system that be a measurable and lasting value for the organization.

Creating Value with Architecture

The design team will first create value by performing sometimes painful analysis of the existing situation with systems, applications, and business processes to create the documentation that describes what exists within the networks, systems, applications, and data stores. This first task is often the hardest part of the job because a lot of existing systems and applications were implemented over time and there's generally no roadmap or adequate documentation of "as built" design information.

In the analysis, the first question must always be this: Is this application, control, system, or software meeting the business objectives? And the second question follows up: Is it as good as it can be? Every application, every data store, every piece of hardware, and every interface requires examination and documentation attesting to the existing condition. The recipe for success is to categorize starting from each application. The end-user interface is where the business work product begins and ends. Architectural teams must approach their work from the end-user application perspective. Both the existing set of applications, or legacy if you prefer, and those features and capabilities desired in the vision that do not currently exist must become the focus and starting point of the architectural design process.

This application-first approach is necessary first to keep the spotlight where it belongs — on the end users and what the system does for them — and second, to facilitate the design team's getting a handle on what would otherwise be a very complex problem to document, understand, and analyze from any other perspective. Just as the accounting profession focuses on following and properly accounting for the flow of money, in the information technology architectural field, the approach to understanding and documenting (accounting for) the data systems design must focus on every one of the pathways that the data (information) takes as it is moved about and acted on to accomplish the organization's work.

For example, to describe the data paths for an e-mail application, you'd begin at the keyboard. The data flows include keyboard to CPU application, to network transport, over network to post office or SMTP (Simple Mail Transfer Protocol) transport send process, and so on. Along the way, every device, device interface, firewall, host, and security sector the data crosses must be captured, described, and documented in detail. Every point where one application passes data to another must be captured. Details of other processes that support the application, such as DNS (Domain Name System) host lookup to allow the e-mail to travel via SMTP over the Internet, must be included in the data paths documentation relating to e-mail. The bird's-eye view is from the perspective of the application. In the building construction design analogy, the details of the plumbing system's design and construction in effect follow the flow of the water. The details of the flows and controls that get hot water to the left faucet and cold water to the right one are the design focus.

The next phase of the analysis must examine the evidence to find the answer to the second question (is it as good as it can be?); determine where there would be benefit from a change in the hardware, software, applications, controls, or business processes; and place a value measure on making those proposed changes. This requires an end-to-end analysis of all of the interfaces and data flows that the system accomplishes to support the business process.

Once an objective measure is made of where changes or new additions need to be made, the team moves to the next phase: researching the scope of possibilities for making the system improvements. The results of exploring what is possible using the currently available technologies, tempered by the constraints that exist within the organization, become the catalyst or beginning bubble model for visualizing the first phase of the desired design.

Documenting for the Desired Design

The first of the two sets of documents represent what currently exists in the enterprise in detail. The second set of documents is the bubble model that represents the desired or target state. The entire discipline of information technology architecture must completely bridge the documentation gap between these two states. It is theoretically the same as the building construction example if you said you have an existing state, a beautifully wooded 10 acres in the Keweenaw Peninsula of Michigan, and a fixed budget. Your desired state is to have a 2,000-square-foot log home on the property, along with a garage and a pole barn that blend into the forest. The buildings should be made mostly from on-site materials and must be built within the budget.

The documentation that allows moving from the existing state to the desired state is brought about by the construction architecture creative design, a process where design concepts are expressed in detailed drawings and specification documents. The building example may be theoretically the same, but in most complex enterprises and technology environments, IT architecture is much more multifarious in nature and requires significantly more documentation and greater detail than is found in sets of building construction documentation.

Information technology architecture requires more than a picture or a diagram of hosts and devices placed in a network to achieve the affirmed goals of its practice in IT systems design and implementation. The architecture team must achieve a level of documentation that leaves no doubt in the mind of the in-house or contracted applications developer or implementer what the systems are to look like, how the application will be developed, how everything works together, and what all the interfaces are. It must leave no gray areas as to how the systems are to be operated, maintained, and when necessary, modified.

The documentation must be complete enough to answer most any question the operations personnel charged with supporting the systems and applications might have. The new developer must know exactly how to fit the new application into the existing environment without creating damage to existing systems or proposing new, alien, or costly-to-support alternative solutions to what was intended. Sure, diagrams depicting the infrastructure are needed, but so are all of the text documents detailed in Chapter 3. Diagrams without the complete sets of supporting documentation are of little value. Collectively, the necessary diagrams, recognition of the policy enforcement zones, and the documentation described in Chapter 3 facilitate and constitute the body of information that is systems architecture.

Enforcing Design Vision through Documentation

In large companies, modern fast-moving enterprises, and organizations where information technology systems and supporting operations are dispersed or where authority is not centralized, enforcement of information systems architecture is a daunting task. Often the accommodating IT staffs, while being helpful in trying to do something better-quicker-cheaper, violate the intended systems architecture, causing increased security risk and adding unnecessary cost to the support phase of an application's life cycle.

Enforcement of completed information technology architecture designs and documentation in any organizations must find its way into the personnel/job descriptions of everyone who plays a role in implementation, modification, operation, maintenance, or application development. In other words, everybody in the IT department, including management, must have within his job descriptions a firm performance link to complying with and enforcing architecture, policy, and standards.

No Legal Enforcement

You find a level of legal enforcement in the field of building construction. States have construction code commissions that establish rules and regulations from laws that control the regulatory oversight of home and building construction. It comes in two modes. First are the building codes, such as BOCA, adopted by local charters and laws and enforced by a body of government trade or general construction code inspectors. The second mode is achieved by licensing home builders, electricians, plumbers, and heating and ventilating contractors, where failure to perform installations to code standards could lead to loss of license. Even though the IT field has, through notable software and hardware vendors such as Cisco, Microsoft, and Novell, offered training and certification, there's no assurance that your design and implementation objectives will be met even when done by certified professionals. Having CISSP-certified staff does not always equate to a system as secure as they should or could be. (CISSP stands for Certified Information Systems Security Professional.)

This places the burden on an organization's management to protect itself by developing a quality in-house practice of information technology systems architecture or by contracting with consulting firms that have established practices with a track record of success. For an organization that cannot afford either option, there is at least a conceptual alternative that has yet to catch on in the industry: third-party plan review. This means that before a vendor proposal is accepted for implementation, a disinterested but qualified third party reviews the details of the implementation to help ensure that the proposal at least meets the objectives. Qualitative third-party design review can help determine if what is proposed by vendors for purchase is at least current technology and efficient if not state-of-the-art for similar implementations.

For those organizations new to the concepts and discipline of information systems architecture as a tool to rationalize what can otherwise become an out-of-control spiral of technology and costs, this is the prime means to get a grasp on expenses and increase the benefit derived from the technology. For those entities that are already heavily investing in the practice, a renewed focus can bring ever-smaller elements under the purview of the process to solve current challenges.

Security Issues Always in Sight

Current design challenges frequently revolve around security issues including protection of privacy, protection of financial data, establishing accountability of access, and sufficiency of the audit capability. The publicity surrounding these topics is driven in part by the Sarbanes-Oxley legislation requiring improved controls and accountability within public companies. The comprehensive solutions to these issues require a higher level of architectural discipline in the design process and operational practices than many of today's information technology systems have.

Keep in mind that this is a complex area often requiring focus on microscopic details that apply to abstract layers of the systems and interfaces. Concentrating on one subset of the bigger picture, such as the security, and approaching design elements from an application perspective makes success possible. That is, resolving to make your applications secure one application at a time will lead to a secure enterprise. Each time an approach works to secure an application, it has the potential to become the pattern for the next round of applications. For example, setting up identity services for the new applications potentially allows retrofitting of the legacy application to use the same service. Establishing the controls inherent in a security architecture design from a priority list one application at a time is the most workable tactic. Using such a methodical approach allows the patterns of the solution to emerge and be leveraged in the subsequent work.

Chapter 2 discusses the individual elements of data and privacy protection that must be controllable for access and accountability. As you read through it, keep in mind that each of the nine elements of data or privacy protection presented there must be evaluated as to whether it should be controlled for access within the circumstances of the data use in your organization. If the answer is yes, then the next question becomes how you can design to accomplish that required control within your architecture at all appropriate levels. Any system's security architecture design will be judged, audited, and qualitatively ranked on how well it can control each of those elements.

Summary

In addition to HIPAA, Gramm-Leach-Bliley, state privacy protection laws, and regulatory requirements imposed in doing business internationally, SOX compliance is just one more reason to use a comprehensive architectural design team and process to create new or improve your current IT systems. IT systems are already complicated, and adding spotty upgrades and patches simply intensifies the complexity without necessarily increasing the security protections. The access controls that should be designed to meet requirements for regulatory compliance may turn out to be the key defense contributing to an organization's very survival from the next big IT worm or hack attack.

The process of formalizing the effort to turn business needs into requirements and requirements into new systems and hardware has value and can pay dividends to the firms willing to trade some legacy systems, applications, and controls for ones designed to meet modern operational and control challenges.

Understanding Basic Concepts of Privacy and Data Protection

Protecting the confidentiality of your own private information and shielding the privacy of the data an organization's management wants to keep secret share common concepts that are parallel core considerations for protecting data of any kind. This chapter introduces them as elements to be considered before progressing with the design of the controls architecture. In the design flowchart, each protection element is considered first as a required need or not in relation to the particular data. Then if controls are needed, to what level or strength of controls over each element is to become a functional requirement within the design.

Privacy laws in the European Union and Canada are in some ways considered to be stronger than those in the United States. In the United States, states vary considerably in what has been passed into law; California is considered to be a leader in legislation aimed at protecting personal privacy. Mushrooming identity theft has caused a huge increase in new legislation at both state and federal levels. From a legal point of view, the legislation of privacy and data protection is a fast-moving target in terms of what must, or could, be done within the current technology environment. Public demand for accuracy of financial information and legislators responding to consumers' requests for legal protection for personally identifying or financial information will continue to challenge technology designs. Plan your systems to accommodate the need to apply changes to the controls as regulation evolves.

The Federal Department of Homeland Security also has an agenda to provide for release of private information that will surely impact both state and federal legislation and that runs counter to what privacy protection advocates desire, further complicating designs when these opposing demands intersect.

What all of this boils down to is that protecting digital information is not an easy job now, and it is not going to get easier anytime soon.

Classifying Data

Data classification is the first topic on which a strategy or agreement must be reached between the organization's business management and the technology implementers before you can move to an appropriate set of controls over access and authentication. The problem can then be framed as how high is the data protection profile and how many end-user profiles does your organization really need to associate with each data classification? Then the question becomes what technical control fundamentals are going to be applied at each data classification level?

It is easy to get carried away with data classification schemes. The complexity some data managers would like to apply may be rooted in spy novels or government bureaucracy; I am not really sure which. Adding layers of classification from confidential, to secret, to top secret, to highly secret, and so on serves little purpose when the technology options to incrementally increase security protection profiles are few. Also, further complexity in the system's environment is both difficult and expensive to establish and maintain. Some classification of data is necessary, but complex classification schemes may not be worth the effort or expense. Safeguarding those data elements and documents that are intended to be protected is where the major focus and allocation of resources should be.

The next few pages explore a simple three-level data classification scheme that easily fits in currently available and on-the-horizon security technologies. The scheme's hierarchy, from low to high, is information specified as:

- Public domain (open)
- Protected
- Restricted

Understanding Public Domain or Open Information

There is very little point in building expensive or difficult safeguards to protect access to information intended for the public domain beyond taking measures to maintain its integrity and accuracy. On a personal level, for example, certain elements of your identity are in the public domain. From the telephone book to high school yearbooks and news reports, newspaper birth announcements to volunteer organizations' member directories, building blocks of your identity are available to the public. There is little that can be done to get information such as your name, address, and phone number back exclusively under your control.

The vast majority of information held by government at all levels is also legally open and available to the public. Citizens and companies need to rely on the accuracy of this information, so impediments to easy access serve no one. Here again the focus needs to be on easy availability and data integrity, not on access controls. Passwords, names or usernames, or e-mail addresses should not be required to get online Web-based access to government information and data. Many units of government operate under the Freedom of Information Act (FOIA). In some cases, this statute prevents requiring members of the public to identify themselves to gain access to the information.

Companies and other organizations often possess information that they either want or are legally required to make available to the general public. By posting that data on the Web, they can concentrate their security measures on the categories of protected and restricted information. Requesting even an e-mail address before granting access to the public data puts up at least a mental barrier to the person who's merely seeking information. Information to which the public is entitled or that you would want to get in front of prospects or clients should be made easy to find and access.

Writing data to this category does require access controls, but would use at least the protection controls discussed later for posting to public information sources.

Understanding Protected Information

The *protected information* classification most simply covers that which you don't want everybody on the planet Earth to know about you. It is information such as a credit card number or Social Security number that you occasionally need to share to conduct some business transaction. You reasonably expect those with whom you share this information to use it only for the purpose you intended and to take measures to safeguard it from unauthorized access as well. Once you have presented your credit card number to a waiter, for example, you expect that he is not going to give it to an accomplice waiting in some third-world country who will then place illegal online orders or transfers until your credit limit is surpassed.

Additionally, you share a lot of personal information — willingly or unwillingly — with the various levels of government, and you expect that it will be safeguarded and used only for that purpose for which you provided it. (Government also originates data that is exempt from FOIA and public disclosure, and may require a court order for access.) The absolute minimum appropriate access controls for this information are a username and password.

Businesses and organizations also have information that deserves protection from competitors and predators. Here is where the security control focus needs to begin in earnest. This type of data is also shared frequently with external entities, so the security concern has to extend beyond the natural borders of the systems in which it's contained.

Understanding Restricted Information

At first glance, the difference between protected and restricted information may not be clear. *Restricted information* is that which is not routinely shared, and its storage, reads, writes, and transport are highly controlled with mechanisms that include chain-of-custody tracking. Its access is auditable. In the nondigital world, restricted information would be kept in a locked vault.

> **NOTE** Audit capability is often referred to as *logging*, although logging is merely storing the information about what device or person interfaced with the data. *Auditing* implies a further level of intelligence, performing analysis on the logs to discover anomalies for additional evaluation.

For individuals, elements of restricted information are those items whose inappropriate release could cause harm, extreme embarrassment, or financial loss or would be considered an invasion of privacy.

Government entities also have data in this classification. Top-secret information, for example, generally requires the highest level of access controls. This data is not routinely released to the public, nor is it required to be released without a court order. Unauthorized release could cause physical harm to citizens or government employees — the true identities and home addresses of undercover law enforcement officers, for instance, need to be protected. There's also data whose disclosure could cause large outright financial loss or the risk of costly litigation. Depending on the financial risk tolerance, government entities may want to start at a level of $50,000 as the beginning financial threshold measure to be classified in this set.

Typical corporations rarely have information in their data stores that could imperil lives like restricted government information can, but loss of trade secrets, production formulas, prepatent research documentation, and financial data can certainly cause harm to a company and losses to its stockholders.

Keeping It Simple

These three classifications — public, protected, and restricted — provide sufficient predetermined security levels of data protection for most systems controls. Additional complexity generally does not add value. Limiting the data's classifications requiring vigorous by-name access controls to two (protected and restricted) promotes a system where the collective protective security measures are stronger and identical, or nearly so, for all data access at that level. Security measures can and should be uniformly designed and applied at each classification level across enterprise systems, whether supporting one individual's computer, a state government system, or a multinational corporation's networked systems.

Regulating data classifications enables the design and systems implementation to be standardized as well.

Essential Elements of Privacy and Data Protection

This section presents a reference framework for protecting data or privacy at its most basic or primal level. What does it mean to protect privacy or information? What exactly are the elements that can, should, or would be controlled in the perfect world? Nine essential elements that will be discussed are as follows:

- Basic protection from any disclosure
- Basic control over what details are disclosed
- Control over who details are exposed to
- Control over how details are used once shared
- Control over the condition of disclosure
- Control over when data is disclosed
- Control over where data is shared, stored, and moved
- Control over why data is disclosed or shared
- Control over compensation for disclosure or use

They provide a basis for thinking about privacy and data protection in IT design criteria.

Protecting against Disclosure

Burying your organization's secrets in a treasure chest on some island in the Bermuda triangle may help keep the information secret and prevent easy access by others, but the problem posed by both valuable data and people is that to be truly effective, they must interact with the rest of the world (or at least with selected contacts within it). So although total protection of confidential personal or corporate information may be viewed as a basic right, it isn't always a practical one. Denying disclosure of any information is not easily achievable, but without a doubt it is the necessary starting point for thinking about protecting important information assets.

The firewall technology rule used to express this sentiment is "deny all" (see Figure 2-1). You first protect important data or information from disclosure of any kind and then grant rights of access only through appropriate controls.

The decision to share the information requires tracing the flowchart to the next sets of choices over the aspects of that information. Access controls for systems housing protected and restricted information must then be capable of denying access on a range from denying everyone to denying only hackers to allowing one or more persons or processes to access.

Controlling What Is Disclosed

When the pizza delivery person arrives, you could answer the door with a mask on your face to protect your likeness from disclosure and pay with cash to protect your bank information or credit card number. To arrange delivery of a pizza in most locales, you have to surrender your phone number, name, and obviously the delivery address. You make a trade-off between keeping such personal details from disclosure and giving up enough of the details to get convenient delivery of the pizza. Figure 2-2 shows an example of permitting specific information.

Individuals and organizations face similar decisions when seeking credit or interacting in modern commerce. Certain disclosures facilitate trade and commerce, while keeping other information closely held protects the organization's economic value.

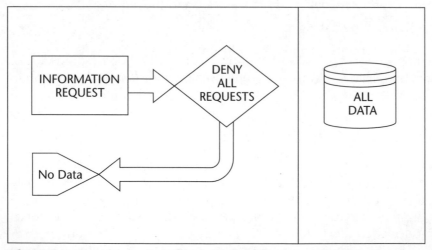

Figure 2-1   Start by denying all requests for data.

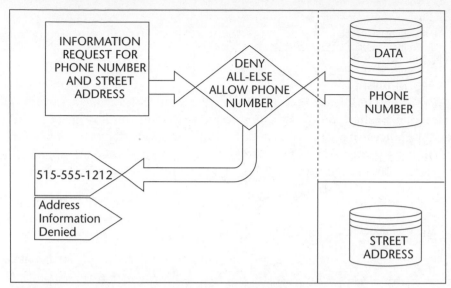

Figure 2-2 You decide what information is disclosed.

The filtering that takes place over which details are disclosed and which are not is achieved through adequate data classification and segregation interacting with IT access control mechanisms. The discrimination relationship between data and granting access rights to meet regulatory requirements for protected or restricted data must control and report exactly what information is released to whom. Systems that cannot identify by name who has access to what information or who is empowered to change a single data field are candidates for failing access control audits.

Controlling to Whom Details Are Exposed

When you applied for credit to buy your first automobile, you may or may not have known that the dealership was going to share your personal information with banks, credit unions, and finance companies to "get you the best deal on financing" and that it would end up in the three major credit reporting agencies and available via the Web to anyone with 10 bucks. The information willingly shared to get credit to buy the car moved from the local dealership to national financial institutions to international credit reporting agencies within minutes. Not much in this scenario about empowering you for controlling who can access your personal information, so it's easy to see why controlling who can get private information is essential (see Figure 2-3).

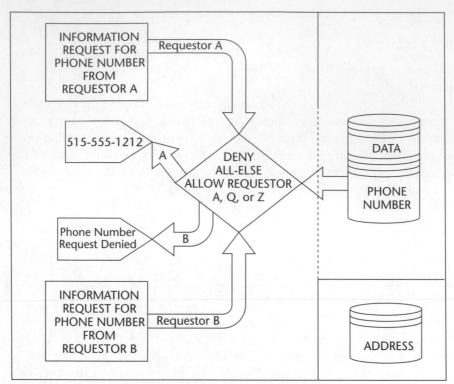

Figure 2-3 You decide who has access to what data.

Companies should not grant one client access to information about another client. There must be some certainty that account information is shared only with appropriately identified account holders or named individuals.

Access controls must be capable of discrimination that is centered on having confidence in the identity of the person who is trying to gain access and, once identified, allowing access only to specific sets of information.

Controlling How Details Are Used Once Shared

Control over how information is used once it is exposed presents the most daunting challenge. Sometimes this aspect can be controlled within the technology; in other circumstances it requires contractual relationships. In some cases, no level of control is possible after the data is released. When buying a car, for example, you may not mind sharing your personal financial information with the car dealer or even the car manufacturer's financing branch. You may not even mind the fact that it is shared with a credit-reporting agency. But you may mind greatly how the information is used beyond that first authorization. Getting offers from companies with whom you have no relationship may not be desired at all, for instance. Having the information out there for the asking by potential employers or insurance companies without your consent amounts to a total loss of control over how the original shared information is used.

Other entities also possess information that must from time to time be shared for the best interests of the organization. Competitive design information shared with a supplier of component parts is expected to be used by that supplier only to make the parts. Sharing information with a competitor or using it for an in-house product without permission destroys the capability of the information's original owner to control the information.

The use of government data may affect more than just the government. One area in federal government sure to come under scrutiny is the new requirement for state departments of motor vehicles or driver's license bureaus to collect and record Social Security numbers for every licensed driver. An SSN should be strictly limited to accounting for your employment tax deposits and applying for your benefit at retirement. All other use of SSNs should be prohibited.

Once information becomes available, how it is used is perhaps the most difficult — and in many instances is impossible — to control. Design for access control mechanisms should utilize features that regulate how information is used to the extent that level of control is possible in any given technology environment. Often the only possible controls over released information are governed by mutual consent or legal agreement.

Figure 2-4 illustrates management of information release.

Controlling the Condition of Disclosure

You should be able to choose whether to share your private information with others. Sometimes, though, an unauthorized intruder takes your information without asking. Espionage, industrial spying, computer hacking, and e-mail eavesdropping are all unauthorized assaults on private or protected data or at the highest level of restricted information. This is lack of every control over the condition of release. Establishing control over the conditions under which information is made available is all about keeping the offenders out by default, allowing access by properly authenticated end users under circumstances of your choice. This means being able to deny access or transactions in unfavorable conditions (see Figure 2-5).

Information technology system controls must filter out the illegal and unauthorized early in the access process to add the capability to differentiate the permissions applied from other control aspects.

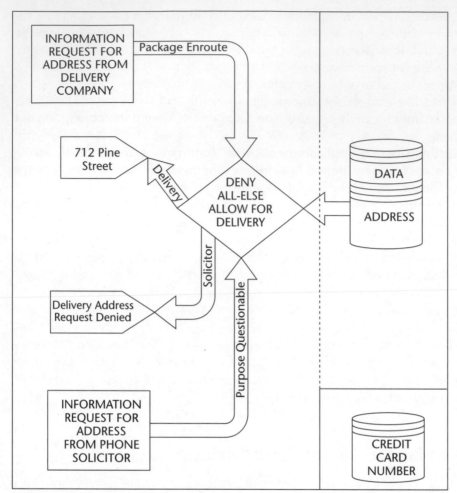

Figure 2-4 You have some control over how released information is to be used.

Controlling When Data Is Disclosed

"Anytime, anywhere, no wrong door, 24/7" are all phrases associated with the World Wide Web that set expectations for access to information and application processes. Production companies get a lot of media mileage by timing the release of films to theaters or to home VCR and DVD markets. *When* data is accessed, released, or modified can become an important point of control. After the fact, it can be an important issue in court cases.

With the 24-hour, 365-day emphasis on Web services' accessibility, the value of being able to control the time and day elements of information release or access availability is often overlooked or downplayed. In certain circumstances it is important to consider controlling by time of day or date. If, for example, a bank customer was an early-riser, up every morning at 4:30 a.m., he could assist the bank in thwarting unauthorized Web access to his account and its information by coordinating with the bank's access control system to allow online banking for his account only from 4:30 a.m. to 5:00 a.m. Access attempts at any other time of the day would be viewed as unauthorized vulnerability scans or hacking attempts and could be dealt with accordingly. With the bank's security team doing some monitoring and working with law enforcement, this approach could facilitate tracking down and prosecuting those attempting illegal access.

Access to internal applications such as employees' self-administration of benefit plans could be limited to groups of employees by day of week or hours during the day. Alternatively, the benefit process could allow universal access but only be made available during normal working hours at the organization's home office.

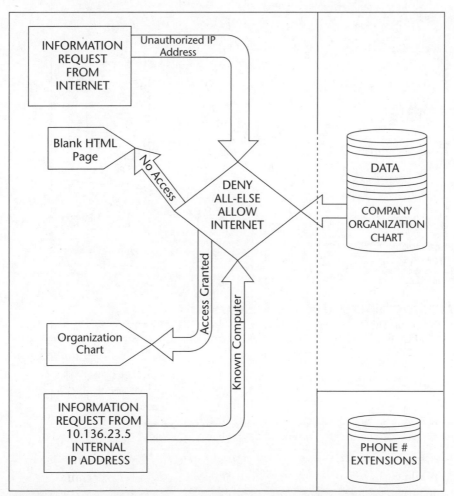

Figure 2-5 An unauthorized IP address constitutes an unfavorable condition.

These are only a couple of examples of the many ways time controls can enhance the security of sensitive applications and data. Selecting the time controls that would be of value in your organization without sacrificing the utility and usefulness of the application is the design challenge.

Time-based access controls should not be considered relics of the past, only used for limiting network access. Controlling access in a creative way by time, date, or day is still a very valuable option for consideration in the security designs of any access model. Figure 2-6 shows how time-based access might work for a commodities broker.

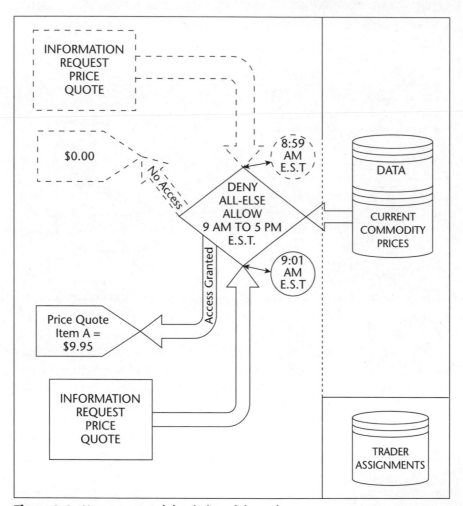

Figure 2-6   You can control the timing of data release.

Controlling Where to Share, Store, and Move Data

If the information composing your identity is stored with you on the deserted South Pacific Island where you live, it will likely move only if you leave the island and take it with you. The options to share the information on the island or to move it off the island with the aid of an empty bottle are presumably under your control. When control over access to data is lost or compromised in any way, that information can be transported anywhere on the planet in seconds, thanks to the Internet. Physical possession of digital data can be put on a keychain storage chip and moved, mailed, or shipped anywhere in the world. (This was always a potential problem in the past with hard-copy data.)

Information systems must be integrated with controlling access and data flow points and with features that enable data owners to control where information is shared, along with where it is stored and where it can or cannot be moved. Designs that fall short of adequate security control in this area or that cannot control these elements at all are simply failed designs from a security point of view.

Figure 2-7 illustrates part of a retail chain's flowchart.

Controlling Why Data Is Disclosed

The element of why data is disclosed is a hot button with privacy-conscious consumers — and for good cause: Identity theft is rampant and results in financial fraud, personal losses, and years of legal hassle for the victims. When cashing a check, most people recoil at a request to add their Social Security number to a check on which the driver's license number is already clearly printed. They ask why a cashier needs an SSN to cash a check. Consumers understand that being asked to show their driver's license at the point of purchase may help prevent fraud.

Having an in-depth understanding of why information is being shared with a particular user, business partner, or other defined entity leads to further evaluation of which of the other eight control elements should be pertinent from an access design perspective. You must actively consider what information really needs to be shared for a stated reason. Often decisions are made to collect and use information such as Social Security numbers merely for convenience in creating an account number at a for-profit service business. Social Security number, driver's license number, and date of birth are the keys to identity theft when properly associated with the public domain information of name and address. When these numbers are needed to support a legitimate business process, they should be adequately protected within the organization's computer systems and accessible only to those people and processes directly using them. Using any of these numbers for a displayed account number is no longer appropriate.

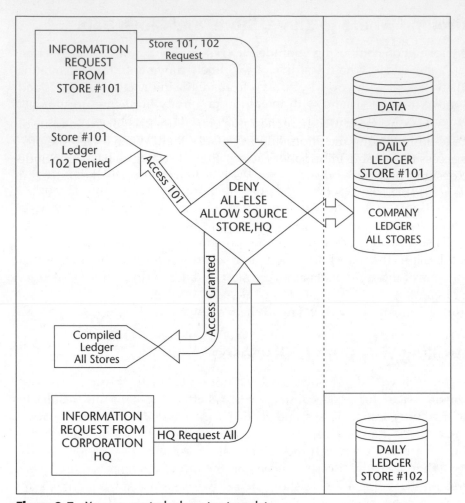

Figure 2-7 You can control where to store data.

Architecture design teams should have the background information or ask why each individual data element is shared. In many legacy systems the answer may emerge that "it was easy, so we used it." Asking the questions before the design begins can reduce the type and amount of data that really needs to be shared and may reduce the scope and effort necessary to protect privacy information.

Controlling Compensation for Disclosure

Even when provided for free, information has value to the person or entity seeking it. When the cellular phone company charges you $2.75 for a phone number, why doesn't the person whose number you wanted get a cut of the directory service fee? When a celebrity allows her likeness to be used in promoting a product, she gets a fee along with added notoriety leading to higher fees. Privacy advocates would argue that the person whose information is in the phone directory should also be compensated for its inclusion. Many Web-based companies' stock-in-trade is charging for access to information.

Regardless of whether the point of controlling access is to protect personal information or a company's intellectual property, the design of the access controls must be considered in light of the value of the data itself or in the value of the trade-off in making the information available at all. When a Web site provides access to valuable information, access control strategies have to include in the design a process to bill online payment systems and verify the cash debit for the access before actually granting access.

For example, a market analysis company may charge different fees to members and nonmembers, as illustrated in Figure 2-8.

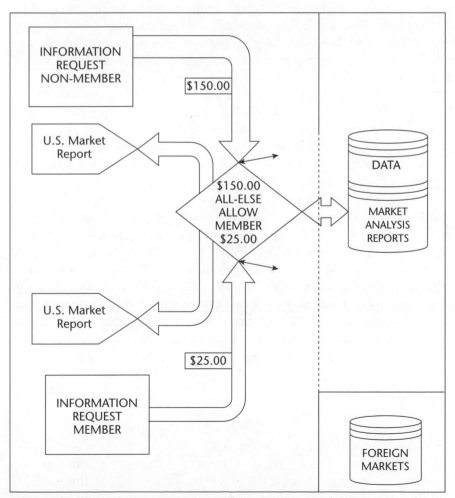

Figure 2-8   You may choose to charge fees to release some data.

Summary

This chapter discussed data classification and three major stages of security for that data:

1. Easy, no-barrier access for public information with great read-only data integrity style controls.

2. Strong, by-name access controls with sufficient authentication to meet regulatory controls and auditability for protected information. This solution is standardized and leveraged across the enterprise.

3. The highest access control standards possible for identity, access control, and authentication that your organization can afford for restricted information. Use them for every system and data store in this category.

Even sophisticated cloak-and-dagger government entities could potentially simplify their data classification schemes and leverage the technology to grant access by realizing that the only thing that needs to change for restricted information access is actually to whom access is granted. More will be said about this in Chapters 6 and 7.

This chapter also examined nine protection/privacy elements, which are considered individually and then combined and considered together to make up the overall data privacy/protection architecture. An access control system design viewed in the context of controlling each of those elements moves closer to being able to protect important information from unauthorized disclosure or modification. Evaluating what can be done given the current technology increases the probability of a more perfect overall design for security controls.

The design goal is to create the control bridges between the identity of a person, device, or application process and its associated authorization and authentication mechanism, and to filter access control to any other device, application, data, or information through any one, a combination, or all of the protection elements appropriate for the information requiring protection. In the current regulatory and audit environment, having one or even a few layers of access controls in place is no longer sufficient. Considering every element in designing security controls will move your organization's information technology architecture toward meeting increasingly challenging compliance audits.

Defining and Enforcing Architecture

As difficult as successfully creating a visionary set of planning documents for an organization's information technology and systems architecture might be, it may turn out to be the easy part of the systems architecture process. The first two sets of documents outline the existing condition and the desired (target) architecture. Much detailed documentation is necessary to bridge the gap between the current condition and the desired or target state.

Compare this point in the process to building a magnificent house. The architects and engineers have seen the land and interviewed the homeowners, taking abundant notes to find out what they want in their new home and how they plan to use it. Now it is time for the architect to create the shape of the living space, begin writing specifications, make materials choices, and do preliminary product selections. If only the discipline and practice of information systems architecture were that easy! Regrettably, IT architecture is nearly always a more complicated set of details than that necessary for the construction of even very large building projects. The difference between the two is, of course, their dimension. A building is physical and can easily be seen and touched. An IT architecture is abstract.

Just as there is a hierarchy of progression that must be observed in building the text-based documentation, there is also a natural order to creating diagrams that further describe and define the architecture. Like piling stone on foundation stone finishes the groundwork before the floor joists can be set for buildings, documents and diagrams are intended to fully substantiate every detail of the entire enterprise's IT systems from end to end.

Developing and documenting the information systems architecture plan should for the most part follow an order that transitions from the very general to the specific and detailed. This chapter presents both the text documentation and the system diagrams in an order of increasing detail. Some deviation to create the minute details first might be OK or even desirable under certain circumstances, but skipping part of the documentation altogether would be like building a house with no roof to keep the rain out or with no doors to enter and exit.

Creating the architecture documentation is difficult but necessary work to build IT systems to quality standards and provide a basis for the management and operation of them over time. Changes, upgrades, and new applications all become easier when you are working from satisfactory documentation.

More important, the documentation serves to enforce a level of discipline on everyone working any facet of IT operations. Implementing and maintaining adequate system security protection profiles and access controls is arduous at best and impossible at worst without sufficient documentation. To reach auditable compliance with Sarbanes-Oxley, HIPAA, the Gramm-Leach-Bliley Act, and other regulatory requirements, every documented node-to-node interface point where you can demonstrate that adequate access and security controls are applied increases the probability of a positive audit report. Knowing that every opportunity to enhance security has been taken brings its own reward in satisfaction for the design team.

Examining Documentation for IT Architecture

The mantra of every IT manager is "document, document, document," yet the reality is that IT projects, operations management, and system change management are frequently under time pressures and adequate documentation is rarely done. Insufficient documentation costs organizations considerably in many ways — it may even be the biggest cost factor, although it is hard to capture its exact value. When an IT staff member has to respond to a request for information about a potential changes with "We will have to take a look at that," it's a clue that adequate documentation is lacking, to be made up for with research that would have been unnecessary with good documentation. The documentation discussed in this chapter is the minimum needed to document

IT systems (that for many of us are too abstract to comprehend without detailed descriptions and diagrams).

The purpose of the text documents and diagrams is twofold:

- To work together to show the whole picture of the design features and aid in the implementation, troubleshooting, operation, and maintenance functions

- To provide sufficient details for design and implementation of security protection features and access controls

The text and diagrams are indispensable to security risk analysis and figuring out better defensive measures to protect systems from harm.

Once the documents and diagrams are completed, it is extremely important to keep them current as changes are contemplated and made. The same level of attention to detail and analysis that went into the original design should be applied to any proposed changes. Any changes made must be documented right away.

Substantiating Business Objectives

The systems architecture team begins its documentation work by capturing and recording all of the business objectives that the operations units of the enterprise would like to have the computers, applications, and technology in place to accomplish. This information may be derived from other documentation about the business, but to put context and understanding into the process, the team must also interview the right representatives of the entity's business operations. Sometimes these objectives are called *business drivers*. Drivers or objectives should be expressed in phrases or sentences such as:

- Our system should be able to process 200 credit card sales per hour.

- Our system must be able to keep all customers' credit card information totally secure throughout the entire transaction process.

- Our online and order-processing system should be capable of nonstop 24-hour-per-day operation.

- The access controls must comply with the access and audit requirements mandated by the Sarbanes-Oxley Act.

Every business objective, statement of need, or business driver to be supported by the information technology system must be documented. As an entity's business operations evolve over time, changes in the systems architecture will have to be made. An advantage of having sufficient systems architecture documentation is that it accelerates the process of updating or improving applications and hardware to meet changing business needs.

The people who devise the entity's processes must communicate early, frequently, and openly with the systems architecture team. Ideally they are also members of the architecture team. That cooperative communication between business operations and technology designers is where the opportunity to use information systems design for economic advantage begins.

After the business drivers are collected, they must be validated through the organization's guiding principles. This step ensures that the objectives are consistent with the organization's culture, values, and current management's viewpoint and direction. Two organizations could have very similar objectives and business drivers yet have contrastingly different pathways to achieve them. Understanding the entity's guiding principles aids in learning the right path.

Substantiating Guiding Principles

An organization's guiding principles should be well known enough to direct the systems architecture team in its designs, and ultimately to direct the operation of the firm's IT department. Unfortunately, many organizations may not have taken the time to capture, record, or publish their standards. Examples of guiding principles include general statements such as:

- If the project contributes to profit or savings beyond internal cost of capital, proceed.
- Board of directors must approve projects requiring payback periods beyond two years.
- Promote electronic access to information and online services without compromising privacy or security.
- Include failover and disaster recovery capability in every critical system design.

Getting to more specificity with guiding principles benefits the architecture team by eliminating guesswork and providing general parameters for the team's decision making. Interviewing people in the organization chain of command all the way to top management is one way to achieve additional valuable insight to what thoughts or ideas are currently guiding or directing the organization. The same is true of government entities. A change in governors or legislative committees can have significant impact on the direction an architecture team could take. For example, the previous department director or governor may have favored outsourcing whenever possible, and the current leadership might prefer developing internal talent and doing things in-house. Nonprofits also change leaderships or boards of directors, and a change in top-level governance likely will lead to at least a different prioritization if not a complete shift in direction for the organization.

Regardless of the type of organization, this part of the process should also capture the outlook on probability for changes in direction of the organization as well as the existing values of what is often referred to as "organizational culture." In every organization there are those informal, undocumented bits of information that employees believe to be true about how the company runs, operates, or makes decisions. These are things that "everybody knows" and are often shared among employees, such as "Everybody knows purchasing will not approve a contract with X, Y, or Z companies." Sometimes these statements are correct and sometimes they aren't. The IT architecture team profits by knowing when those statements are true because it aids in making choices that will be in tune with the company's management. Architecture teams often propose what might be considered drastic changes in systems design, so the collective management's propensity to accept change is also a very good thing for the information technology architecture team to know and understand.

Values directly relevant to the information technology development and operations within the organization must also be discovered and documented in detail. The chief information officers, the chief security officer, and others closely tied to the operational processes, applications, and systems are prime sources for discovering the relative importance placed on qualitative design elements. This aspect of the guiding principles aids the design team when it is necessary to make trade-offs affecting the design elements. For example, if "reliability" is most important, losing "ease of maintenance" may be the trade-off.

It is helpful to put some associative structure around these statements by grouping them logically. That will help show the relationship of guiding principles to the decisions that impact the design criteria one way or another. Here's a list of some example methods you can use to group your statements:

1. Base on organization's mission, vision, and values statements.

2. Relate to architectural model.

3. Base on organization charts and responsibilities.

4. Base on business processes.

5. Collect them all first, then sort into unique logical categories.

6. Categorize based on a connection to desired outcomes.

7. List and do not categorize.

8. Connect to policy domains.

This list is not necessarily all-inclusive, but it is a starting point. A combination can work best; numbers 1, 6, and 8 may be the best grouping of guiding principles for larger organizations, for instance.

Substantiating Policies

IT policies are the precursor statements that begin to bring form and shape to the architecture and establish and control the boundaries necessary to achieve the vision of the information technology architects. Policy is at least inferred, if not directly derived, from the set of guiding principles. In any case, statements of enforceable policy cannot conflict in any way with guiding principles. There may not always be a direct relationship between a needed information technology policy and any one guiding principle.

Policies are high-level statements that are directive in nature. They begin to define desired behaviors of management and staff, the supporting technology, and how operational processes arrive at similar outcomes from variable inputs.

Policies are broad statements of general conditions rather than gritty details, and once decreed are rarely modified. A policy statement for wireless network access, for example, could contain the line "Wireless networks access points at all locations will require a username centralized management model for granting access rights" or "Only the network support group will install and maintain building-to-building wireless connections." Both of these sentences are broad, short on details of how, and, barring a drastic change in the organization, may not warrant any change for a number of years.

Policies require evaluation soon after implementation to determine if they are achieving the results expected. You also want to ensure that they are not causing any unintended harmful or undesirable consequences. Policy documents should also be reviewed sometime between two to five years after publication to make certain they are still relevant and needed.

Substantiating Standards

Each information technology policy provides the basis for the more in-depth and detailed technology standards. The standards help to define the restrictions or limits and refine the usefulness of the applications and systems. Standards differ from policies in that they outline the details of the technologies used and describe the specific use of identified technologies, developmental models, deployment techniques, methods, and rules.

For example, a standard would define how end users on the Internet can access company resources using VPN (virtual private network) technology. Standards are used to define operating system configurations, application development models for applying security controls, how applications will interface with stored data, and what encryption or hash will be used for IP (Internet Protocol) transmission of protected data. Many organizations cut short the work associated with developing standards by only going as far as defining what software is permitted for use. Needless to say, that does not go nearly far enough to assist in the required level of detail needed.

Setting standards is hard work and requires involvement by persons knowledgeable in the various technical areas for which the standards are intended. Their comprehension of the technology must be deep enough for them to know, appreciate, and be able to articulate the consequences of choosing one alternative over others as choices for standardization are made.

Because they are more detailed and closer to the products in use, standards call for more frequent reviews than policies do. Certainly if one software product is replaced by another, the standard that led to the original product choice needs to be reviewed.

Substantiating Procedures

Procedures flow from policy and standards. In this context, a procedure is a way to accomplish some task, often presented as an order of steps that need to be taken. Procedures start to characterize what or who does something and when the specific courses of action are taken. If it were necessary to shut down an entire computer server room with multiple pieces and types of equipment, a procedure would cover which pieces of equipment should be turned off first as well as the correct order for powering them back up again. For example it may be necessary to power up DNS and DHCP (Dynamic Host Configuration Protocol) hosts before turning on Web servers.

There are those who like the idea of combining standards and procedures, but I suggest keeping them separate if for no other reason than procedures may need to change much more frequently than standards typically do. Also, procedures are often done by work area or roles within an organization and may need to be adjusted as staffing levels change or with reorganizations of operating sections or divisions.

Substantiating Best Practices

Procedures may or may not spell out instructions for following best practices. Whenever best practices can be foreseen, however, they become a part of the architecture by design. When they are developed later in the systems or application life cycle, they still need to be recognized and documented as a part of the system design or operational plan. When system architectural changes are proposed, best practices being used have to be considered. How will the changes impact the best practices? Will they also need to be modified?

Best practices that are brought in from an external source require adaptation to the context in which they'll be used in your organization. If, for example, a best practice is to always use the operating system vendor's minimum security recommendations for configuration, then the adapted best practice must include your configuration elements that need tighter security over the minimum recommended.

The National Security Agency publishes some unclassified security best-practice documents at www.nsa.gov/snac. (The one covering configuration of Solaris 9 is 107 pages.) When using documents like this from outside sources, it's critical to chronicle the recommendations from the full document you are using as well as those that, for operational reasons, are not being followed. Further, recording exactly what the final configurations — right down to the final syntax — look like for your servers is a critically necessary step in incorporating the best practices adapted for your unique systems.

Best practices — whether from external sources or internal development — are good only for a finite amount of time. External standards bodies and organizations that publish best practices are expected to be on top of the need for changes. Always ensure that you are using the most up-to-date best practices.

Substantiating Reference Lists

Sometimes standards, procedures, and to some degree best practices incorporate information that needs to be updated on very frequent cycles, maybe hourly or daily. The reference list is how to handle posting the changing information. The standard or procedure can cite the list, perhaps even specifying the URL (Uniform Resource Locator) where it can be found. A reference list is also used to identify the personnel positions, operating groups, or roles that play a part in daily operations named in the policies, standards, and procedures. The names of the people in your organization who are allowed to authorize a VPN connection for a road-warrior employee, for example, should be maintained in the list of sanctioned requestors. Table 3-1 shows a brief sample reference list of authorized agents.

Table 3-1   Example Reference List

REFERENCE LIST OF VPN AUTHORIZING AGENTS (REVISED NOVEMBER 2005)			
DEPARTMENT	**AUTHORIZED AGENT**	**PHONE EXTENSION**	**E-MAIL**
Accounting	John Doer	1-8876	Jdoer
Finance	Sally Mooer	2-7788	Smooer
IT Opns	Ralph Soper	2-8191	Rsoper
Front Office	Bev Secare	2-7676	Bsecare

The reference lists in a large organization may require wide availability yet the capability to post changes to such lists must be tightly controlled to prevent compromise.

Substantiating Guidelines

All of the documentation to this point is instructive in nature. Each one should leave little doubt as to what the architecture team has in mind. Each level further narrows the scope of the design and operation of the information technology systems. As you move down the group of documents, you see that they leave less room for discretion in how the systems should look, function, and work together. Guidelines are the tools that allow room for the creative art needed within systems and provide space for discretion both in implementation and in operations.

They permit some originality and judgment within limits that are not in conflict with the policies or standards that preceded them. The limits are contained in the guidelines. A good example of the nature of guidelines is troubleshooting lists or charts. Guidelines are general and suggestive in nature; they aren't precisely stated requirements in the way standards are.

Guidelines are best used where there may be more than one good or acceptable way to do something. In a practical sense, they become optional paths to a desired outcome. (Please refer to Appendices for examples.)

NOTE Each of the documents discussed in this chapter plays a specific role within the architecture. Each also has its limitations. For example, when it comes to access controls, there is little room in today's regulated companies for guidelines. Access controls must be derived from strong policies, detailed standards, and tightly defined procedures. If your company is trying to use guidelines for handling authentication and access controls, there is great risk that audits will result in findings that fail your control strategy.

Substantiating Security Policy Domain Definitions

Security policy domain definitions are the final set of IT architecture documents, which has become one of the most important. Incidents of identity theft, lost privacy information tapes, hacking successes, poor security control, a scheme based on excessively broad concepts of required security and so on. I could go on and on giving examples of these newsworthy security failures that clearly point out the enormous need for far better security definitions.

Far too many organizations have not achieved adequate definitions. Some have not done it at all. Having a firewall for this or that does not even come close to meeting the bar for successful definition and enforcement of security domains. Every time your security fails, your security domain was effectively breached or did not exist at all.

In a broad sense, a security domain can be defined as any physical area, communications channel, device, network zone, application, data store, or logical focus where security policy is different for that instance over any another like thing or its counterpart. For example, suppose you have an IP network with a firewall that enforces rules on data traffic passing through its interfaces to create a unique security zone in the network on each face of the firewall. If the firewall has unique sets of rules for each of three data ports, the networks attached are then three different security domains. The firewall itself is also a security domain from a configuration point of view. So a three-port firewall requires four security policy domain definitions. But you are not done yet. The physical access to the firewall space creates the need for a fifth security policy domain treating who is allowed to access the building and room housing the firewall equipment.

The security of equipment such as firewalls demands creating a policy domain for whom and what can access it, read logs, or make changes to configuration settings or firewall rules. Every place, device, node, application, router — you name it — for which security is different, could be different, or should be different, requires going through the painstaking process of describing the associated policy domains in rigorous detail.

HANDLING ADVICE AND SUGGESTIONS

Should you take and incorporate advice and suggestions into your architectural design? After all, anyone involved even remotely with computers, networks, and applications has some degree of anecdotal or unique technical knowledge and is willing to share as your designs and systems take shape. The answer is maybe, and the maybe depends on your passing the suggestion through the entire sieve of process and documentation that makes up the architectural design process. Each idea must be vetted from the top at business objectives all the way down to guidelines. If it fits into the architecture and adds value, the idea should be considered on the merits of the value added. If it conflicts with the architecture, it should be rejected.

In exceptional cases a suggestion could be really new — new in that the architecture team missed the area of concern altogether. In those instances you should consider an adjustment to the architecture, again by starting to scrutinize the idea for value from the very beginning of the design process.

Only by getting to this thorough level of detail can you fully understand what security is in place or what is possible to achieve with the given technology. Your organization's security architects or operational chief security officer must take this painstakingly detailed approach to securing your systems or likely fail at protecting your data and systems' security over time. Any security method that takes a broader approach may already have failed. Regrettably, hacks are not always discovered the instant when they occur.

Examining Diagrams for IT Architecture

The well-worn cliché "a picture is worth a thousand words" isn't wasted on people involved in information systems. Some technicians can barely communicate without a whiteboard and marker. A good descriptive set of diagrams really is worth its papers' weight in gold! The complexity of networks, computer systems, applications, data flows, and logical operating relationships makes it very difficult to document systems in an easy-to-understand way. Anyone who shows you one picture and says that it is the organization's information systems architecture is fooling no one. A too simplistic view leaves out essential details and does not help you understand a network or a particular security policy domain's relationship to others. The main purpose of diagrams is to show contexts and relationships that cannot easily be conveyed in the text documentation sets. The documents and diagrams must work together and complement each other to aid in the observer's understanding of the system and its operation.

Detailed diagrams provide graphical information about the interfaces, points where the risk of compromise can be countered by applying access controls or other appropriate security measures. Comprehensive designs are necessary to satisfactorily meet the control objectives mandated by Sarbanes-Oxley and other mandated regulations.

Creating the diagrams highlights the opportunities for the application of access controls and security measures. It is no longer sufficient to apply control measures for one layer such as network access or operating system access and not apply controls at other levels when it is possible to do so. Over time, auditors will find such weaknesses in security design and report them as adverse findings.

The size, reach, complexity, and sophistication of an organization, along with other factors, all play a role in determining exactly what diagrams and how many instances of diagrams will be necessary to fully express an information system's design. The following categories of diagrams are quite obviously helpful in achieving sufficient detail of the information systems architecture:

- Geographical/location
- Hierarchical infrastructures
- Networks
- Logical grouping N-tiers
- Device interfaces
- Application logic
- Host-to-host data flows
- Contained process flows
- Web sites
- Security sectors
- Security policy domains

They provide a starting point for you; you may want to add or, for smaller organizations, subtract from the list, or perhaps combine some of the categories.

Diagrams should also be considered for their value in aiding the full description of the existing condition and in providing transfer of information from the architect to the implementers of the IT systems. Their lasting value is to those who provide daily operations and support to your systems and applications. Additionally, the documentation is of value to the change control process. As changes are made, the documentation should be updated in the same way as-built drawings are updated in building construction or remodeling projects.

The diagrams fully delineate every characteristic of an organization's entire information technology systems, from end to end. The descriptions help both technical and nontechnical audiences understand the systems and relationships. This visual documentation aids in implementing new systems and applications. Troubleshooting is facilitated by the details showing the interfaces among locations, systems, or program logic. Security risk analysis, design of access controls, and implementation of security policy domains are all made possible by sufficiently detailed diagrams that complement the text documents.

The following sections discuss these diagram categories.

Diagramming Locations

The number and size of geographical and building location diagrams will vary widely from one organization to the other. Multinational organizations will have diagrams much different than those of a small local company. These diagrams provide top-level views and need to capture information about communications links, operational divisions, place names, and what resources are present or required at the remote locations. They begin to tell the story of the scope and reach of information technology resources already in place or help mold design decisions about what would best be placed where in new designs.

Figure 3-1 shows an example diagram of the locations, communications links, and network firewalls of a company with three locations in the United States and two foreign sales offices.

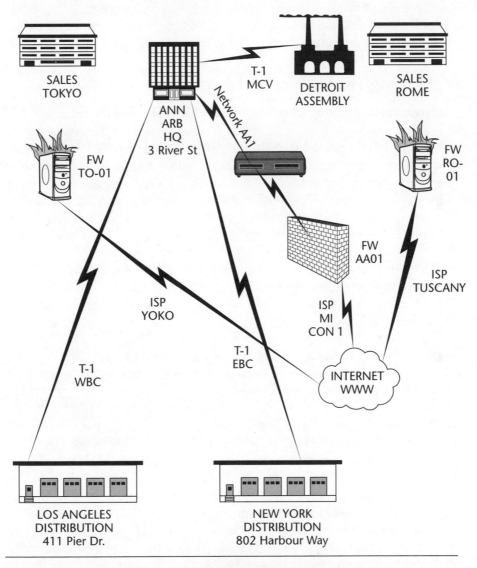

SALES TOKYO

T-1 MCV

DETROIT ASSEMBLY

SALES ROME

ANN ARB HQ 3 River St

FW TO-01

Network AA1

FW RO-01

FW AA01

ISP TUSCANY

ISP YOKO

ISP MI CON 1

T-1 EBC

T-1 WBC

INTERNET WWW

LOS ANGELES DISTRIBUTION 411 Pier Dr.

NEW YORK DISTRIBUTION 802 Harbour Way

COMPANY INC.
Locations - Communications - Firewalls
Sheet 1 Revision 3

Figure 3-1 Diagramming locations and communications links.

Location diagrams are the highest-level drawings that show the wide area, metro area, and building-to-building networks. Every communications element that the organization's IT staff is responsible for should be included for every company location. The size of your organization size and the choice of paper size dictate how many sheets are necessary to show all the routing equipment and location firewalls controlled by your IT staff. Equipment and intercity cabling run by others (such as Internet service providers or phone communications providers) can be represented with a cloud figure. The other drawings (discussed later) will flush out in greater detail the picture of the infrastructure and computing equipment at each specific location.

Diagramming Hierarchical Infrastructure

Hierarchical infrastructure diagrams (hereafter called infrastructure diagrams) can be one set of many individual drawings or multiple layers on the same drawing in computer-aided drafting (CAD) software files. They represent each location in greater detail than do location diagrams. The diagrams for a company with many offices and production facilities require more layers to describe that an organization with only two sites needs. Infrastructure diagrams need to have sufficient drawing sheets or layers to map down to the next level of detail necessary to identify locations for computer server rooms and communications closets, and to depict all the equipment the spaces contain, such as backup power supplies, servers, network devices, and similar supporting equipment. Every piece of computing and network equipment for which the IT staff is responsible should be represented somewhere on an infrastructure diagram.

> **NOTE** The term *infrastructure* refers to buildings, rooms, trenches, equipment, hard goods, and similar items with physical structure. It does not refer to people, processes, or applications.

Infrastructure diagrams graphically show what equipment is where and what telecommunication and utility power links serve each location. The final layer of infrastructure diagram is the room layout and, where a lot of equipment is present, the mounting rack layout. The mapping of the location, buildings, rooms, closets, room layouts, and, when needed, rack level layouts is useful for many purposes beyond design, such as in dispatching repair teams, during emergencies, and in disaster-recovery operations as well as in space planning and management. The diagrams also must reflect electrical supply and air-conditioning and environmental controls. The example infrastructure diagram in Figure 3-2 shows the equipment, equipment names, and host IP addresses for that equipment for a receiving and product distribution center in Los Angeles. It also shows the dual-use T-1 data network and Internet Protocol phone connection back to the home office location in Ann Arbor.

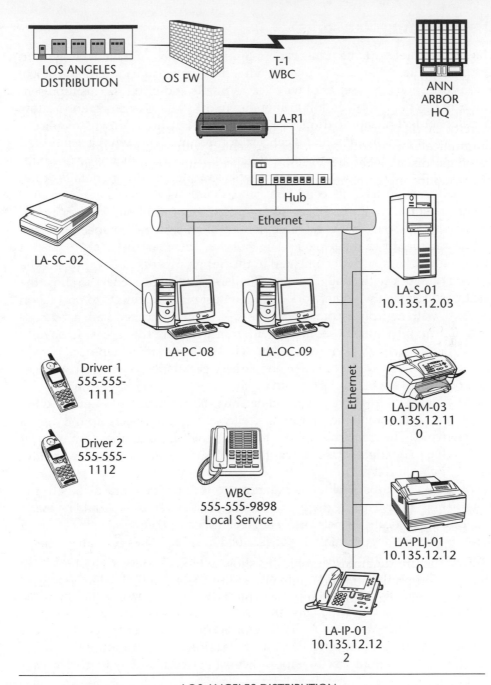

LOS ANGELES
DISTRIBUTION

OS FW

T-1
WBC

ANN
ARBOR
HQ

LA-R1

Hub

Ethernet

LA-SC-02

LA-PC-08

LA-OC-09

Ethernet

LA-S-01
10.135.12.03

Driver 1
555-555-
1111

Driver 2
555-555-
1112

WBC
555-555-9898
Local Service

LA-DM-03
10.135.12.11
0

LA-PLJ-01
10.135.12.12
0

LA-IP-01
10.135.12.12
2

LOS ANGELES DISTRIBUTION
Infrastructure - Equipment
Sheet 2 Revision 2

Figure 3-2 Diagramming infrastructure equipment.

Diagramming Networks

The focus of network diagrams is on mapping the flow of data over communication media, whether an Ethernet wire, fiber-optic cable, Internet Protocol over power lines, or a series of wire access points and bridges. This representation is the data and communications network. Many organizations allow installers or technicians to drop off a router and just plug in downstream connections and equipment with no concern for documenting what is connected where and to what equipment and to what specific port on that piece of equipment. The practice of not building networks to adhere to design details or not documenting the as-built conditions and details is not acceptable from a design perspective. It also is not acceptable to the troubleshooting or repair process, and moreover it is not acceptable from a security perspective. How would you identify a rogue device?

The network must be documented in the design process or in capturing the existing network with enough layers, details, and reference blocks to show the exact particulars of what network card in a host server connects to port n2 on a switch, with an uplink connection to port n12 on the router, with a T-1 connection to an ISP (Internet service provider) or whatever the case is. To be fully useful, network diagrams must contain detail sufficient for a help-desk person a thousand miles away to direct an on-site service person to switch an end user from port n2 to a working spare port on the same device or to one nearby.

Every device that moves digital data must be documented — every wire, every host, every appliance, essentially everything that makes up the digital data network. The same rule applies to fiber networks and other communication media: Every detail has to be captured. Many sheets or CAD drawing layers may be required for more complex organizations.

The drawings must include annotations to link the network details to the location and infrastructure diagrams. Enough cross references should be made that it's easy to locate the network details for a specific communications wiring closet. Sufficient documentation as described here facilitates centralized help-desk and support functions. The drawings should be cross-referenced with callout boxes to show the drawing names or drawing file numbers to facilitate finding the additional details when the quantity of equipment or the complexity of the situation requires many drawing sheets to cover all the details. Figure 3-3 shows a Web proxy segment of the network separated from the Internet and internal networks by routers and firewalls that control the allowable traffic. The callout box identifies the next network segment and drawing as 10.135.24.xxx.

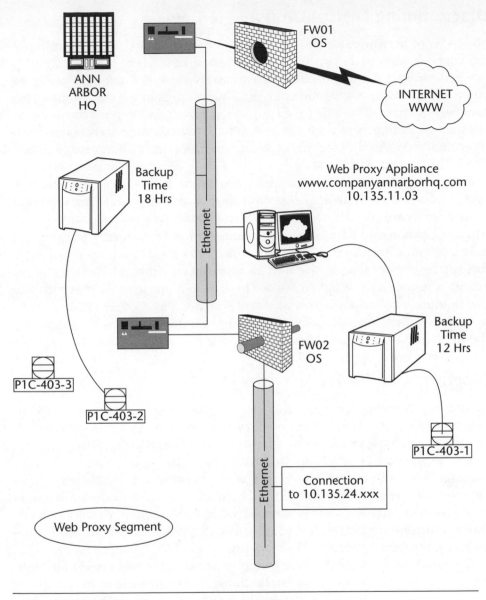

ANN
ARBOR
HQ

FW01
OS

INTERNET
WWW

Backup
Time
18 Hrs

Ethernet

Web Proxy Appliance
www.companyannarborhq.com
10.135.11.03

P1C-403-3

P1C-403-2

FW02
OS

Backup
Time
12 Hrs

P1C-403-1

Ethernet

Connection
to 10.135.24.xxx

Web Proxy Segment

4th Floor
Room 403

ANN ARBOR HQ
Network 10.135.11.xxx
Sheet 4 Revision 1

Figure 3-3   Diagramming a Web proxy network segment.

Diagramming Logical Grouping N-Tiers

N-tier diagrams provide logical rather than physical views. Logical groupings are made of systems and services that perform like kinds of functions. This is referred to as Nx-tier architecture, where each N represents a logical grouping or cluster and x represents the number of logical tiers in the design. In a Web hosting environment of N5, for example, tier N1 might be the Web front-end appliances performing load balancing; N2, the Web servers; N3, common services such as LDAP directories and credit card processing; N4, content services; and N5, back-end databases.

The N-tier set of diagrams represents what happens within an interconnected information system, and is often employed to explain to management or to a nontechnical audience how the host systems work together or where a new application will fit into the environment. This delineation and grouping also aids other functions within the design process, including analysis for security needs. Because these diagrams are used for different audiences, they are often redrawn for simplicity to use in presentations to show how a particular application works with a degree of abstraction that reduces the amount of detail. The final level of detail needed for the more technical documents should include each specific host by name within its respective tier.

Diagramming Device Interfaces

Device interface diagrams get deep into the details of what is connected to each interface port on every computer, router, hub, or appliance in the network and to any other devices to which the connection is linked. The individual port connections could be called out in a table placed in the drawing on a larger diagram or be in a diagram of their own when the shear volume of connections requires a larger amount of space for the details. Device power supply panel locations and circuit numbers as well as battery backup power supplies should be referenced at this level of detail so that power problems can be easily traced for each device.

Figure 3-5 shows a print server and all of the devices connected to it. Each device is labeled with the port or slot number that it connects to on the server. The laser printer in the diagram, for example, is connected to the second parallel port in slot six on the print server. Power connections for the devices are also shown with labels, such as the one for the laser printer (P2-203-1), which says the power for it is supplied through panel 2, in room 203, and that it is circuit breaker 1.

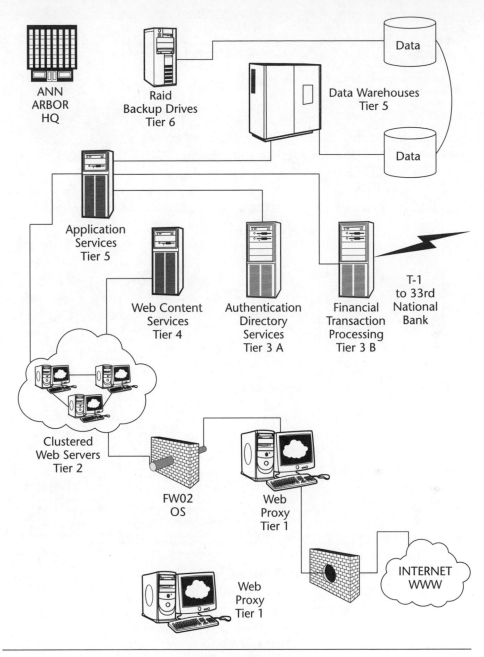

ANN ARBOR HQ
Web Services Tiers 1-6
Sheet 2 Revision 2

Figure 3-4 Diagramming Web services tiers 1 through 6.

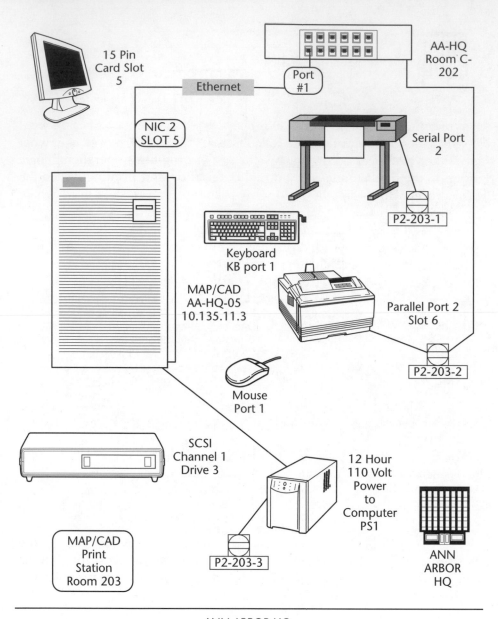

15 Pin
Card Slot
5

Ethernet

Port
#1

AA-HQ
Room C-
202

NIC 2
SLOT 5

Serial Port
2

P2-203-1

Keyboard
KB port 1

MAP/CAD
AA-HQ-05
10.135.11.3

Parallel Port 2
Slot 6

P2-203-2

Mouse
Port 1

SCSI
Channel 1
Drive 3

12 Hour
110 Volt
Power
to
Computer
PS1

MAP/CAD
Print
Station
Room 203

P2-203-3

ANN
ARBOR
HQ

ANN ARBOR HQ
Device Interface MAP/CAD Print Station
Sheet 2 Revision 2

Figure 3-5 Device interfaces for a print server.

Diagramming Application Logic

Application logic diagrams depict an application's process logic across the entire system. The information shows the nodes where the application's data is exchanged and acted on and briefly describes what happens at those nodes.

The diagram begins with the application startup and shows the points where information is keyed in, all of the program's decision points, and what other processes or applications are called for data responses, as well as at what stages those interfaces occur. It shows all of the program's operational logic right up to the final storage and output to reporting and printing. When the logical process flows are shown, analysis can be done to determine where security risks occur and what can be done from a control perspective to enhance the security protection profile for the application.

Figure 3-6 illustrates the high-level application logic between hosts when an end user attempts to look up the status of an order on the company's Web site. An LDAP directory clearly is used to authenticate the user.

Diagramming Host-to-Host Data Flow

Data flow diagrams detail the movement of digital data by each application, including every protocol, port number, encryption method, source port, destination port, and IP address — basically every data call that is made from one host to another. Everything about each communication call must be documented to capture the movement of information by the applications to accomplish the work of the programs.

Web-based programs that provide dynamic information based on input requests from an end user provide the best example of how one host, the Web server, can call out to a number of other hosts for information from databases. The Web server collects the replies from the database hosts and provides the template arrangement to present the collected data back to user's Web browser. The host-to-host diagram would map out all of the data paths to the database servers. The information would be used in the security controls design to limit the data flow so that the hosts are only allowed communication along those necessary paths and from and to each other. This can be done with controls in routers, in isolation firewalls, or with managed ports on a switch.

Figure 3-7 shows the data flow associated with processing a credit card authorization between the application services host computer and the financial transactions host. The IP addresses, connection port numbers, form of encryption, and hash algorithm are defined in callout boxes.

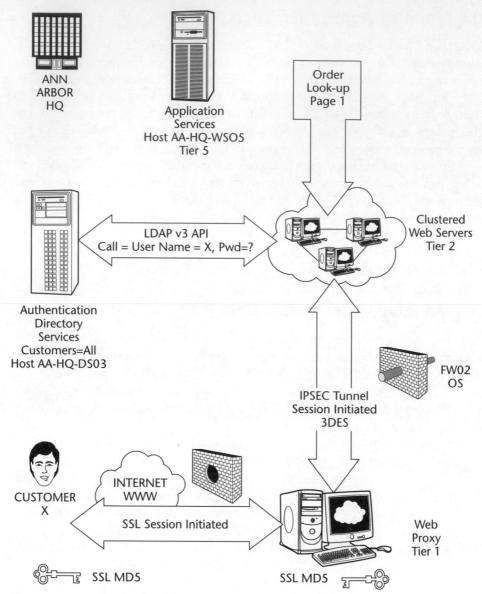

Figure 3-6 Application logic for order status authentication.

Diagramming Contained Process Flow

Contained process flow diagrams detail those processes and procedure calls that are confined to one piece of hardware and restrained within one operating system.

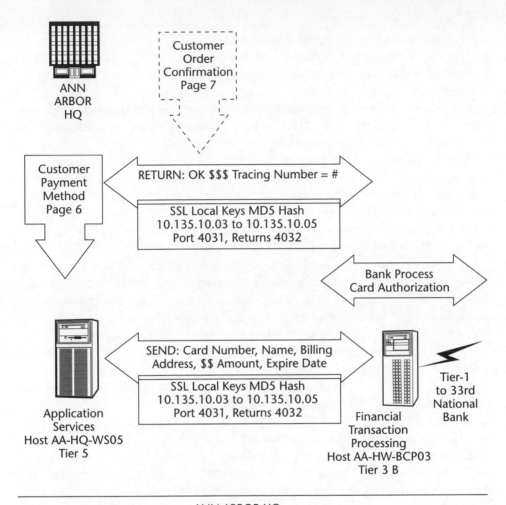

ANN ARBOR HQ
Data Flow - Web Customer - Credit Card Authorization P=6
Sheet 2 Revision 3

Figure 3-7 Credit card authorization data flow.

In N-tier systems where Web servers are communicating with other servers, calling for a process to take place and expecting a result, the logic associated with each host doing different things is fairly easy for people to comprehend. In environments where one host computer system's applications are multi-threading or spawning processes within that single computer system, the logic and tracking of what each process is doing is more difficult to understand. Contained process flow diagrams reduce the potential for confusion by detailing the communications flow between the various processes of the applications running on that host.

This type of diagramming adds value by clarifying design issues and aiding in the implementation process. It also adds value with security analysis to identify conditions of risk on each host. For example, a single host server may be running a Web server application and also have a few databases on it. A hacker might attempt to use the Web server application to launch a compromise to other databases on the server. Mapping out the internal process flows in the server will help expose the potential points for security weaknesses so they can be countered in the security controls design.

A process flow to check inventory for one item selected from an online catalog is illustrated in Figure 3-8. It shows that if inventory for that item is greater than zero, process 288 runs, returning the item count balance from the database. A security analyst would see that SQL (Structured Query Language) is present within the application and that additional analysis of the controls affecting SQL access to the database is necessary.

The design and implementation of an information technology system require documentation fully describing the system and every one of its subsystems and subcomponents in detail. The documentation — particularly the application logic, host-to-host data flow, and contained process flow diagram sets — works to help identify security weaknesses and what can be changed or modified to protect the integrity of the whole system. The view necessary for the security analyst to succeed requires an evaluation to take place one application at a time, and the documentation must be sufficient to completely explain the inner workings of all the related parts.

The collection of documents and systems diagrams presented here forms the basis for creating adequate documentation. Unique environments and special cases may require that additional views — diagrams or text documents or both — be presented to explain the situation. Technology specialists can quickly learn the details of complex integrated systems if you have created quality documentation for their review.

Diagramming Web Sites

So much of what is done today is fronted to the end user from Web pages, even from many of the mainframe legacy applications. Documenting the design of the Web site first assists those involved in the site creation and development process to ensure that the site fulfills its planned purposes. The documentation also provides a basis for analysis to eliminate security weaknesses. Future changes to the site content and applications are also facilitated by good documentation.

At least two kinds of diagrams are necessary to illustrate the inner workings of a Web server. One represents the general layout and cascade of the pages that make up the site, and the second points out the site's applications and embedded logic flow.

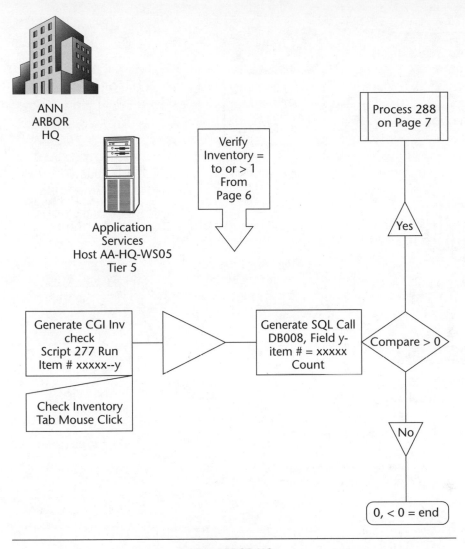

ANN
ARBOR
HQ

Application
Services
Host AA-HQ-WS05
Tier 5

Verify
Inventory =
to or > 1
From
Page 6

Process 288
on Page 7

Generate CGI Inv
check
Script 277 Run
Item # xxxxx--y

Check Inventory
Tab Mouse Click

Generate SQL Call
DB008, Field y-
item # = xxxxx
Count

Compare > 0

Yes

No

0, < 0 = end

ANN ARBOR HQ
Process Flow - Inventory Check
Sheet 2 Revision 4

Figure 3-8 Process flow for checking inventory.

Figure 3-9 shows the beginning design layout for the Ann Arbor HQ Web site. From the company's home page there are paths to divisions of the Web site that contain groups of related information. The next level of drawings would show each division with its subgroups of pages.

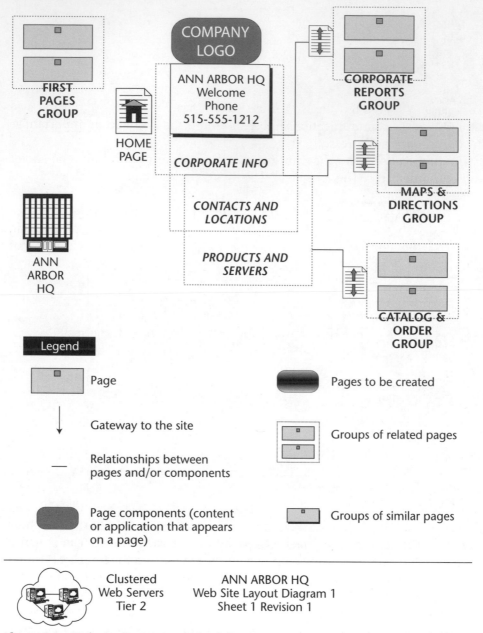

Figure 3-9 Web site front-page design layout.

Web site logic diagrams are similar to the application logic diagrams covered earlier in the chapter. A simple Web site that does not have any embedded application programming or dynamic content derived from databases from end-user queries would not need the logic diagrams.

Diagramming Security Sectors

Describing security sectors requires two types of diagrams. The first shows the physical security boundaries as an overlay to the location diagrams. Managing access to physical spaces is a necessary element of providing adequate access controls, particularly in terms of internal risks. Designing controls over physical access to spaces that house servers, digital data storage, supporting systems, networks communications hubs, and routers is every bit as important as the digital access controls.

The physical security diagram for a small company with only one server and equipment room would be an easy task, probably just one drawing. At larger organizations with multiple locations and technical staff that work at more than one location, defining and controlling physical access to areas housing servers and network equipment takes more effort. For example, defining the physical security sectors on building floor plans would help ensure that card readers or biometric devices control all access points to restricted areas.

Security sectors take on characteristics similar to the data classifications discussed earlier: spaces are open, protected, or restricted. Publicly available data could be in an open hallway or reception area with little risk. Protected data requires limiting and controlling access. As a practical matter, deploying the same solution to the protected and restricted spaces may do the job as long as there is a capability for a differentiation to be made between who can and cannot access the restricted spaces.

The second type of security sector diagrams maps out the data network areas controlled by groupings of similarly restrictive security policy.

In the traditional networking sense, security sectors (also referred to as zones) include the logical groupings of connections on the organization's network and typically take in the intranet, Internet, WAN (wide area network), and the area in front of the firewall, which is sometimes called the DMZ (for demilitarized zone). Although the conventional approach to security sectors provides a starting point, creating additional specific-use network data paths from the sectors, with more restrictive controls for each branch, can enhance security. For example, routing employee VPN access from the Internet through different firewalls and equipment than the company's Web site data traffic would provide for more restrictions on both paths.

Groupings by network security sector add value in a larger sense and will continue to be used because they are somewhat descriptive of the category of users being provided with connections at that node. The sectors are based on very broad definitions related to trust derived from the access and security policies applied to control them. The Internet is often labeled as Sector 0, and considered hostile territory; there's no trust in its connection point. Sector 1 might be the label for the DMZ, which can be somewhat trusted, if some access rules on the router in front of the first firewall are applied to protect the organization's assets connected in it. As the defined zones get closer to the most protected back-office data storage and databases, they're designed with more protections and are considered more trusted.

There is no set number of security sectors; each organization and systems environment varies. Sector numbering becomes larger or smaller the relative trust increases or risk lessens, with, again, the Internet trust level being zero, or totally lacking in trust. The most trusted network sector has the highest number. Keep in mind two points during the design and documentation of these sectors: They are broad groupings, mostly of clusters of connections, and they are general in nature. Further specifics of the security criteria have to be dealt with on a much more granular level that combines the use of security policy domains with the device interface diagrams. Each device interface presents some level of security risk, so security policy domains must be related to each interface along a network data path. Where the security threat must be thwarted by applying a unique and more restrictive security policy, the application of a policy change creates a new security policy domain.

When partnering with other companies that may connect directly to your extranet (a network node connecting business partners), be aware that the risk increases when you do not have complete control over who is accessing your network. Logical numbering of a partner sector could be a negative number to reflect that risk. The risk increases as you grant end users not vetted or controlled by your identity management process some level of access to your systems. By default you are not treating the data traffic from your business partners' networks with the same scrutiny as traffic from the Internet.

The diagram in Figure 3-10 shows eight security sectors present at the company's Ann Arbor headquarters. Each cloud represents a segment of the entire network that is in another drawing showing all the equipment and servers connected in that segment.

Diagramming Security Policy Domains

Security policy domains are made up of all the rules — often excruciatingly detailed — that contribute to preserving system, application, and data integrity; maintaining confidentiality; and sustaining availability. Their documentation includes diagrams and text recording of the rules base. This term is usually applied to firewall rules, but it conceptually fits all policy domains when translating security and access policies into the rules that control the domain.

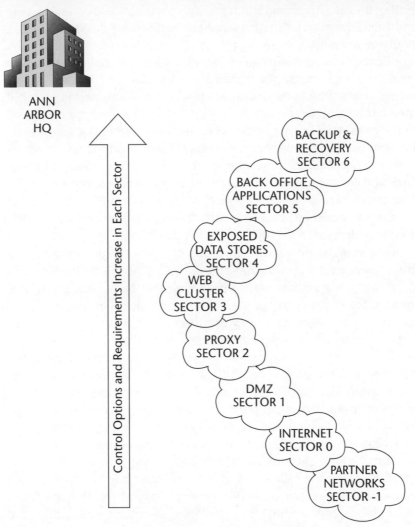

Figure 3-10   Security control sectors- Digital/Sheet 1 Revision 2

Policy domains are often specific to a single particular firewall, router, host system, or network. Any device, interface, or application can be a separate and distinct security policy domain. When security policy domains involve more than one interface on a single piece of equipment or multiple pieces of hardware on the same network segment, it is appropriate to complement the text description of the security policy domain with diagrams. The diagrams and text need to be cross-referenced to each other so that between them it is clear what is allowed within the domain.

Security policy domain diagrams predominantly amount to overlays on the infrastructure diagrams that define the security restrictions placed on a given cluster of equipment, networks or segments, or applications. Equipment, devices, or application clusters with nearly identical security policies make up a security zone. Keeping security policy domain diagrams as drill-down layers from the security zones when you document in CAD systems facilitates rapid retrieval of needed information.

Security rules get very detailed in that they include elements such as data transmission protocol, port numbers, and identification of specific Internet Protocol addresses. Graphically representing this information in the diagrams with text blocks or callout frames increases the utility and usefulness of the drawings. The fewer places one has to look for the information, the better. However, having the details in both the text documentation and in the diagram adds to the update effort when changes occur.

The rules captured in the policy domains are not limited to purely technical elements. Any change in the applicable security policy profile of how data is transmitted, stored, used, shared, monitored, logged, or accessed requires identification and documentation of an additional new policy domain or revisions to an existing one. Physical security profiles must also be a part of defining the security domains. In smaller organizations, the physical security domains could simply be an overlay on the location or infrastructure diagrams. Larger organizations may need multiple diagram sheets and may want to include the locations of security cameras and access card readers.

The capability to identify and properly document the organization's security domains is essential to a successful information technology security program. Intimately knowing what the security policy domains look like and how they interact with the entire information technology systems environment is critical both for any architectural effort and for managing current operations.

If your organization's systems require security, use all of the resources needed, both in the systems' architecture effort and in getting a handle on the existing systems' environment. The security failures you read about in the news and trade journals relate directly to failures in understanding, defining, documenting, and implementing adequate security policy domains. Do not take shortcuts in defining security policy domains. Common problems to avoid include oversimplification, lack of any definition of security policy domains, and domains lacking the necessary detail.

The diagram in Figure 3-11 shows the security policy domain for a single router port that attaches conference room network connections and a wireless access point to the company's Internet connection. The routing controls defined in the callout box summary limit the access available to these connection points to the Internet, and allowing only some specific exceptions to internal network IP addresses. The policy domain diagram's purpose is to provide a visual mapping of where on a network or device a given security policy domain is enforced.

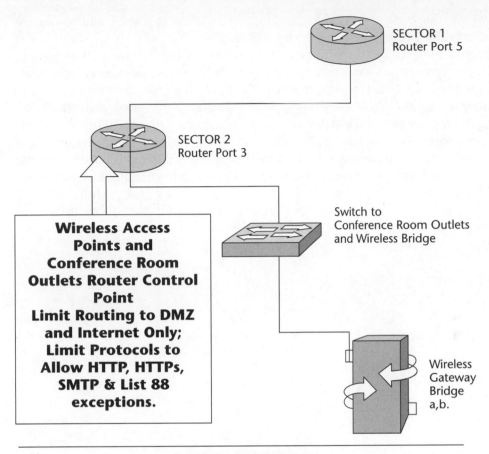

SECTOR 1
Router Port 5

SECTOR 2
Router Port 3

**Wireless Access
Points and
Conference Room
Outlets Router Control
Point
Limit Routing to DMZ
and Internet Only;
Limit Protocols to
Allow HTTP, HTTPs,
SMTP & List 88
exceptions.**

Switch to
Conference Room Outlets
and Wireless Bridge

Wireless
Gateway
Bridge
a,b.

SECURITY POLICY DOMAIN
SECTOR 2 Domain = Conference Rooms - Wireless
Sheet 1 Revision 2

Figure 3-11   Conference room and wireless security policy domain.

Summary

The text documents and diagrams should fully represent the architecture of your IT systems. Not creating and maintaining at least the minimal level of detail described in this chapter contributes to confusion, miscommunication, risk, increased operation and maintenance costs, and an inability to rapidly respond to changing demands on your systems and applications.

Providing adequate IT security and access controls to meet all of the external regulatory requirements requires attention to detail. Giving careful consideration to the interfaces where access and security are possible increases the likelihood that your systems will rank well in compliance audits and that your risk of compromise will be reduced. Don't let the systems for which you are responsible become easy targets for hacking.

Achieving quality architecture documentation takes time and resources. The current state of external and internal security threats alone may be enough to justify the architecture effort even if the external regulatory forces requiring adequate security controls do not. Also to be thought about is the risk of litigation for failure to protect privacy information. The prospect of having a first-rate system design, owning the capability to respond rapidly to changes, and the potential for a competitive advantage help make the case for providing the resources for building the architecture process in your organization stronger than ever.

Combining External Forces, Internal Influences, and IT Assets

As you start putting together the information that will influence the design requirements and framework for access controls in your organization, collect the information first, and then consider the external forces (environment and regulations) that necessitate access controls in systems design.

If your organization is complex and involved in many lines of business or in more than one country, your concerns for creating controls' compliance will go beyond the requirements of Sarbanes-Oxley. It is important to collect the external influences from all sources and to dissect them to find the similarities and differences in their requirements. Your architecture team must then create one design leading to an infrastructure that meets and supports the externally imposed requirements.

The next step is to weave the external influences in with the identified business and operational needs (drivers) derived from the collection of documents defining your internal requirements. Then consider both internal drivers and external forces within the confines of the infrastructure (current investment in or budget for improvements in networks, systems, and applications) that you have or plan to put in place. Finally, take into account the larger philosophical values held by your organization's management group that will influence how the security controls architecture ultimately looks. These big-picture influences cannot be discounted as you work toward the finite details of the access and security controls design.

This chapter examines the internal and external requirements that must be met in your organization's infrastructure.

Examining Framework Influences

Each organization operates inside of a framework of influences that include environmental factors, legal and regulatory issues, and internal and external politics. These influences are all details of the framework. It is essential to understand the framework from the perspective of the limits placed on the organization by the external influence dynamic. It is particularly important to consider the controls that may be needed in the near and long terms as a result of operating in response to these factors.

For example, it is fair to say that both the state and federal governments will continue to pass more restrictive regulations on business, requiring greater accountability. For practical enforcement, they can only require compliance to the realistic limits of the technology. Although current regulations may not require audit control finite enough to track a single bit change in a critical data field, the application tools you are using today can do so. The recommendation in that case is to design to incorporate that feature in your current application environment if it can be done at little or no appreciable cost.

Anticipating the trends from external influences can give your organization competitive advantage later, save costs in not having to do re-designs, and position your IT systems for immediate compliance with multiple sources of audit criteria.

Let's take a look at the influences that impact various types of organizations.

Evaluating the Public For-Profit Environment

For-profit publicly traded companies are framed by high degrees of transparency obligations, as well as accuracy in financial reporting and auditing requirements, and are constantly under scrutiny for their profit performance and growth. Larger companies with greater financial resources will likely find the costs of applying adequate controls to satisfy these influencers a small percentage of their total revenue. Because bigger companies are more likely to operate across borders, they may face a higher level of regulation but may still benefit from leveraging design solutions.

Smaller companies will discover that their costs for controls are higher as a percentage because they do not have massive revenues to spread the costs over. Economies of scale do play a role, particularly if the security controls are designed from the ground up to leverage across the requirements placed on the entire organization. Meeting the aggregated requirement with only one design approach provides that leverage.

A small company's overall security framework for compliance with access controls over similar lines of business will look very much like a larger company's if they are both designing to meet the same regulations. The only differences in the final infrastructure may be no more than a requirement for the larger company to handle more volume.

Publicly traded companies, large or small, will have to design equally featured access control frameworks from an authentication, authorization, and access control perspective. Only internally imposed requirements or cross-border regulations may add to the mix.

Evaluating the Privately Held For-Profit Setting

There are still many external regulatory factors placing requirements on privately held companies, and the threat of litigation from inappropriate disclosure of personally identifying or HIPAA- (Health Insurance Portability and Accountability Act) related information is just as risky for them. This category of companies may not be under the same microscope examination, but nevertheless the companies must pay attention to the factors that will influence the adequacy of controls.

Smaller companies may also be very dependant on keeping trade secrets and protecting intellectual property and, as a result, may need to place a higher value on adequate controls to protect the company's assets.

No matter their origin, control requirements can be satisfied within the same design framework.

Evaluating the Government Sector

Every week, the news media reports some dreadful story on the inadequacy of data protection and failure of internal access controls within the federal government. States also have horrific shortcomings in keeping citizens' data private. Local units of government in a rush to make things easily available on the Web have all but ignored steps to control inappropriate access to what should be private information.

Governments at all levels are prime targets for hackers and crackers because of the large amounts of aggregated personal data held in trust by them. It's easy for a thief to use information from a public database to steal a financial identity.

The same framework, designs, and infrastructure that protect private enterprise financial statements from unauthorized access can be used to protect government systems. When you reduce the design requirements to the lowest common denominators, the requirements are similar from one type of organization to another.

Evaluating the Nonprofit Sector

Although faced with a requirement for accurate tax exemption reporting, the nonprofit sector is not quite as highly regulated as public, for-profit companies. Still, the IT architecture team must be fully aware of the regulatory and constituent factors that that will influence designs. Nonprofits are a rich environment for potential identity theft just because of their membership lists. They may well be having difficulty finding the financial resources to build adequate controls and defenses for their computer systems.

The depth of external criteria leading the nonprofit sector's requirements for security controls may be shallower, but if those organizations have open, protected, and restricted data, their access frameworks will contain the same design details as the for-profit and government sectors. They need a similar infrastructure to protect their digital resources.

It's All in the Details

A portrait frame is not an integral part of a displayed oil painting, but it can make or break the effect the painting has on the viewer. When a painting's frame is carefully selected so that it and painting to work together, they become nearly inseparable in the eye of the beholder. The IT architecture security and access controls designers are on the opposite end of the challenge spectrum. Like it or not, they are dealt a multifaceted framework in which to operate. The framework is very much in place, and they must be fully aware of the implications of its existence and impact. Their framework is also likely to change on the side of additional control requirements over time.

I cannot emphasize enough the importance of taking the time to seek out the framework's details and document them to benefit the design team's work. Multinational companies, for example, need to know exactly how operating security access controls and protecting privacy information differ across borders. This knowledge enables designers to find the toughest common denominator and design to that standard, or to isolate and design to the exceptions if that strategy proves most cost-effective.

Within the United States, Sarbanes-Oxley, HIPAA, and the Gramm-Leach-Bliley Act (the Financial Modernization Act of 1999) all play important roles in determining what must be included in access control, identity accountability, and audit features for computer systems that support operating your business. Companies that do business across state borders must design access controls and privacy protection strategies that will meet the regulatory requirements within all the states in which they do business.

Sizing Up the Framework

After the design team has garnered all of the internal and external influences, it must turn each of the details into finite technical requirements for the design of access controls and data protection measures.

To begin the process, list the legal and regulatory requirements as the top bar of the framework. Then translate each law or regulation into the technical requirements.

The desires of internal constituents also deserve consideration. Employees may want to choose whether their personal information held by human resources can be shared over the Internet, for example. The technical requirement for that would be an on-off Internet flag in the directory that controls access to the employee HR (human resources Web applications. External constituencies may want to post information to company message boards on such matters as global warming or environmental cleanup. A company could facilitate the message board on a by-name basis to build good will and get some positive PR with green-sensitive groups.

All organizations and their IT architecture design efforts will be enhanced from taking the time to recognize outside influences (see Figure 4-1) that inevitably becomes expectations surrounding the design work. These expectations can be translated into design requirements when practical. There is also benefit in knowing ahead of time which ones cannot be reasonably met.

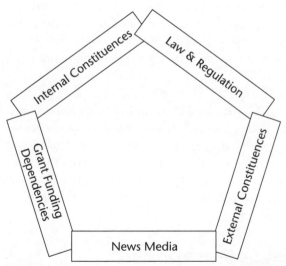

Figure 4-1   Influences create a framework for IT designs.

The array of framework elements must be translated into thorough requirements of sufficient detail for the technical staff to understand what must be done within the programming tools and within the applications and programs.

Understanding Business Drivers

After considering external influences, the architecture design team must capture the effect on design of the internal business drivers as completely as possible. Using more technology to solve every problem in an organization's portfolio is not always the answer. Business drivers are multifaceted. Drivers such as international competition, external regulatory power, and growing stockholder influence can impact the direction of a company on a large scale. Those types of external drivers filter down into technical requirements for an IT architecture team to develop.

Other business drivers originate within the IT division and, if allowed to proceed, not only influence the technical design criteria but have the potential to exert a positive influence on a company. Often these internal drivers are discounted, set aside because management is too quick to try to tie them directly to the financial bottom line with some return on investment criteria.

The most popular buzzword in IT discussions and trade journals lately is ROI (return on investment). Some very necessary investments in technology may never have a traceable and readily quantifiable return. Some investments will only keep your company in business and the returns (gains) will have to be found elsewhere. Providing an ROI case for every technology investment is difficult at best, particularly for those investments whose successful result can only be expressed as, "Our data was not stolen and our systems have not been hacked."

Consider the perceived value of security investments. What factors force security requirements in your organization? In most companies using computer systems, the adequacy and effectiveness of overall security controls and the capability to audit the accuracy and propriety of financial processes and reports are at least in part reliant on the success of the entire body of computer controls. How do you quantify an ROI on investments that improve overall security of access controls and protection of valuable data when management's perception is that the data is already protected?

Using Security Controls as Business Drivers

In the year 2000, security discussions often started with the question, "How much security is enough?" That was soon followed by, "How much security can our organization afford?" And then by, "What is the return on investment in security?" If your company is still having discussions like this on the topic of digital security, it is time to take stock of how the world has changed since 2000.

Having sufficient security defensive measures and adequate access controls is no longer an option for systems on any network. Government seems to add more regulatory and oversight standards every day. The auditors and associates sent from audit firms to check your books are becoming much more technologically astute and are attending the same security seminars that only IT staff was present for in the past. The body of knowledge of what constitutes adequate protection of data is also expanding rapidly across all sectors of the economy.

The awareness of security breaches is propelled across all sectors by the news media because organizations in every sector and division of the economy fail to some classic hack or have been infected by malicious code or, worse, victimized by internal wrongdoing gone undetected for a long time. Privacy advocates continue to lobby for additional required measures to protect personally identifying and financial information.

If all of that isn't enough, the civil courts are becoming the battleground for fault finding when organizations' security is breached and harm finds victims because control methods and mechanisms proved seriously wanting.

Security concerns alone render sufficient reason for using a formal architecture design process and a highly disciplined approach to protect information technology systems, networks, and applications. Reactionary approaches to security design place the hackers at an advantage and the IT staff in a no-win downward spiral of iterations of discovery, patch, and run.

Security is hard to measure. The minimum acid test must be as follows:

- Is the security as good as it can be?
- Have you afforded sufficient resources to expect to be successful at protecting the data?
- Has the security investment been worth it?

There is no ROI in failing to provide adequate security controls in your organization regardless of the sector or business you are in. Regardless of how your company goes about evaluating improvement projects and new IT initiatives, do not get caught in the trap of failing to do what is needed to protect digital assets, because the ROI is hard to find and quantify. Accept that security controls and protective measures are one of the external forces, and do all that can be done within your available resources to get it right. In the process, try to avoid the flavor of the week products that waste resources and deliver little added security value.

Using Increased Efficiency as a Business Driver

Expectations that IT projects increase efficiency apply to all manner and types of organizations. New projects, applications, and software products are often presented to management clothed in the garment of increased efficiency.

Elements that enhance effectiveness, however, do not always translate directly into dollar savings. For example, employee stress levels strained by a high volume of calls may be the reason an organization has extraordinary turnover in frontline help desk support staff. Adding self-administration of forgotten password resets from a Web page could cut help desk calls by two-thirds, reduce call volumes to average levels, and lower employee stress levels. Help desk staff turnover would return to normal levels, training costs for new staff would be reduced, quality of service would increase, and overall employee satisfaction with the IT department would improve — all of which may not have been evident to you when first considering the ROI for deploying the self-service password Web portal.

In selling an investment to management, there's no reason to make leaps of faith on what efficiency the project may bring, but it is sensible to at least list the secondary benefits that might accrue from doing the project. That list can be presented simply as potential benefits in addition to the hard values that are easily quantifiable.

CAUTION Any ROI formula that stretches time frames excessively for IT projects should be carefully scrutinized for risk factors because technology may change more rapidly than the formula expects.

Using Profit as a Business Driver

IT improvements and projects from IT architecture efforts that propel ROI above zero and add to the bottom line of the organization are the most desired. Because returns cannot be guaranteed, such projects bring additional risk factors along with the profit potential. Secondary benefits are not an applicable consideration here; the ROI analysis must be on hard, traceable returns that are expected to result in direct increases in after-tax profits.

The methodical application of the IT architecture process can easily identify this type of project and improvement. Improving security and access controls within projects of this nature need not be cost-justified on their own merits. The controls' costs simply become part of the necessary investment to move the project from plan to production.

Using Competitive Advantage as a Business Driver

Do you think that having the best possible data protective measures, access controls, audit compliance, and privacy protection measures can bring your organization a competitive advantage? It can if the consumers of your services know about it and the news media reports on it. Failing to attain adequate protection could certainly put you out of business — consumers tend to aban-don organizations with negative reputations from an inability to meet the publics' expectations for security.

Seeking IT projects that will provide competitive advantage requires empowering the visionaries in your organization to engage in "no bad ideas" discussions. Then take each of the resulting ideas through the IT design process to identify those with sufficient merit to consider for funding and implementation. Clearly this can be interesting for the staff involved and valu-able to any organization focused on future performance.

Using Risk Reduction as a Business Driver

Risk reduction as a business driver includes those strategies that reduce, miti-gate, or avoid the risk factors regardless of the way risk is quantified. Reaching a zero state of risk for a modern organization is improbable if not impossible. IT designs can support or enhance the risk reduction strategies in play in an organization. Strategies are often combined to reduce the risks, mitigate the effect of risks should they occur, and attempt to avoid risk in certain projects altogether all at the same time.

One of the best ways to show business management the risks the company's current technology environment is facing is to do "friendly intrusions." That is, hire a company to hack into your systems, if possible, to expose your weak-nesses and data. Not every organization is willing to do this (nor is every IT professional, for fear of being fired). When system vulnerabilities and data are exposed, the risks appear more real, although no less difficult to apply an ROI to combating the weakness. If the company president's Social Security number is hacked, of course, the risk reduction measure's message may get through without having to attach a dollar amount.

In some cases, attaching a dollar figure to risk reduction initiatives may be possible. The cost of mitigating the repairs after a computer virus attack may be known, for example, and so might the dollar value of the many person-hours it takes to repair desktops and the lost productivity of business staff resulting from poor access controls that allowed the virus to vector into the systems. What is not known is the dollar value of controls that prevent the infection from happening. How many viruses will not enter the systems in the future remains unknown.

Using Values as Drivers and Boundaries

Boardroom values become drivers, boundaries, or both for the IT architecture design team. In any case, the design team must be cognizant of them. The less intangible or idealistic values of an organization such as "don't build it if you can buy it" and "avoid solutions that add to staffing levels" are conceivably major influences on the IT architecture. There is no point in designing an infrastructure that is outside of what management would support. The design team needs to be aware of the company's existing boundaries, whether cost- or business risk-related, and have a good idea of what is possible to achieve and what solution sets to avoid.

When a company values a high level of control and is willing to be responsible for its own information technology systems, there is a strong bias for doing things in-house. Contractors and consultants help internal staff along on new projects when needed, but the ultimate control and responsibility for daily operations or new implementation projects rests within the CIO's staff, and the boardroom values the capability to control outcomes.

Another organization's management may have the opposite values and may want to outsource most or all of its IT operations because of a belief that with the outsourcing goes the responsibility. While responsibility for the duties associated with daily operations of IT systems may be easily distanced from management through outsourcing, the liability for the adequacy of controls and privacy protection may not be fully transferred. Contractual relationships include having satisfactory language to define your needs for the security components.

The organization's values certainly will influence how IT design objectives are accomplished. The IT architecture team must take the time to become knowledgeable of the management values and accommodate those influences in their processes. Even if outsourcing may be the guidance received, it is still necessary to figure out and articulate the objectives and requirements in total to include in any procurement contract or service agreements for external services. In the same way, a company placing a high value on using business partners to help achieve short-term objectives may lead to doing a staged implementation of the design with multiple sources of outside assistance over time.

Understanding Infrastructure

Certainly, designing an entire IT system's infrastructure from the ground up is the dream job of every CTO (chief technology officer). Rarely do such opportunities present themselves, though. In most cases the company's CTO and IT design teams start with what is already in place. Inherited infrastructures are often hard to rip out and replace because computers, applications, and networks have to support the added business with its existing processes for some number of months.

Organizations facing the need for improvements may be heavily invested in existing infrastructure. Parts of that infrastructure may have been planned, while other parts may have been added simply as an outcome of decisions that occurred over time with no real spotlight on a vision for what it should become.

As you begin sizing up infrastructure, reflect on how the following essential considerations will play out in your design elements:

- Life cycle of devices
- Security policies
- Physical access controls

Assessing Device Life Cycles

Infrastructure is the hard goods in the IT space. It is those things that are physical or operate at a physical level: the servers, networks, routers, switches, and even the desktops, notebooks, and handheld equipment. Nothing lasts forever, so each of these items of infrastructure has an expected life cycle.

Things that influence the life cycle are the availability of in-kind replacements, spare parts, and factory-authorized support. Operating system and firmware support also affect the length of the life cycle of infrastructure items. As you classify and categorize the items in your design or existing environment, some thought should go to calculating a reasonable expected service life of each component. (Categories are discussed in the "Exploring Infrastructure Categories" section later in the chapter.) The expected service life for items in each category enables you to plan a replacement cycle for that category of goods, making budget forecasting easier.

Each time equipment replacement occurs, there's a potential impact on the architecture functionality because newer, better, faster, or improved versions may allow for added features that were not practical with the earlier versions of the equipment. Consideration for the influence of device life cycles on the various components of infrastructure should lead to a replacement or upgrade schedule. A plan may put desktop replacements in year one, servers in year two, application software in year three, network equipment in year four, and so on as a starting point. That approach gives a resident IT architecture team an opportunity to get in front of the challenges that will come with changes to each of the categories.

Applying Security Policies

Each major category of infrastructure also provides the prospect of applying general and at times specific security policies or access controls across the entire category of equipment. End-user access to notebook computers, for example, will likely involve a very different access control method than allowing an administrator to change a router configuration. User ID and password may be OK for access to a notebook with word processing software. The router configuration changes may warrant a two-factor authentication in addition to the user ID and password.

Examine the broad categories of devices for beginning the policy process to help manage and apply protection to the entire group.

Evaluating Physical Access Controls

Physical access controls are also applied to each category in the infrastructure. The controls could range from antitheft straps and locks for notebooks all the way up to requiring retina scan for access to client/server rooms.

Your controls may require that all endpoint switches and hubs be behind locked doors, with each port on the switch as a managed access point correlated with a specific desktop. The more detailed and specialized security policy domains may require more barriers and higher controls.

Always develop policy from the general (applies to all equipment in category) to the specific (applies only to a select group of exceptions where the policy may increase or relax access control). Limit the exceptions to one or very few, and have good reasons to support the need for the separate treatment. Be sure that relaxed levels for one group do not compromise the security profile for the other items in the category.

Exploring Infrastructure Categories

Designers are often faced with the economic reality that they must use as much of the existing infrastructure as possible in any new implementation project. The challenges in revising and reusing the current infrastructure are not insurmountable and can still potentially lead to adequate designs for authentication and access controls. Each infrastructure category has its some of its own conditions and trials. What are these categories? Here's a basic list them:

- Handheld devices
- Notebooks and portables
- Desktop and tower computers
- Host systems
- Networking components

It isn't an exhaustive list, and your organization may be much more or less complex. Your IT access control architecture design team is responsible for how controls will be orchestrated within the categories.

It is OK to decide that one category or another in your environment does not need to have controls applied, but do not decide that controls aren't necessary without understanding the implications and risks of that determination.

Assessing Handheld Devices

It may be difficult to think of small, portable handheld devices as part of infrastructure, but they are. You at least need to recognize very portable processing equipment in terms of surrounding their use with policies in a security policy domain. Then you need to enforce the policies.

This category includes all of the little USB memory chips (flash drives, key drives, and so on), as well as cell phones, PDAs (personal digital assistants), and any hand-sized computing devices — basically any small device with the capability to process, store, or transmit data.

This is a high-risk category for two reasons. First, small items can easily "walk off." They are easy to pocket and easy to lose. Any data on these devices is liable to find its way to outsiders, whether by theft or by accident. And second, it is difficult to apply meaningful controls to these devices, and they don't yet come bundled with outstanding security features. These devices should hold company secrets only if the files are password-protected and encrypted.

People in a hurry to get home may forget the precautionary procedures to password-protect and encrypt a spreadsheet saved to a USB memory device, so the biggest challenge is training users to take the steps needed to protect the information. That training is critical if your company values its data.

Assessing Notebooks and Portables of All Sizes

As with handheld equipment, heavier, fully functioning portable computers provide means for data escape. They also frequently are the inroad for malicious code from road warriors' use of public wireless hot spots.

The more developed operating systems on modern notebook computers provide built-in access control and security features. The boot-up firmware can be password-protected, and eventually use of a token card in a USB slot may become commonplace as an additional security feature. Security can be layered in at the firmware boot-up and OS boot-up; passwords can be required to access an application; data file access can be password- and encryption-protected when stored. If keeping the data in the device is important, all of these will be done for starters.

Adding features such as personal firewall software, virus protection software, and spyware detection software will improve the security control profile for protecting portable computers. Using host-scanning features to verify system integrity when those devices are back on the organization network is also a good practice to protect the stay-at-home devices and internal company networks from the introduction of malicious code.

Assessing Desktop and Tower Computers

Larger personal computers share many of the features mentioned in the previous section. No need to list them again. As with notebooks, added access protections such as password-protected idle time-out screen savers can also be deployed on these devices to enhance security.

In most corporate environments, desktops and docked laptops are used to connect to networks and enterprise-level applications where additional controls can limit access to networks and isolate access to file areas and print services. Every security feature available in the desktop environment needs to be considered in relation to both the devices and what each end user will see or share with other users once the access is granted.

Assessing Host Systems

Client/server hosts, file and print servers, database servers, data marts and data warehouses, and mainframes all promote similar concerns regarding access controls. Controls have to incorporate all the various types of uses the devices accommodate. Will access be through an intermediary device, such as an appliance? Will the appliance handle user identification and authentication, or will end-user access be granted right to the host device operating system?

Design of access controls for this category of devices must take into account hosts accessing other hosts through applications, and end users accessing host operating systems and applications, as well as the needs of the system administrators and application developers. The help-desk staff could be another group whose controls must be considered. Do they get to see protected data or not?

As with the previous categories, each opportunity for applying an access or security control must be considered for implementation. Always default on the side of using all control points the hardware, operating systems, and application software provide. In a sense, your organization has already paid for those on the systems you are using.

Chapter 10 discusses how this control environment is integrated and simplified to the extent possible.

Assessing Networking Components

The IT architecture team assigned to design network security for an existing network may have a much harder time implementing adequate controls strategies than someone designing an all new networks with the most current equipment. Networks have many varied characteristics that at fundamental levels allow for increased or decreased levels of controls. Opportunities to apply controls differ substantially based on the age of the networking equipment. Other characteristics such as routed portions of the network in contrast with switched portions allow for different control technologies. If the network is shared in a cloud configuration with other organizations, you may have to conform to the control rules imposed in shared-use agreements.

Each time the characteristics of the network change — from wide area to local, for example — the control possibilities change as well. Even within a switched environment, some equipment designs allow access management controls right to individual ports. Routers can also be used as firewalls with additional software and configuration parameters, increasing the range of possible controls.

Summary

Success increases and time to deliver decreases for an IT design team that begins with external forces, internal influences, and the existing infrastructure investment in technology. Mid-level details and then the finer levels of detail follow these major influences. Always try to move the team's treatment of the work from the general to the more specific.

Start the platform-specific design effort by beginning with those closest to the end user and moving up the tiers from appliance to mainframe appropriate. Begin network design in the same way, by focusing on the end users' needs and building the network to the hosts in depth. Be sure to keep the opportunities (the nodes) where access controls can be applied prominent in the documentation. The nodes are critical points for detail design coordination for the controls and any intended implementation of identity management and provisioning. Take advantage of every practical opportunity to implement access controls or authentication measures.

Chapter 5 discusses the essential components of security that are applied to the infrastructure controls highlighted in this chapter.

Simplifying the Security Matrix

The success of modern IT systems security controls rests in seven essential elements that compose the security matrix (see Figure 5-1):

- Identification
- Authentication
- Authorization
- Access control
- Administration
- Auditing
- Assessment

The strengths of each matrix element in your access controls design and implementation are combined to determine the overall strength of your system's security profile. Weakness in any element impairs your security.

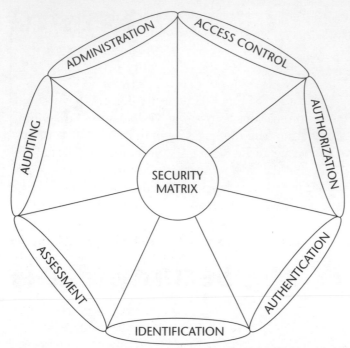

Figure 5-1 Security matrix elements combine to create the overall security profile.

These seven topic areas are the substance in which information technology security originates. Even among some security professionals, the definitions or roles of these essential elements of security are not universally understood. For example, one area of that is often misconstrued is the limits of today's technology for providing nonrepudiation from authentication methods. Online financial transactions and business processes seek assurance that the person logged in is the one whose identity is being used. In legal terms, the assurance sought is defined as nonrepudiation. The level of trust that can be placed in any authentication method is not absolute regardless of the technology. Some methods are better than others, and it is important to grasp the remaining risks for the choices made.

This chapter clearly defines all seven elements of the security matrix, sets their boundaries, and explains how they are combined in creating more secure access controls, as well as how they work interactively to enhance overall system and application security.

Understanding Identification

In the impersonal space of the Internet or on a company intranet, how can you be certain the end user is really who he or she claims to be? How do you know the purported identity is valid? Similarly, with a hacker's ability to spoof IP addresses, devices with firmware capable of mimicking MAC addresses, and just about any firewall's capability to NAT (Network Address Translation) IP addresses, how do you achieve certainty in the identity of a device to be granted access rights to another device on your secure network?

How much confidence do you have in the true identity of a person or device trying to gain access to your applications? How much reliance are you willing to place on that identity being the true identity? Keep in mind that your systems only see the digital username and whatever is presented as a digital credential. Anyone could be at the distant end trying to log in to your systems with stolen or guessed credentials. It is important to differentiate between the true identity of a device or person and a username as a representation of that identity.

Do not confuse identity with any of the other elements in the matrix. Someone or something is simply purporting to be someone you want to deal with through your networks, computer systems, or applications by entering a username the system is supposed to recognize. Build your acceptance of any class of usernames on the up-front vetting of users and a process to issue unique usernames. There is a very low limit to how much confidence can be placed in the identity element by itself. If the syntax of your usernames is known, for example, then guessing one is made easier.

A Case of Mistaken Identity

A mid-Michigan radio call-in show receives a request for some Moody Blues songs. The caller has a strong Scottish-sounding brogue and identifies himself as Sean. He says he is calling on a cell phone from his limousine as he's traveling from Detroit to Grand Rapids. The DJ, a young woman, is excited about talking with a celebrity, a superstar (namely, Sean Connery) and plays the songs the caller requested; in the interludes she talks about her favorite big-screen flicks in which he starred. There is only one problem; that day Sean Connery was somewhere in the British Isles.

To give the DJ some credit, it did sound an awful lot like him, but it simply wasn't him. It was a classic case of mistaken identity. The credential that was presented — the sound of a voice with a distinctive brogue — was not sufficient to be certain of the identity of the caller.

Exploring Paper Credentials

Identification is all about lifting the mask and finding the unique person or device hidden under it. A person's identity — those things that make one person unique from everyone else — begins with parentage and is refined by culture and life experiences.

A collection of paperwork and databases are created over time to collect information about who you are and what you have done. The state issues a birth certificate, and a birth certificate is used to obtain a Social Security number. Teenagers generally need both of these forms of identity to obtain a driver's license or check-cashing identity card in their state of residence.

Your birth certificate, SSN, and driver's license do not make you unique. They are merely representations that are recognized and usually accepted as credentials verifying that you are who you claim to be. Each of these documents can be forged easily, yet for practicality in commerce, they are accepted at financial institutions, convenience and retail stores, and any place where identity may be checked or challenged.

The process of creating these paper credentials includes someone else certifying the identity's reliability. Doctors sign birth certificates, parents or guardians sign young drivers' first license application forms, and the Social Security Administration trusts parents' application information for issuing an SSN to a child. This is an old method. Centuries ago, for example, a letter of introduction introduced someone sent far from home for the purpose of commerce. A known person signed a document saying the presenter of the document could be accepted as an agent of the signor.

NOTE In the past, many surnames assigned to people dealt with conferring identity. John, Jacob's son, for example, would become John Jacobson, while Peter, the local baker, might become known as Peter Baker, and Edward, a stonemason, would become Edward Mason. Similarly, a man named Geoffrey who lived in London in very early times and might have moved to a small village elsewhere in Britain would've become known as Geoffrey of London or simply Geoffrey London. Charles, who lived by the brook, was eventually know as — you guessed it — Charles Brook. This simplicity of identity worked well in local areas and sufficed when people traveled only short distances.

It is impossible to look at the paper identity credentials half a nation or world away, so credentials in which some level of trust can be placed must be used to create digital identities in the Web environment.

Vetting All New Users

In the digital arena, identities are handled with no greater inherent reliability than paper credentials are. When a new person is hired into your organization, a human resources staff member accepts the SSN, driver's license, high school and college diplomas, and identity cards as positive enough proof that Molly is who she purports to be. Even if she is not really Molly, these documents are usually accepted at face value as sufficient proof of a valid identity.

Scams against for-profits, nonprofits, and government bodies often occur because these documents are faked. How can you be sure of an identity? Well, you cannot always be certain. The risk of mistaken identity can only be reduced. To do so, expand the vetting process to verify the accuracy and increase the reliance you can put on the data making up the identity. Among other things, you can check other sources of information and compare that with the information the new hire presented on the application. For example, you can

- Actually call the references listed.
- Call landlord references.
- Check credit bureau reports.
- Check law enforcement or court records and online criminal records.
- Check online background search sites.
- Verify phone numbers (can be done online, along with reverse lookups of phone numbers to addresses).
- Verify professional licenses on official state Web sites.

Online search tools make checking someone's paper credential validity easier than ever. Encourage your HR department to use the online services when it's appropriate. For sensitive positions, of course, your company may want to do a formal investigation.

Only after your organization's vetting process is completed should a new hire be granted any access to systems containing confidential categories of information. Temporary access to protected resources for unvetted users is very risky at best.

Exploring Digital Identity

The United States is not yet to the point of issuing everyone national ID cards with RFID (radio frequency identification) chips inside, so for practical access to systems and applications, your organization's HR office likely requests some form of digital credential for each employee from the IT department.

A digital credential is no different from an ID card in the physical world. It's used to represent the person for access to end-user workstations, networks, and computer applications. The digital ID is simply the username or user ID (a username is often referred to as a user ID) — a series of keystrokes that is unique to your organization and can be used to purport an identity to the networks, computers, and applications.

The digital representation of a person's identity is no different from one in the paper world. The risks are nearly identical, and a user ID can be compromised in some of the same ways a driver's license number can be. A user ID can be guessed, stolen and used by someone else, lost, or forgotten.

Some IT systems use other digital ID means, such as magnetic swipe cards, RFID chips, and similar technologies, which are not necessarily any better for representing identity. These technologies are better used as a part of the authentication discussion. They are practical as identity information only in that they may save the steps of entering the user ID into a keyboard. They do nothing to enhance the concept of identity because there's really no difference between a username being typed in or read from some card. It is still just someone on the distant end of a wire purporting to be some identity that your systems and application are supposed to recognize and grant some services to.

Identifying Devices

Research each device you intend to use or in which you're already invested, and learn what features are present in the hardware, firmware, or software that run it that can present the device's identity to the network or to other devices. Determine if using them can increase the overall access control and security strategy for your systems and applications.

TIPS FOR INCREASING USERNAME SECURITY

Here are some steps that can be taken to enhance the credibility of an access user ID:

- Use a very wide field for entering the user ID in login screens even if the IDs require fewer keystrokes. This makes a hacker's attempts more difficult because the length also has to be guessed.

- Require your system and application end users to keep not only their usernames secret but the syntax secret as well. If a hacker does not know the required orderly arrangement, attempts to breach through with a valid identity will be more difficult.

- Do not use lame, easy-to-guess combinations such as last name and first initial as starting points for usernames.

- Use a different syntax for each group of users to make internal attempts to breach user identity more difficult. Do not select obvious patterns such as appending to user Dave the letters "acctn" because he works in accounting or to Mary "purc" because she is in purchasing.

There is little or no cost involved in implementing these ideas, and by doing so, the user ID becomes more passwordlike. The fact that it is a kept secret, there is no apparent like syntax and no obvious connection to a person's identity information, and no two employees with the same job share a same syntax all help to complicate attempts to inappropriately co-opt a coworker's username.

The newer the devices you are using, the more likely identity features are available. List the features presented for each device, and establish whether there is value in using each of them in your environment; have a good reason to reject their use. For example, a router can be configured simply to route network traffic, to move data packets to the correct communication pipelines. That same router may be capable of supporting IPSec or 3DES encryption of the traffic, or may support inline intrusion prevention. Some routers, properly configured, can also function as a firewall. Frequently systems are breached because manufacturer's available features were not used, despite those features having no negatives attached to their use in the IT environment. Don't let that happen to the systems for which you are responsible.

Understanding Authentication

Authentication is all about increasing the level of confidence that can be placed in an identity, source, or message. A message can be wrapped in authentication methods to ensure that it is kept secret and has not changed en route to its destination. The focus of this authentication is on identity and source, because these aspects relate directly to access and security controls.

The level of confidence you can routinely place in the identity of an end user, device, or system-to-system process is based on the authentication method. Identity answers the question, who are you going to try to authenticate? Authentication deals entirely with how you will accept the username as having a sufficient level of genuineness that access to networks, host systems, applications, or data can be granted.

Vetting a user determines if the digital identity about to be issued is to someone whose identity data can be considered accurate. If the identity can be trusted sufficiently, a username is assigned to the person. A username could be thought of as the person's digital persona. A correlation is made between the identity and the networks, systems, applications, and data that are going to be made routinely available to that user. With the username as the starting point, various methods of authentication must be decided and imposed on it.

The authentication method imposes a barrier on access. In the physical world, you lock things — doors, offices, file cabinets, and so forth — and issue keys or combination numbers to open the locks. High-tech methods for physical access use thumbprint readers and eye retina scanners to grant access, which, in effect, makes you the "key" — it is something that you are or is a part of you that gets you in the door. Banking systems allow you to get money from cash machines when you identify your bank account by swiping the card through the reader and authenticate with a PIN (personal identification number), often called, rather redundantly, a PIN number Your garage door opener at home may open when you enter a simple PIN in a keypad. All of these examples apply a method of authentication to grant physical entry to something.

Access authentication methods can also be combined, providing multiple barriers to entry. For example, you may require a key for the first lock, a combination for the second, and a retina scanner or perhaps a swipe card for the third.

Concepts for authentication in the digital environments are not much different than the physical environment. The most common way authentication is imposed is to have a username used in conjunction with a secret password. When someone signs up for an e-mail account from one of the Internet's sources for free Web mail accounts, for instance, an automated process is used to test the suggested account username against existing usernames to ensure it is unique to that e-mail domain. After a username is established, the account applicant enters a password that meets the provider's password creation policy, and an account is created. There is no vetting; anyone can get an account and pretend to be anyone he or she wants to be as far as the identifying information goes.

Those e-mail accounts are examples of a nonexistent identification vetting process followed by the use of the most common authentication method, a simple user-selected password. The password is intended to let only that user, whoever he or she is, back in to use the system to send and receive e-mail, but of course anyone entering the correct username and password can access the account. Use of a free-for-all enrollment process such as this should be limited to accessing only zero-risk resources and data.

Authentication methods used to access protected resources begin with some confidence in the identity of the end user and are applied in ladder fashion, with username and password on the first rung. An added method, such as a PIN with username and password, takes the second rung. As the methods are added one rung at a time (see Figure 5-2), confidence should increase that the end user is who or what he/she/it purports to be. Strengthened confidence in the authentication is also thought to increase nonrepudiation from a legal perspective.

NOTE Some would argue that 100 percent nonrepudiation is not possible with electronic methods. The reality is that when legal disputes arise over who really did or did not trigger the online transaction, it is decided by the courts on a case-by-case basis from the evidence available.

The increase in security beyond the use of a two-factor token card in the top two methods is somewhat subtle because how they are actually deployed contributes to their power. If, for example, digital certificates are issued to the end user by a third party whose vetting of identity is less than perfect, confidence would naturally be less. Similarly, if in the deployment, bio scan data is simply used to input username identity information and the actual authentication method is a password, it adds little beyond convenience.

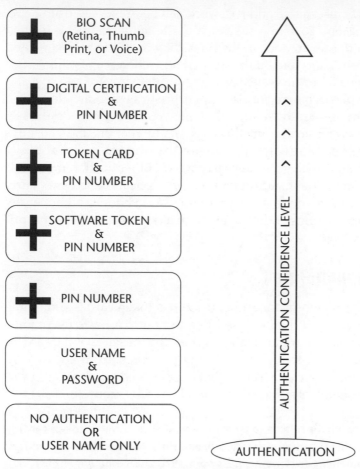

Figure 5-2 Authentication methods increase confidence levels.

Although not the easiest to set up, the token card is predicted to become the gold standard for authentication in the near term (two to five years). Its strengths are explored in Chapter 12.

Using Username, Password, and PIN

A number of methods and products are on the market to improve the confidence in authentication of end users beyond username and password. A very simple addition is requiring the use of a PIN to access applications once a user has been authenticated by username and password to a Web portal or sign-on screen.

Some products can help by associating a biometric reader, such as a retina scanner and record, with the username. If the retina scan does not match the stored information, the username and password can be prevented from being forwarded by the local host to gain system access. The retina scanner is likened to having the key to the storm door in the physical world; the username and password open the inner door only if the storm door (retina scan is successful) has already been opened. Products such as biometric devices also add cost and implementation complexity; there are also support issues when they fail, often requiring site visits by IT staff to repair.

Adding layers of authentication methods assists in keeping the bad guys out while facilitating your increased confidence that the true person is provided the access required. The username/password authentication method is very inexpensive to implement. Adding a PIN for application access is fairly simple as well. All are based on requiring the end user to know, and hopefully remember, some simple strings of data to enter on a keyboard at the appropriate points in the sign-on process.

Using Token Card and PIN

Sometimes referred to as two-factor authentication, a token card is something that you carry with you and is often used in addition to a basic username/password/PIN combination. A card reader verifies the presence of the card, or the user enters a time-generated random string of numbers from a view window on the card. An authentication server that is associated with that card verifies that the random-number string entered by the user is accurate.

NOTE The term *two-factor* relates to a user's *having* something (a token card) and *knowing* something (username, password, and PIN). The two factors could also be *knowing* something (username, password, PIN) and *being* something (biometrics' optical scan, for example).

There are basically two types of token cards. One type has a magnetic strip much like credit cards and bank cards. Other cards in the same category may use a small, embedded chip that returns a signal to a card reader. Card readers are often used at entryways to buildings, usually with a PIN, to grant access. Regardless of the card's underlying technology, the end user is required to carry something that a hacker would not have. If the card is stolen, the thief still must know or guess the PIN to gain access.

As you evaluate card products, be sure you fully understand what their different technologies are actually doing. It may help to equate the features to the physical: locks, keys, combinations, and code word pairs. A card reader that merely saves an end user from keying in identity information may not necessarily add any security value. Don't confuse convenience of use with added security.

The second type of token card adds a time-dependant feature. The card has an embedded clock that constantly spools off to a digital display window what appears to be random numbers. A username identity is associated with the card, and the user must enter the token-generated number plus a PIN into the keyboard when requested to do so. A calculation is made from a seed record associated uniquely with each card against a time clock to match the card-generated number, so that a token number is valid for only about a minute. The card is time-synchronized with an authentication server that is capable of calculating what the number should be.

There is five-way connection with timed token cards: A username identity (1) is associated with a token card (2); the user must enter the token-generated number (3) plus a PIN (4); and a calculation (5) is made from a seed record associated uniquely with each card against a time clock to match the card-generated number. The authentication is dependant on knowing the username associated with the token, knowing the username's password, having the token card to acquire the random number, and knowing the PIN.

It is the level of complexity that makes this one of the best available methods of authentication. Newer variations of time-dependant token cards can be plugged into a port on a computer to relieve the end user from having to manually enter the random number the card generates. It adds a degree of difficulty for implementation because you need to include the authentication server, its maintenance and management, license fees, and administration of the issue process. There is also an implementation development requirement to integrate use of the token cards with networks, servers, and applications. Random-number token cards simply make hack attempts very difficult because a would-be hacker is trying to guess at a moving target — the ever-changing random number string. (And the hacker would also need the card's username/password/PIN combination to get any use out of the card.)

Using Software Tokens

An alternative to having the end user carry around a random-number token card is to use a small software application that can be loaded on various types of end-user devices from handheld to notebooks to desktop computers.

The software performs a similar job to the token card. When a computer or device is first placed on the network that is hosting the authentication server, it is synchronized from the authentication server. After the initial synchronization, the computer or device can generate its own random-number string from the software that will match the calculation expectation of the authentication server.

The end user is still required to enter a PIN to complete the process.

Using Biological Scans

Biological scans include any scanner or reader that can match a scanned biological feature of an individual such as voice prints, fingerprints, face recognition, or retina with an electronic record of a previous scan. A scan can be associated with username and user password, and can also require a PIN entry as well to add confidence.

This method has not garnered widespread acceptance because of the additional equipment need, and perhaps because quite a few people think that bio scans are little freaky, and some consider them downright objectionable.

Scans change authentication to include presence (being there). Add them to something you have (token card) and things you know (password and PIN), and you've got a pretty good authentication system. On a confidence scale, though, how big a difference is there between having a token card and a PIN and being there for a bio scan with a PIN? Not very much difference; certainly not always enough difference to justify the additional equipment required to do bio scans.

Using Digital Certificates

Digital certificates with public and private key pairs are another way to authenticate a username. A third party issues digital certificates to both parties (users or devices) involved in the transaction while implying some vetting of both parties' identity. A common use of digital certificates is to authenticate to a Web site. The Web server will have a digital certificate loaded with a publicly available key. The end –user's computer will have a certificate loaded that is invoked only when the password is entered correctly, after which the Web service grants some trust in the identity of the user.

To use the digital certificate as an authentication process to verify that a particular end user is on the other end, a certificate is loaded on the user's computer. The certificate is launched for use in the interaction between the user and a host Web server with a PIN or password, proving that at least there is a person on that computer who knows the password. Hopefully, it is the person whose username it is purported to be.

Understanding Authorization

The end users on your systems have been assigned unique identities. Your security design determined which authentication methods are to be used at various access points. Now the association between an end user and right of entry becomes a one-to-many mapping of relationships between usernames and the networks, computer hosts, printers, applications, and data stores to which users can be granted access.

Various influences converge to create the map for any given user. Location, workgroup, job assignment, security clearance, need to know, matrix team assignments, system domains, application access needs, and assigned projects could each play a role in determining what a particular user should be granted authorization to use. The decisions are business or operational in nature; technology plays a low-key role at this stage. The technologies applied to achieve authentication, authorization, and access controls are facilitators and/or limiters in determining how closely the business and operational needs for access boundaries around a particular user or groups of users are met. Beyond the particular technologies chosen for your design, the specific products used to implement the technologies will also have an impact on the quality of your access controls. Be careful to fully evaluate every aspect of competing products to ensure that you're selecting the one that most fully satisfies your design goals for finite access authorization differentiation by individual user.

The IT system administrator should not have input into the authorization process. Which resources an employee is granted access to should be entirely a management decision. The complete authorization process should be documented sufficiently so that an audit trail for each user clearly shows what use rights have been grated to her.

Figure 5-3 illustrates an authorization map of all the resources available to username CoFINSmth. The upper left quadrant shows the Web-enabled applications available to that user. The upper right quadrant shows there is only one firewall rule restricting this person's Internet access. The lower right quadrant shows that his access to the company's intranet is limited to one file folder and a printer at the company headquarters building. Finally, the lower left quadrant shows all of the local LAN devices available and assigned to this user. The presentation and recording of this type of information for your end users does not have to be done graphically; text will do, or a database can be used. Help desk personnel benefit from the use of the graphic because it can quickly show them that user's authorization profile and they can focus quickly on the problem area.

The authorization process defines in a finite and precise way what any username will have access to. It's fine to grant use rights to generic resources to a group of users. Such resources include printers, fax portals, collaborative file areas or folders, and applications that result in read-only access to data files. Generic items are ones that are not subject to external regulatory influences. Once your information or devices cross the line from general-use items to protected, it is no longer appropriate to grant everyone in the same OU (organizational unit) container unencumbered access to data such as company financial reports, confidential data, or privacy information.

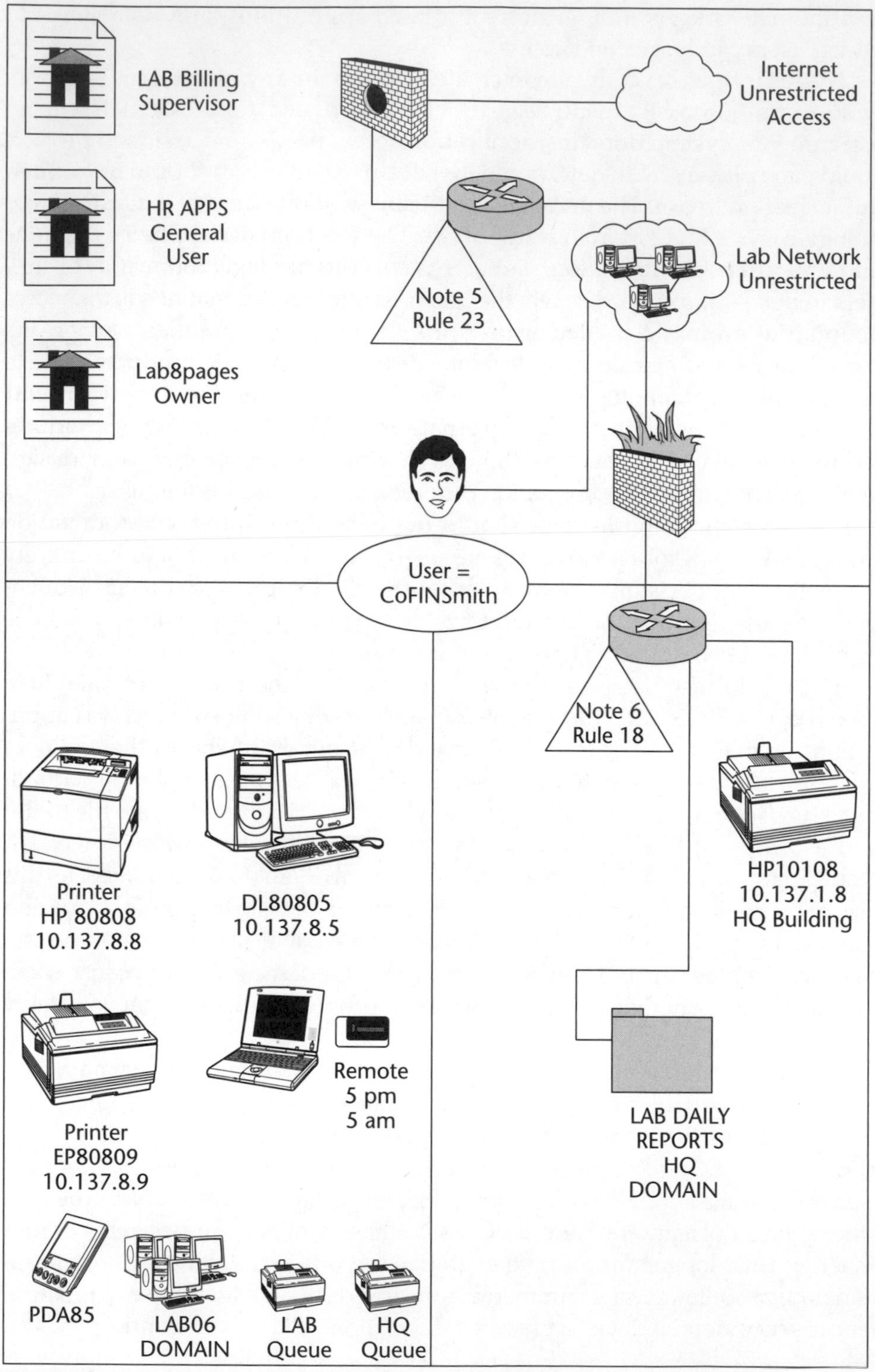

Figure 5-3   A graphical authorization map for CoFINSmth.

Sarbanes-Oxley and other external regulations requiring adequate controls render container-based security obsolete for auditable records as well as for data, personal medical information, and personally identifying information. Authorization must be designed and technically implemented in a way that can control access rights to a single field in a database or a single file in a data storage area. If your authorization and access controls cannot do that and at the same time provide an audit trail as to who may have made the last change in the field or file, they are hardly adequate in the current regulatory environment, let alone the rules that may be promulgated in the near term.

Take stock of your current access control situation, particularly the quality of your authorization process and how well your existing access controls are capable of enforcing the rights granted. Very few existing implementations establish a distinct, tightly controlled relationship between individual end users and finite data elements. For example, it would not be appropriate for any supervisor in the company to see every employee's Social Security number in a human resources application. Privacy advocates would argue that even HR staff should not be able to see it once entered into the income tax reporting data field.

Understanding Access Control

The output of the authorization process becomes the design input requirements for the access controls. Access controls enforce the requirements that flow from the authorizations by allowing the access rights granted by authorization or preventing access that is deliberately denied. In designing access controls, you will find some factors, normally out of your control, that either limit or facilitate your achieving the finite controls identified in the authorization process. Many of the software products and programs in use in your organization have innate access control features and work with APIs (application program interfaces) that easily fit your design criteria; there also are some products and programs that will challenge you to have custom interfaces developed. The same is true when you are designing a system from the ground up. The state of the available products requires purchasing from and perhaps working closely with a list of vendors. No single vendor is likely to have products to meet all of your design needs.

Frequently your access control needs will require that end users be able to access OS-level services such as file space access and print spooling. Each OS (operating system) has innate access control mechanisms to enable an end user or other computer device to access services hosted on it. Likewise, NOSs (network operating systems) can be configured to grant access and use of network services and devices to end users who are identified, authenticated, and authorized. Built-in directory services are usually the vehicle that provides access controls to an OS or NOS.

In other computer environments such as mainframes and large server applications, databases or simple access control list are the checkpoint for determining what services and applications a username is authorized to access.

You can layer various levels of access controls. For example, you could require a login process (a username and password) first to get to the network services, and then require a username (which can be different from the login one) and password to access a particular host computer, followed by requiring a token card and PIN to access a confidential application on that host. At each step in the example, the access control barriers are innate services. The username would typically be stored in the network directory, with a password. The OS would similarly store the username (could be different) in the host OS directory, and the application controls would store a username or refer to a service directory and may also include a requirement to use a token card in an access control list on an AAA server. Current environments are often complicated, with a single user's access information stored in a directory or list in every device and application to which he may need access. The complexity contributes not only to an onus on systems administrators but to mistakes and access control failures as well.

Meeting the access control objectives of the authorization process in a complex computing environment becomes a chase of details, usually orchestrated by a string of system, database, and application administrators. The details are sufficient in number to make this process subject to human errors and reliant on periodic housecleaning to keep the administration of the access controls current.

Access control criteria relevant to keeping the data that directly impacts the financial reports is of particular interest because of the requirement to audit the adequacy of IT access controls and comment on it in public financial reports. This necessitates the management of public companies ensuring that the IT staffs have implemented adequate access controls. The level of control required moves the discussion to defining specific auditable connections between username access rights and specific data.

The access controls to meet today's requirements must cause the entire IT system of an organization to become like a maze with automatic doors that open compartments of devices, data, or services only for authorized and properly authenticated usernames. This is illustrated in Figure 5-4. To the unauthorized username, the devices, data, or services do not exist — they're totally blocked. Read-only users are presented with a glass window they can read through, but they cannot change the data. The controls must be able to turn the maze into a tunnel to one data element if that is all the username is permitted to see or change. To hackers, the maze would not even exist.

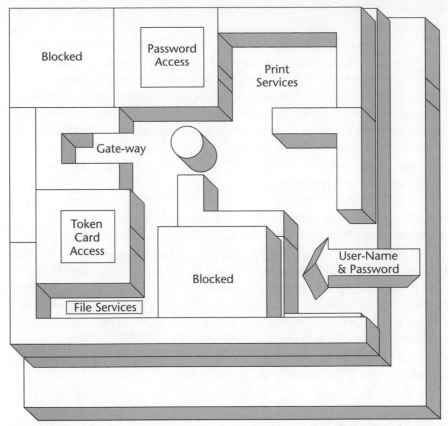

Figure 5-4 Fully implemented access controls create a thee-dimensional maze.

Now picture the maze as a building of an unknown shape with possible doors in the floors and ceilings to move up and down on the various layers when authorized. The last characteristic is the magic of being able to skip users over layers without them ever knowing how many layers were skipped.

To meet audit requirements, every time a door opens for a username, it is recorded in a log along with what is changed while there. If you can visualize this imaginary maze, you are very close to understanding the complexity of control required to be deemed adequate.

The next two chapters discuss the basic features that are required to reach the ideal described in the maze analogy.

Understanding Administration

Documentation may not be the most popular word in IT circles but it is perhaps the most important. From how your information is protected to how you will recover from malicious code — and everything in between — needs to be documented. Then the processes and procedures must be adhered to by everyone on your IT staff with operations, administration, or management responsibilities. Security and controls administration is not just the responsibility of the CSO and those who report directly to her. Everyone with any IT responsibilities must do their part to protect networks, computer systems, and data stores.

Security management procedures include such simple things as adding usernames, creating or changing firewall rules, and issuing tokens. They define the administrative component of security. Administrative procedures must be well documented, universally understood, and followed to the letter. Failure to follow them creates the weakest link in the security system and serves to negate all the good design intent, implementation effort, and product expense that went into building and maintaining the access controls.

If the documentation for your organization's security administration is not up to par, begin by correcting those things for which the mere lack of documented administrative procedures may cause harmful consequences to multiply from a potential negative event. To help prioritize, ask yourself and others in your security circle what would be the worst thing that could happen because certain steps, processes, and procedures are not recorded anywhere. Then get a collective estimate on the probability of each case occurring. The product of those answers leads you to the items to work on first. You want to reduce the most hazardous shortcomings as quickly as possible.

Understanding Auditing

Auditing IT systems' access and security controls for either quality measures or regulatory compliance begins with assessing whether security administrative procedures are in place and if they are being routinely followed within the organization. Focusing on the technology components alone does not show the whole picture of strengths or weaknesses in an organization. Auditing will include tests for compliance with the internally developed policies, processes, and procedures. In fact, internal auditors may benefit the organization by using the whole body of documents outlined in Chapter 3 where operations or administrative activities require adherence to the documented requirements. Getting a good look at whether the IT organization is doing what those documents demand provides an opportunity for corrective steps before the external compliance auditors begin testing.

Internal auditors and self-auditing by IT staff should make management well aware of the shortcomings with internally imposed requirements long before any third-party auditor has negative findings. Over time, external auditors examining the organization as a function of a regulatory reporting requirement will become increasingly efficient at determining which of your practices constitutes adequate IT protective measures for meeting the regulatory requirements.

The IT portion of the regulatory compliance audits will become more central to the public reporting as it becomes clear how dependant most modern organizations are on the underlying IT technology and computer applications from the front line to the board room. Errors can become exponential because financial data is often aggregated from many divisions or combined from multiple locations on its way to year-end reports. Audits must be geared to find the weaknesses at every level where data that may need monitoring and repair is created, stored, or moved. If, for example, a national fast-food chain were to have control weaknesses in its point-of-sales software across 600 store locations, a $100 error per store per week would have a serious impact on the company's bottom line.

Your own auditing process should focus on finding weaknesses in your existing access controls. For example, if your controls allow an employee access to the Approved checkbox on an expense voucher, that could be problematic. An internal auditing process should find and correct this type of situation. In a good design, the application would never present that view with the checkbox, and would require the supervisor to enter a PIN to approve payments on the screen presented to her.

Proof that your access controls are working is crucial to passing compliance audits. The following sections discuss activities that not only enhance overall security in an organization but position your IT shop to provide proof to external auditors that your control and authentication strategy are succeeding at keeping the unauthorized out of your systems.

Using Logging

Ask the members of your IT staff if they have an audit program in place. The wrong answer is, "Sure, we keep system logs." Turning hardware and software manufacturers' built-in logging features on where it makes sense is a great starting point. Purchasing additional or supplemental logging products where doing so fills a hole in a sensitive area is also good. There is nothing interesting or exciting to the average IT person in these logs. Having someone read through the logs, though, may only succeed in making the reader ready for a coffee break. The raw data in the logs can show glaring discrepancies but eyes-on reviews do not always find the more nuanced hacks or abuses of access rights.

Further auditing analysis is dependant on having logging turned on where the metrics the logs produce are significant or where reviewing logs provides forensic value. What at first appears to a log reviewer as a small periodic anomaly and chalked off as a "false positive" may very well be a patient hacker with a script hitting your systems a few times an hour every day for a year.

Logging by itself adds little worth. The logs must be analyzed promptly and must provide important information to make the whole process worthwhile.

Evaluate every opportunity for providing a logging procedure in your networks, computer systems, applications, and databases that may present valuable knowledge in near real time, from periodic forensic evaluation, or from long-term trend analysis. Document your reasons for turning available logging features off, particularly if best practices in similar environments indicate they should be turned on.

Your logs must be subjected to analysis tools to find all of the incongruities — big and small — and then you have to use the intelligence gathered to take corrective actions to reduce or eliminate the risks that logging detected. Select log software analysis tools capable of mining through the logged data and connecting what may appear as random data into patterns that could expose threats to your systems. At this time, it's probably necessary to select analysis software for the various logs from multiple vendors who separately focus on analysis of specific logs such as firewall activity and Web server access.

Using Monitors

Monitoring is a real-time activity. Either someone is paying attention to a runtime process or there is some sort of probe ready to sound alarms when abnormal conditions are met. Real-time monitoring may be incredibly important when access to back-end systems is available over the Internet. IDS (intrusion detection system) monitoring coupled with alarms to a rapid response team empowered to take defensive measures is slowly giving way to IPS (intrusion prevention systems), where an intelligent IDS application takes immediate defensive actions and then notifies you through an alarm. The IDS action could be as simple as turning off a port on a firewall that is being attacked. A strategy for the near future requires use of both systems because IDS product offerings are maturing and IPS is still in its infancy and not yet capable of replacing IDS entirely.

Here's an example: A potential customer of an online mortgage company signs in on an SSL connection, enters his personally identifying and financial history information, assigns himself a username and a password, and waits to hear from the loan officer. The username and password enable him to check on the process while his loan is being considered. Say that the mortgage company holds his information, whether his loan was approved or not, for a year and keeps his account login active. The account login includes an automatic lockout feature that engages after three failed login attempts in 12 hours. Joe Hacker in Southeast Asia learns this the first day he tries to breach security on the portal by making multiple attempts to log on with phony credentials. The mortgage company does not monitor the portal entry point, believing that the three-strike lockout is enough security. During the course of the year, Joe Hacker can attempt to breach security by sending two logon attempts for each of hundreds of usernames per hour every day across the Internet to the portal — totally undetected. This hacker can try thousands of possible username-password combinations over time. He needs to be right only once to compromise an admin login and gain access to everything on the server.

With the use of scripting and previously compromised Internet hosts, one hacker could be attempting low-profile compromises against all the Fortune 1000's Web-connected hosts. How many of these companies will have IDS in place that recognizes the two logon attempts as a potential security problem? For security reasons, the answer may never be known, but you and your company need to be wary of calling anything found by IDS a "false positive" or "harmless anomaly"; there may be no such thing.

When real-time monitoring is done, it has to be capable of detecting the patient hacker's approach. Monitoring for three failed attempts is going to help you find only your own customers who have forgotten their passwords. Monitoring choices for sounding alarms must be very carefully considered. Focus the monitoring on areas with a capability of mitigating the highest risks and oversee the weakest entry points as your first priority.

Any risk your organization faces, whether from internal or external sources, that is not dealt with by your overall system of access controls diminishes your claim that your SOX compliance strategy and access controls are adequate. Perhaps your initial security designs did not cover every node that can come under attack from potential wrongdoers. IDS can become one more way to discover ways to improve your overall controls. It isn't just for monitoring anymore. The intelligence data generated from IDS should be input right back to the beginning of the design process to seek ways to improve controls at every opportunity discovered.

Using Detection

In addition to intrusion monitoring, many computers and network devices have alarm bells and whistles to get your attention when things that have gone wrong are detected. When alarm information is forwarded, it is not always security-related — but it could be. Thinking that only the paranoid don't get hacked will cause you to want to have alarms for all events looked at by security staff, but their seeing every alarm event is probably not necessary. Alarm events that are in no way likely to be security events should be separated out from the ones that could be.

Hardware and software host-based detection varies from product to product, so much so that it isn't feasible to cover them in this book. A general course of action is to turn on every event detection capability your hardware and software systems provide. Then you have to determine what to do with the resulting information, how to filter it, and how to use it. This is a challenge for your architecture or network management and monitoring staff. Detected events such as a redundant fan failing merely need to be logged for later analysis; other detected events should be processed by staff immediately. Separating available alarms into action categories requires careful consideration by experienced staff.

Evaluate the possibilities for host-based detection features in your existing infrastructure and applications. For new designs, alarm features may influence your choice of one product over another. Study the features and determine their value. As always, justify shutting down what is already available and document your reasons for doing so; err on the side of using more rather than fewer features.

Systems that have detection and automated alarm events that could flag potential security failure events should move to the top of the list for activation and security staff notification. When a buffer overflow event occurs on a Web host, for example, detection alarms can notify you of its occurrence. The question is whether the overflow was caused by a harmless event, by a successful hack, or by some malicious code that's found its way into your network. Host-based detection features can automatically inform your operations center of many events — so many events, in fact, that the alarms and information forwarded can lead to sensory overload for your staff. It may be helpful to send normal alarms such as "fan out" or "drive failure" in drive arrays to an operations desk and then carefully separate those detection alarms on security protection levels to be forwarded or copied out to security staff for immediate analysis.

Discovering OS hack attempts, application or database security breach attempts, and system- or data-destructive employee behaviors involves adding some form of intelligence to your monitoring and detecting processes. It is often necessary to store the log information gathered from all sources in a log data warehouse and run an analytical program against the data to find matches for the anomalies that you wouldn't usually notice when reviewing the logs. Analysis programs matched to the logging software program often seek only the known, high-profile risks. Detecting security problems *before* they become well known in the industry is an enormous challenge.

Thwarting damaging behavior from insiders is also a huge problem. If your systems have weaknesses, it is important to be the first to know and to be as proactive as possible to eliminate the risks. A well-thought-out approach to detection will help. Access controls designed to support separation of responsibilities such that the originator of a refund cannot approve the refund check can facilitate monitoring and detection when an originator attempts to do so. The inside security threat is real in organizations of all sizes, so it's well worth designing event protection into applications and turning it on. Think in terms of proactive prevention as a strategy over reactive processes that correct after the fact. If employees are aware that negative behaviors such as attempting to access authorized data can be detected, that alone provides some deterrence for a potential rogue employee.

Using Reporting

Reporting strategies have to be matched to the needs of management. It is way too easy to be caught up in providing the same metrics time after time. A ship's captain wants to hear "Everything checked and squared away, sir; ready to sail" from the crew. Those responsible for IT systems and particularly those accountable for the security aspects want a similar message.

Reports must be interesting, meaningful, and useful for decision making. Managers tend not to care that every day you are getting a thousand attempts from the Internet to breach your security as long as none gets through or degrades network performance. The one attempt that got through is the one everyone should care about because in it are the clues to actions that will ensure there is no second successful breach through your access controls. Reporting on successes is an appropriate thing to do, but the focus of reporting should always be leading the question "What needs to be done next to eliminate the threat?" or at least to reduce the risk presented by the threat factors. Thinking like an electric utility may make the point. It would be a rare utility customer who cared (or perhaps even noticed) if the lights stayed on with electricity supplied at 117 volts for the first hour every morning and supplied at 116.5 volts the rest of the day. Every customer cares if the lights go out, or go so dim you can't read by them.

Your reporting plan must similarly focus on the problem areas and potential problem areas until they are managed completely out of your risk pool. The security reporting elements for validating metrics relevant to SOX authentication, authorization, and access controls become a subset of your entire security reporting criteria. Generally speaking, the report outline begins with a threat category, specifies the risk presented by that threat, and then breaks out into the items that are actually measured. (Remember that you are measuring the end items so that over time you can respond to them and reduce them to zero or near zero.) If Internet hacking is the threat category, for example, your detection probes outside the firewall could count overall intrusion attempts.

The risk presented would be a successful unauthorized login. The host systems or a monitor on your host system would count failed access attempts by tracking logins in two end-item categories: unauthorized usernames and failed passwords (with correct usernames). The outline of such a report would look something like this:

<u>Internet Hack Attempts</u>

Intrusion Attempts	120
Access Attempts	120
Failed Logins	100
Failed Usernames	26
Failed Passwords	74

If analysis were to show that all of the intrusion attempts are from a network IP address in Southeast Asia, one action that could reduce the numbers in the next reporting period would be to block that address at the ISP router.

The objective of reporting is not simply to show the numbers; the numbers are to be used to focus on mitigation or preventive measures to take. Over time, preventative actions should reduce the items needed in the reports. If you have totally eliminated a risk and its corresponding threat, there's no reason to keep it as a reporting category. That doesn't mean that monitoring and detection for those items should be turned off; it simply means they no longer need to be on the report. Should a new vulnerability lead to an event in an eliminated reporting line, reporting must be done again, along with corrective and mitigation steps and actions to eliminate the threat.

Understanding Assessment

A *threat* is the potential for harm to your organization. *Risk* is the possibility that a threat will cause harm in some manner. Cutting to the chase, your designs for access controls and overall security are for risk reduction, to ensure that threat is reduced to zero or as near zero as possible. *Assessment* is the process of assigning probability value that your systems' defenses will be breached or harmed by some threat.

In a way the whole discussion about probability is minimized if the one-in-a-million attack succeeds, resulting in the theft of 10,000 identities from your data store. At that point, no one in your organization's management chain is going to care about probability.

Here are some steps to assessing your organization's system vulnerabilities:

1. Define and list all the threats contributing to vulnerabilities.

2. Classify the threats into two main categories: the ones that can be eliminated and those that, for operational reasons, cannot.

   Yes, some threats can be totally eliminated. Turning off all possible connections to the Internet and getting rid of phone lines and modems removes the threat of outside attacks. These are extreme examples, to be sure, but there are subtle strategies that succeed in eliminating threats as well. Fronting Web applications with proxy server technologies, for example, keeps the inexperienced hacker focused on the wrong device.

3. Perpetually reevaluate the remaining threats for possible elimination as new strategies and tools become available to do so.

4. The ones that remain become the to-do list for future elimination. Prioritize this second list, and provide some discussion points in cost-benefit evaluations.

The goal is always to eliminate the threat. If that cannot be done, take steps to mitigate the harmful effects if your systems should become a target. Those that cannot be reduced to nuisance levels are the ones that must be monitored constantly and consistently to contain any damage when you are targeted.

There is no particular foolproof formula or approach to doing assessments. The steps presented here are merely a guide; you must decide what works in your environment. Keep in mind that it is only a prioritization process to determine where to focus resources. Always use the same numbers when placing a comparative probability in your assessments. The probability numbers you assign may be subjective, but do not change them from one reporting period to the next (at least not without justification or an explanation to management).

Summary

A successful approach to designing or evaluating security controls must always consider each element of the security matrix. The elements are of equal importance and work together to enhance the whole security profile. Ignore or shortchange any part of the matrix in your access control design considerations to your systems' security detriment.

Developing Directory-Based Access Control Strategies

The access controls design issue essentially begs the question of how best to manage the five-tier relationship among identity, authentication, authorization, access controls, and the protected targets, including networks, computer systems, applications, and data, based on the assessment of risk for those assets. Furthermore, how do you design access controls to be managed in a way that reduces the administration burden and makes finite auditing evaluations possible?

Figure 6-1 illustrates that a grant of access is similar to passing access rights through a pipe partially blocked by the "filters" of five security elements, with the pipe itself made up of the administrative and auditing elements that influence each of the others on the way to getting to protected resources. You certainly can see why security protection measures are so highly detailed.

This chapter introduces directories, the LDAP (Lightweight Directory Access Protocol) standard API, and meta-directory functionality, all critical to implementing a comprehensive access control strategy. Their most important features are highlighted, and an example of the necessary analysis needed prior to deciding how they are best used is presented. Chapter 7 presupposes basic familiarity with these topics, making this a must-read chapter if you're not already familiar with directories and the LDAP standards. The IT architecture design principle that places a high value on defining security policy domains is revisited from Chapter 3 to demonstrate how it begins to influence decision making.

With all the negative press recently associated with security breaches, you'd think there is no way to successfully protect information from inappropriate access channels. On just about any day, a scan of the consumer news media sources yields many reports of system breaches in all types of organizations. Reviewing the computing and communications trade journals nets similar results, with more details included of what went wrong. If there is one area in which an organization should cast off a reactionary "fix it or patch it" mentality, this is it. In the long term, for e-commerce, there is a lot riding on how well organizations of all kinds deal with the subjects of identity, authentication, and access controls to protect information and keep it within a sphere of managed control. Failure to achieve sufficient success over the control of private and financial information could result in the zeroing out of public confidence in online transactions of all sorts.

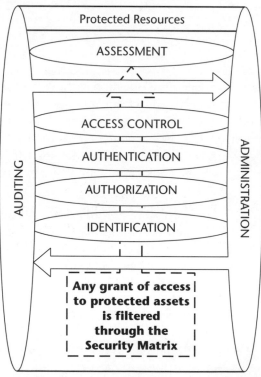

Figure 6-1   Access establishes a controlled relationship between an identity and a resource.

There is as much at stake with the challenge to be in command of access control strategies as there would be if the SSL protocols' inherent security features were totally compromised. Either event could stop electronic commerce as we know it. Fortunately, the hardware, tools, software, and reasons to improve access controls are all available on the technology smorgasbord today. Creating an access control strategy that works in the unique environs of your organization requires adding a dash of art to the science and technology available. The next few sections discuss how the use of directories and their features are certain to be integral to your successful access control strategy.

Directory technology evident in products that are compliant with LDAPv3, the common schemas that are published, and the capability to use meta-directory features to move identity-related information from one storage point to another can be leveraged in a complementary fashion to improve a system's access security profiles.

The topics in this chapter are important to the development of an access control strategy. There are other excellent books (including *LDAP Directories* by Marcel Rizcallah John Wiley & Sons; 1st edition (June 15, 2002) and *Novell's LDAP Developer's Guide* by Roger G. Harrison, Jim Sermersheim, and Steve TrottierWiley; Bk&CD-Rom edition (January 15, 2000) that cover the finer details of LDAP and directory topics. The focus in this and subsequent chapters is on how the features evident within these technologies are best combined and used to improve access controls within an organization with a complex IT infrastructure.

Exploring Multiple- versus Single-Directory Paradigms

Is having only one access control directory better than having 10? Or is having a hundred better than having 10? Over the past five or six years, the discussion for larger organizations around directory services has gone from asking, "Why can't we just have one vendor's directory for our access authentication?" to "Wouldn't it be wonderful if all the different operating systems would interoperate so we could pick one platform for directory authentication?" to where many are today: "You have to accept that you are stuck with many different directories, right?"

Opinions vary considerably on this topic, with many information technology specialists being caught in one-directory-for-everything as the ideal place to be. Systems security thinking is, of course, still evolving. This discussion must be settled within the greater context of how best to meet security concerns with implementation criteria that actually serve to keep protected data within a managed sphere of control. The reality for most organizations is that multiple directories (see Figure 6-2) are going to be evident in their IT infrastructure for some time into the future. Given the current state of the situation, the challenge for today's access control designers is how to best use directory services with as few instances of directories as possible in a way that enhances security and tightens access controls. (This chapter and Chapter 10 provide you with valuable insights for sorting out the specific needs of your organization.)

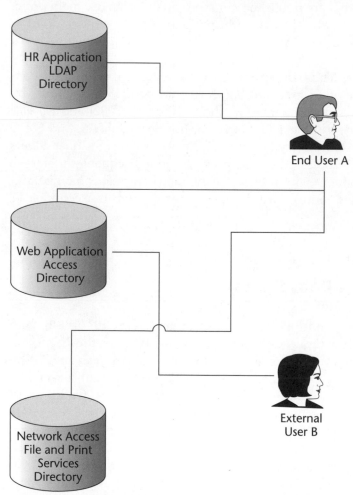

Figure 6-2   Multiple directories are typical.

Examining Directory Services

Directory services provide identity information about end users or devices that can facilitate finite access controls by the user's username or device name when referenced by a gatekeeper such as a network operating system or a host operating system. The capability of a directory to store and rapidly retrieve identity information when requested is the keystone to access control architecture.

The idea of putting information into one place so it can be quickly found and used is not new — paper directories have been used for generations. Electronic directory services and the standard LDAP API can be used together, along with the capability for a meta-directory, to move directory information where it is needed to form the hub of a modern access control strategy.

Using Hard-Copy Directories

Historically, hard-copy directory services have been the underlying "technology" that facilitates finding bits of valuable information and then doing something with the information. Examples include telephone directory books to find phone numbers and city directories to find addresses for businesses and residents. Each hard-copy directory makes the next logical step easier — the directory service provides information for the next step in the process, such as making the phone call or visiting the business. A level of reliance has been placed on the information provided in the paper directories as to its accuracy. In each case, the information has been collected and placed in the directory service by others; their collection process is trusted even though the user may not know how the information was collected.

In the same way that a paper directory can be used over and over again and for different needs, digital directories can be referenced and used in the control strategy any number of times as a user moves deeper into the applications holding ever more sensitive data.

Using Digital Directories

Directory services in IT systems are used to apply access controls. They store the important bits of information that have been logically associated with a collection of resources. Resource information stored in a directory could contain entries for such objects as end users, devices, and applications. The directory can also be used for establishing relationships among the data entries. End users, for example, can be associated in a named group.

Directories are designed to allow API calls to quickly wade through the hierarchy of information and return the requested data quickly. It is this capability to quickly return information for use in another program's process that makes directories ideal for storing relatively large amounts of identifying information about end users or other system resources.

The primary access control role for directory services is to store all of the information that the actual gatekeeper mechanisms use to grant or deny access. A directory is queried for information at any necessary number of junctures as an end user places demands for various services: An end user is challenged for username and password when booting up a workstation; access to network resources is granted when the appropriate username and password combination is provided to the NOS, and Web applications require a username and password to function. In organizations with a heterogeneous computing environment, this may mean storing different username and password combinations in three different directories. It's a situation that creates a *purpose-driven* directory environment. Figure 6-3 illustrates how complex these authentication paths can get.

Having one directory service for each purpose produces a relatively inefficient situation from a support and administration perspective. Entering data into and managing and supporting these directories takes time and drains resources. From a security standpoint, it adds complexity, making audits and additional control elements more difficult to apply. Co-mingling the information for each unique end-user population into each purpose-directory makes it harder to secure the data stored there. Having all the authentication information in one directory means that the data flow must travel across zones and security policy domains, opening data paths that increase security risks and the potential for compromise of the directory itself along with the application host.

Casual implementation approaches to the use of directory services are a big part of the security problem companies are experiencing, but directories are also a way to facilitate tighter controls. A rational approach to using the power of directories in an efficient manner is the crux of the challenge of designing and deploying adequate access controls. Shifting from a purpose-driven directory paradigm to a population-specific directory model is the first step in raising the sufficiency of directory services in a way that enhances overall system security. Deploying population-specific directories appropriate to the organization's unique categories of application end users enables the building of tighter security domains incorporating customized access controls for the population. When an end-user population is defined and placed in a directory based on the users' need for access to similar applications with similar levels of access rights, very finite controls can be designed to meet those specific requirements. An entire security policy domain definition can then be used to enforce the controls at every juncture in the system that relates to the access and security needs of that population. Chapter 10 provides more details on using population-specific directories.

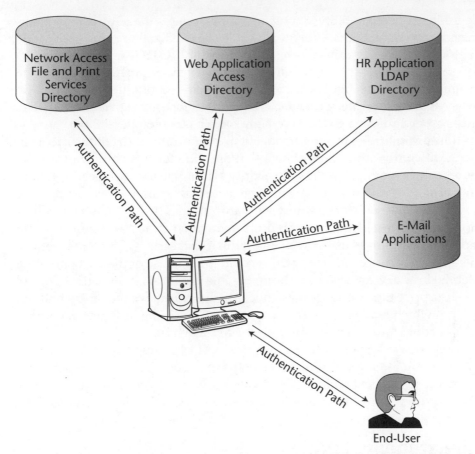

Figure 6-3 One-directory-per-application access control keeps many directories busy.

Examining the Interoperability Challenge

Because most organizations are using multiple operating system hardware platforms and a complex mix of software application products on them, there is a pressing need to continue using existing implementations while tightening security profiles. Accomplishing this requires attention to the details involved so that each application's security profile is as strong as possible.

The fact remains that previous decision making by CIOs resulted in the use of multiple operating systems in larger organizations, in turn resulting in multiple instances of directories and, in some cases, countless access control lists. The concept touted to justify the implementation of different OSs and hardware platforms and software vendors was "we use best of breed." Unfortunately, there is little built-in interoperability among operating systems made by different customized software vendors. There is also little standardization at the application level for how security controls are applied within COTS (commercial off-the-shelf) software. As long as there is more than one vendor providing products in the same space, there's little capability for systems or products to work with other systems or products without a lot of special effort on the part of the IT staff. Industry standards are needed to provide some basic interoperability.

In-house application programmers often approach the issue of security controls in different ways. Many things that are difficult to totally control contribute to different approaches to security within custom applications. Staff turnover and variations in logical approaches, for example, are among the many things that can work against standardization. The use of an IT architecture design approach mitigates this problem by producing a customary way to handle access controls using available industry standards. Of all the options presented for access controls — which could include use of the host operating system's directory, an access control table in a database, or an access control list — an application designer may choose to use one above the others without regard to which may provide the best security. The same designer may make different choices from project to project even when using the same software development tools. Standardizing on a single API and the way your organization will deploy its use of directories helps to rationalize the approach from one project to the next and creates an internal standard for how applications will be secured. Access control is too important to leave to design by chance.

Understanding LDAPv3

The x.500 directory structures standard, which was endorsed by both ISO (International Organization for Standardization) and ITU (International Telecommunications Union), gave rise to the development of LDAP as a simplified way to access directories using TCP/IP (Transmission Control Protocol/Internet Protocol) and a common API. LDAPv3-compliant directories are used pervasively on the Internet today to provide services for controlling access to networks, operating systems, free e-mail, and Web-hosted applications.

The body of LDAP standards provides a path for sharing information from one software vendor directory to another directory through LDIF (Lightweight Directory Interchange Format). Schema definitions have been developed within the IETF (Internet Engineering Task Force) RFC (Request for Comments) process to define common directory entries for an end user in an LDAP-compliant directory. A common user definition is the inetOrgPerson

LDAP object class defined in RFC 2798 and updated with additional matching rules in RFC 3698. LDAP directories are hierarchical and contain defined object classes for each entry and an entry's attribute definitions. These features make the base object class extensible to allow the inclusion of custom categories of entries to a parent object class that were not in the beginning basic definition.

The features of LDAP directories that are important to the designer of the access controls are that they are:

- Based on standards
- Accessed by using TCP/IP network protocols
- Capable of being shared to other types of data repositories
- Customizable to include additional information

In the directory space, the effect of the lack of interoperability and vendor cooperation is sufficiently minimized by the LDAP standards. Directory and related software products that are LDAP-compliant become the means and method to satisfactorily bridge the interoperability gap.

Understanding the Meta-Directory (Meta-Functionality)

A good definition for a meta-directory is this: a higher order directory that is in the presence of others and capable of communicating with other directories. It also can provide a changed view of the information contained in them. The capability to use a directory to collect information into a whole from subsets of information is of great interest to the access controls designer. Using a directory as a hub to move information from itself to other directories or to dissimilar storage points becomes the basis for identity provisioning to different systems.

Using the Aggregated View of Multiple Directories

The term *meta-directory* is used to describe a directory that combines or aggregates information from multiple directories into itself or provides a point for a common view of the disparate directories. A *meta-view* allows all the information contained in multiple directories to be accessed from one place.

This adds convenience but reduces security enhancement options. The typical implementation of a meta-directory as the single directory for all authentication and access control reduces the security domains related to directory services to one. Your ability to apply additional controlling elements is extremely limited when all authentication calls are done with a single directory or single meta-directory model, which, unfortunately, is often presented as ideal by many vendors. It does at first present the appearance of convenience until you try to engineer out some of the risks of having multiple populations with differing rights accessing and using the same directory.

The one-directory model also usually leads to the need for a more complex schema development. The choice between using a meta-directory as the authentication point or simply using the meta-functionality to move information from one directory or data store to another leads to very different security policy domain definitions. When one meta-directory is used as the authentication point, options for enhanced access controls are reduced from what you would have with population-specific directories being serviced by a meta-directory acting solely as an identity-provisioning resource.

Figure 6-4 shows a meta-directory collecting user identity information from three specific-use directories. Using aggregated data for provisioning to other repositories is discussed in detail in Chapter 10.

Using the Information Exchange Point

Complementary software associated with meta-directories has features used to place information from one directory's entries to another directory by using descriptors called *tags* to customize how the data is translated correctly from one to the other. This capability to apply some process logic to the transfer of directory information gives rise to the whole topic of identity provisioning of services throughout an organization's IT infrastructure. Identity provisioning software allows one instance of identity information contained in the meta-directory (often called the *identity vault*), which can be passed to every point where identity information is needed and stored. A stored password for file and print services, for example, can be provisioned (moved) to the e-mail authentication directory. Provisioning also standardizes the identity data needed in the different directories or access control lists.

The features that facilitate the exchange of data from one directory to another can also be used to exchange information from one directory with other storage points such as databases. The capability to use some business process logic and filtering with a meta-directory as the central hub to move information from place to place is important meta-functionality. The business logic features in the provisioning tools can be used to change the format of the information when a different one is needed by another directory or storage point. For example, an IP-phone speed-dial directory may not want the dashes between the area code, exchange, and the last four digits of the phone number and the voice mail system may need the dashes to work properly. The provisioning software, once written to make the conversion, would always use the correct format needed by the storage point as it moves directory identity data from one storage point to the other.

In Figure 6-5, the distribution of directory information is dependant on software that provides the capability for customized rules and filtering and can be used with small real-time synchronization applications that provide the interface to target repositories. Each vendor providing provisioning software uses its own name for the application interfaces.

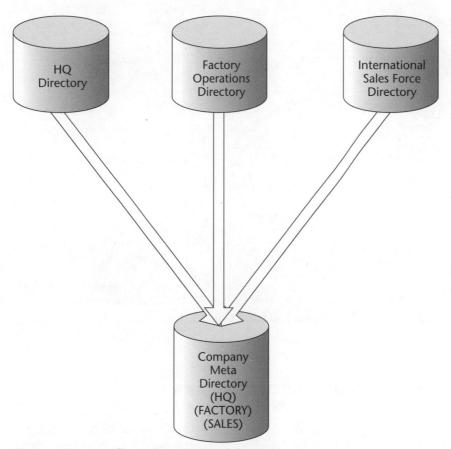

Figure 6-4 Meta-directories aggregate information.

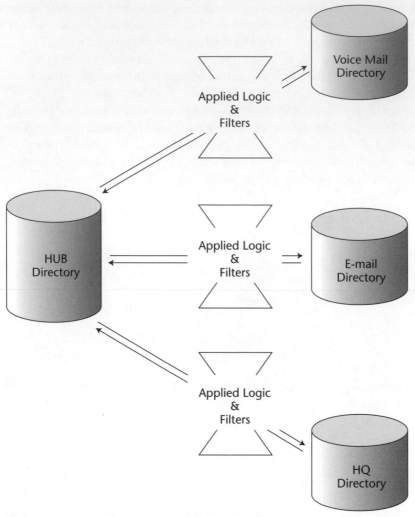

Figure 6-5   Meta-directories provide hub share points.

Revisiting Security Policy Domains

Directories, LDAP standards, and meta-features are all useful in the own right and have been designed and long used to solve problems in their area of direct functionality. The power to improve the security profile of the entire access controls spectrum comes in combining them into complementary interoperating systems and deploying them in ways that improve the overall security policy domains in an inventive fashion. The combination of using meta-directories and service directories, within the context of the LDAP standards, and leveraging meta-functionality to move consistent and accurate information where it is needed is the foundation of a successful access control strategy.

Take a few moments to go back to Chapter 3 and review the section on security policy domains. The art in creating your strategy is taking these three fundamentals and placing them within the concept of security policy domains. Better security policy domain definitions, coupled with implementing the definitions to the practical if not theoretical limits of the technologies involved, is how security is improved.

As you think about designing some of the shortcomings of existing implementations, it's easy to conclude a need for more than one security policy domain surrounding your directories and access controls. What would be the right number for your organization? If your access controls are required only on one application for one purpose, the security policy domains and population-specific service directories will be few in number. If your company is international with hundreds of lines of business, your security policy domains could still be as few as 10. The security needs and requirements for access to similar applications typically determine the number of unique population directories you will use. For companies with international Web access applications, the language spoken or differing privacy laws also may have an impact on the decisions for creating additional specific-use population directories. The security policy domain definitions direct how the access controls, identity management, and provisioning are to be implemented and perform their respective functions. They also determine the locations, features, and rules that are associated with other elements such as installing firewall measures to protect the directory components.

Begin the process of determining what directories are needed for access controls by putting the focus back on the context of security policy domains. Some whiteboarding or sketching may be helpful as you evaluate the options. As with any evaluation within the greater security environment, each element in the security matrix must be considered individually and collectively. Strong complementary relationships may exist at a few or all junctures within the matrix.

Using a Checklist

Start with this basic checklist and add to it:

- **Identity** — What populations will be served?

     Do the different populations require different resources?

     Does dealing with external populations change the risk profile?

- **Authentication** — Will all be authenticated at the same level of trust?

    Will nonrepudiation be a consideration?

- **Access control** — Once authenticated, will all users have access to the same resources?

    Does every end user need access to every data element or just a subset?

- **Authorization** — Will the same underlying business process provide authorization for appropriate access?

    What is the relationship between the population(s) and the protected data?

- **Administration** — Will the administration of the directory entries be a manual process?

- **Assessment** — What rudiments of risk will the assessment require the controls to counter?

    How valuable are the target assets that are to be protected?

- **Auditing** — Is each population's access going to be subject to conforming with externally imposed audit requirements?

    Will auditable access logs be required to show every access to financial reports over the last three years?

As you answer these and similar questions about your organization's unique requirements, some patterns of similar or equal requirements should begin to emerge.

Fictional Case Study: Governor's Brew Coffee Shop

To illustrate the security policy domain approach to your strategy for directory services, take a look at Governor's Brew, a hypothetical coffee shop on Mackinac Island. Here are the coffee shop's answers to the checklist questions. Watch to see if patterns develop.

- **Identity** — What populations will be served?

    Owners

    Managers

    Employees

    Preferred Customers

    Customers

Do the different populations require different resources?

> Yes; employees need to do daily cash point of sale only.

> Manager's; point of sale, financial reports.

> Owners; is same as managers plus bank deposits.

> Preferred customers; use credit, debit card with point of sale and fast-track-pass ordering.

> Customers; credit and debit card with point of sale.

Does dealing with external populations change the risk profile?

> Yes; system holds identifying and financial information for preferred customers.

- **Authentication** — Will all be authenticated at the same level of trust?

  > No; more trust with owner, then manager, then employees.

  Will nonrepudiation be a consideration?

  > Yes; for all financial components.

- **Access control** — Once authenticated, will all users have access to the same resources?

  > No; different resources by different groups of users.

  Does every end user need access to every data element or just a subset?

  > Each identified user needs a subset, except the owner, who needs `all` accesses to available information.

- **Authorization** — Will the same underlying business process provide authorization for appropriate access?

  > No; different manual processes are required.

  What is the relationship between the population(s) and the protected data?

  > Relationship based on ownership and/or responsibility for data.

  > Ascending scope of responsibility increases from employee to owner.

- **Administration** — Will the administration of the directory entries be a manual process?

  > Yes; but no entries are made for nonpreferred customers.

- **Assessment** — What rudiments of risk will the assessment require the controls to counter?

  > Multiple risks including financial loss, loss of good will, and liability for loss of identifying information.

How valuable are the target assets that are to be protected?

Daily cash receipts, potential loss from liability.

- **Auditing** — Is each population's access going to be subject to conforming with externally imposed audit requirements?

    The access of three populations — owners, managers, and employees — needs to conform. Customers and preferred customers do not actually input any financial information (other than the preferred customers' credit cards).

    Will auditable access logs be required to show every access to financial reports over the last three years?

    Our best practice is to archive the logs with access security applied to them for at least three years.

The most obvious possible solution is one directory for all populations. Another option is one directory for each of the four processes (purposes): a directory for point of sale, one for financial reports, one for access to bank deposit records, and one for access to preferred customer records. A third option is one directory for each of the four end-user populations. Any one of the approaches could be made to work, so the question is, which one provides the best mix to meet all objectives and offers the potential for tighter security controls within an identified security policy domain? Or does some other amalgamation of identity information fit better?

Exploring Solution Options

Examine all available options before deciding on a solution. Here's a quick analysis of possible solutions for the coffee shop example:

- **One master directory** — One directory dictates only one security policy domain surrounding the directory. This is not optimal because there are different trust levels between the workers and customers. This also amplifies the problem areas in each of the next two alternatives.

- **Four purpose directories** — One for fast-track-pass preferred-customer ordering, one for point of sale, one for financial reports, and one for banking report access. For the owners to get the access needed, they are entered in all four, managers are entered in three, employees in two because during off hours they want fast-track-pass ordering, and preferred customer are in the fast-track-pass directory. This leads to four policy domains with mixed populations and limits the ability to isolate resources and data flows on the network. It also makes it very difficult to define the policy domains.

■ **Four population directories** — One directory for owners, one for managers, one for employees, and one for preferred customers creates four policy domains all requiring access to all the same resources. This approach breaks down because all data flow across the network to the same network segments and defines any additional; controls such as limiting routing paths or firewall placement and strict firewall rules become limited.

■ **Two rationalized population-specific directories** — The solution driven by security policy domain considerations recognizes that owners, managers, and employees are accessing similar resources.

> The preferred customers access one device and one application that can place their standard order and bill their debit/credit card for payment. They have no need to directly access the other features of the point-of-sale system or access any of the financial tracking or reporting applications. Their access is based on proximity of their electronic card at the card reader and knowing their credit or debit card PIN. A clear opportunity arises to isolate and control data from and to a single point-of-sale access point: one specific population in which each person has identical needs for access and resources; hence, one directory and one security policy domain for them.

> Owners, managers, and employees share similar resource needs but are separated by need-to-know on some of those resources. Managers and owners sometimes work the counter, so everyone needs point-of-sale access. The best fit is one population-specific directory for everyone directly involved in the company. Couple that directory with an additional access control authentication requirement for the high levels of trust needed for access to financial reports. Employees authenticate with username and password; managers authenticate with username and password and have to enter a PIN when authenticating to financial reporting applications; and owners authenticate with username and password, with PIN for financial reports, and a two-factor authentication mechanism such as token card with a time-sensitive number string to enter the banking application. The resulting two population-specific directory approaches with two security policy domains would be the best match for the coffee shop.

Looking for Patterns

The coffee shop example is simple and not all inclusive of the details, but it illustrates some of the analysis that should take place before deciding on the access controls architecture for your organization. The patterns that emerged were that preferred customers had a one-to-one match to a single resource. The company insiders were one-to-many resources separated with different levels of trust. The two patterns fit into two well-defined security domains. The resulting security policy domains netted one relatively simple domain and another with more complexity for the authentication requirement.

Two LDAP-compliant directories would be used. The preferred customer directory and the company directory would begin with the inetOrgPerson object for users with only essential data fields filled in. The preferred customer directory schema would have to be extended to include objects to link to the pass cards with the credit/debit card and standard order applications. The need for meta-functionality is minimized in this example but could come into play in a bigger way if there were multiple locations for the same company and a network that connected the stores, or if other digital data sources were used to prepopulate the preferred customer directory.

Summary

In building from the concepts discussed in this chapter to more complex access control environments like yours, continue to analyze within the whole of the security matrix. In the next few chapters, the importance of directory services, LDAP standards, and the use of meta-functionality will become more evident as the difficulty grows with the increasing scale of the resources requiring protection and when designing to serve a larger number of end users.

The design of the auditing component is highly dependant on knowing what the completed design for access control will look like. Closing all audit gaps likely requires a mix of products whose choices also are dependant on the design and products selected for implementation. Choosing audit methods and products too early could result in placing too many constraints on the design of the controls up front. Awareness of the various products and what points they can audit is helpful but should not override the other considerations. Said another way, do not compromise the quality of control achievable to enhance audit capability.

Integrating the Critical Elements

To build a successful access control infrastructure, critical elements must be brought together in a logical framework based on appropriate relationships between them. These essential components are as follows:

- Identity management
- Authoritative sources
- Identity vaults
- Service directories
- Identity provisioning

As with verification sources for paper-based identities, digital identities must be derived from an authoritative source that you trust. The identity information is stored in a meta-directory, frequently called an identity vault. Software tools that use the identity vault as a storage and distribution point add features to manage the identity information and use it for provisioning accurate information to other repositories. To provide one methodology for authentication and access control, you must provide each distinct population served with a corresponding service directory as the focal point for managing its authentication and access controls.

This chapter discusses the concerns and challenges you'll face in your design details that define the relationships between these elements. The requirements placed on access controls by finite authorization criteria — often needed for compliance with externally imposed regulations — have increased the detail necessary in a successful design.

Putting Security First

Security controls have historically been added as an afterthought. The first personal computers and DOS operating systems had little in the way of built-in security features. Networking changed that somewhat by including a network login and password to access the file and print services available on the local area network. Many commercial software packages focused on applications' features, bells, and whistles, and did little to improve security. Early databases and data file storage went to disk unencrypted and were readable with a simple TYPE file command. Network setups often included groups in which everyone had access to the files, and there was no easy way to audit who had accessed or modified a particular file.

Evaluating Security Features

Security features for hardware, operating systems, and applications are considerably better today, although they aren't always taken advantage of in the implementation and deployment phase. There is considerable room for improvement in the way many software packages deal with security. If your organization and IT department are serious about security and controlling access, every security feature available in the software packages you are using must be evaluated for the benefits derived from their use. Every time a decision is made to not take advantage of a built-in security feature or control, record the risks and the justification for not doing so as part of the architecture documentation. These features have been bought and paid for, except for the person-hours to integrate them; it only makes good sense to fully evaluate their benefits and use them when they enhance access control or accountability.

The lack of finite controls today demonstrates how much of an afterthought security has been in the implementation process even when the security features were present in the software. Beginning with the DOS operating system, third-party vendors offered security products as add-ons to fill requirements for providing access controls to early desktop computing environment. Another factor that becomes apparent to even casual observers of technology environment security is how complex the security profile for any one end user is in most organizations' complex computing environments. Figure 7-1 shows a small sampling of the different levels and ways security control points are appropriately applied to an end user.

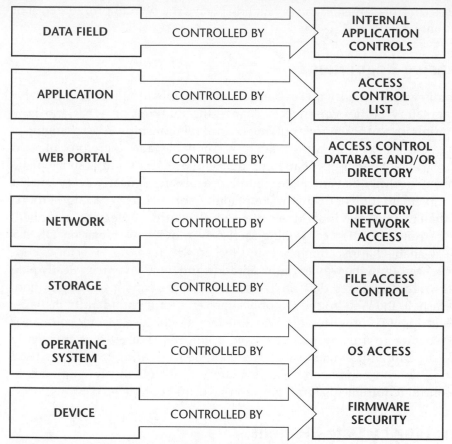

Figure 7-1   Access control levels create complex profiles.

The complexity of levels and lack of coordination between them are root causes for security failures. The simple principle of what-can-go-wrong-will and each additional control point compounds the probability that something will go wrong and weaken overall security.

Today, a more refined approach to making more sense out of identity-based authentication, authorization, and access controls is possible. The tools and the expertise to greatly improve access controls at all levels are in the IT market-place right now. Knowing what to ask for is far too often the missing element. The human tendency is to answer the question that is asked, so knowing the right questions to ask is what gets you the proper information. For example, the answer to "Does my application include access control?" may be yes. But for the follow-up question, "What about the storage for that application's data files?" the answer may be no, meaning that there is not adequate security for all access control elements. Any weak link breaks the overall profile's level of protection.

Increasing Regulations

The points where security access controls are possibly applied are still evolving. Regulatory bodies continue to change the thinking on what and how many points are sufficient for applying control relationships. Also changing is the character of who is appropriately accountable and therefore allowed access, a group of end users or an individual end user. SOX audits soon will be uncovering not only that adequate controls are missing at nearly every level in some implementations but that accountability spreads to very large groups rather than to identified individuals when weak control strategies are applied.

The current trend for controlling is clearly moving to focus on DEALS (directory-enabled application-level security), in which service directories control access rights all the way to the application and, whenever technically possible, the right to isolated data fields within the data of any given application, particularly in the Web front-end applications environment. Identity management and identity provisioning, which leverages the use of one source for identity data across many platforms and applications, are terms frequently used as descriptors for major components of the facilitating technology used to reduce sign-on complexity. The regulatory trend obviously continues to drive control requirements for application-level and data-level controls.

Controlling by Data Element

In the future, controls will have to be equipped with the capability to manage from the directory information access to any one data element within that application in relation to any particular end user's rights. What is rapidly becoming necessary for compliance is a one-to-one relationship between a user and any one or a few data fields within the larger database. Differentiation only down to a group of end users will be OK for some global access controls, but certainly will not meet the need to control access to protected assets or financial data. Group- or container-based access controls for financial data are already obsolete. In many instances, controls will have to be designed into application controls that couple access rights to data in a manner that establishes a one-to-one time-stamped, auditable relationship with a data object for each person authorized to change the data.

If you use the seven-layer OSI networking model, you must now add an eighth layer (data elements) to your security framework. In the N-tier computing models used today, applications are frequently on different hosts than the data storage for those applications. Controlling access rights beyond the files to identified data fields reduces the risk that an operating system or application layer hack will be as successful. An alarming number of external hacks appear to occur at the application or operating system level. Extending the reach of access control as deeply as possible helps counter the risks from these hacking attempts.

Figure 7-2 illustrates the fine-grained requirement. User ID C in the diagram is the only one able to change the data in data field X; user IDs B and C can change all the other fields, and all three users can read the database. It is as if the access controls are weaving threads from the users to the data where the woven strands of cloth are sometimes braided together for shared access and at other places along the way branch out of the bundle for a while to touch certain resources and are returned to the braid to share again and are finally terminated at some unique end-data points.

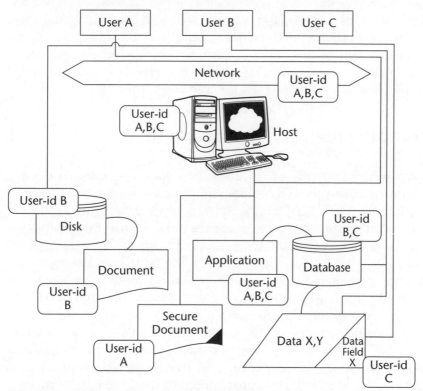

Figure 7-2   Finite access controls to data fields.

Improving Accountability

The capacity to link end users to one or more specific data fields increases accountability and facilitates improvements in auditing. The scope of auditing software tools today is too narrow. There are some excellent auditing capabilities at a few levels of the technology, but the silver-bullet software package that audits at every point where access controls are applied has not arrived yet. The intelligence within auditing software for analysis of the logging facility at access control points also needs to be improved upon. The final stages of the controls' design need to tackle auditing by selecting tools that get as close as possible to all-inclusive auditing of any end user, while at the same time detecting the larger pattern of anomalies and hack attempts.

Of course, security access controls have to be applied at every possible level. Some reduction in the complexity to cover those levels is also a desirable feature to include in the design goals. This chapter shows how the five main topics in this chapter cover how their complementary features of identity management, authoritative source, identity vault, service directories, and identity provisioning are leveraged to support the business processes with control requirements that reduce the complexity without compromising overall control. It explains how the facilitating features built around directories are used to manage identities over a life cycle from an authoritative source of information and then to use the identity information to provision services and access controls.

Understanding Identity Management

As you know, a digital identity can be associated with a person or a device. Even with biometrics involved, computer equipment is not really capable of identifying a person or another device with 100 percent certainty. The software is only going to recognize a pseudonym for the person. Most frequently, this pseudonym is a username or user ID; different terms for the same thing.

End users as well as their usernames have a life cycle with the organization's computing systems. Identity management is all about recognizing the changes that take place in the relationship between the end user and the IT systems she uses and managing that relationship based on those changes. Generally, a user ID is created when someone joins the firm and should be removed quickly when that person leaves the firm or possibly when she's transferred to other locations. Over time, the relationship is altered by job requirements, promotions, changes in duties, and transfers to different work units, as illustrated in Figure 7-3. Various applications and files are typically required to support that individual's work, from e-mail to business processes, as changes occur. Adding, removing, and altering these accesses are the actionable events within the end user's life cycle for the identity management system design.

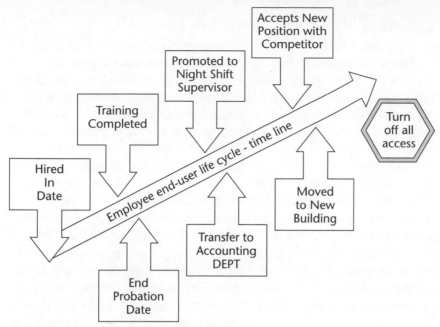

Figure 7-3 Employee end-user life cycle events.

Clients and customers frequently are granted access to Web-based applications and are also given or are self-enrolled for user IDs and passwords, creating another distinct group of users that must be administered and managed in some fashion. The customer-client relationship is also subject to changes over time and is also driven by life cycle events. As you begin to define the dissimilar populations that require access to your organization's IT resources, it's necessary to define the life cycle and events that will require changes to be made for that population of identities. Events that affect the end user's access requirements and privileges are then monitored and may become input into the identity vault and the provisioning process (discussed later in this chapter).

Understanding Authoritative Sources

To acquire sufficient trust for an identity, it's best to use a reliable starting place for that information. A phone call to the help desk is probably not adequate justification to add a user to protected systems in a large organization. Finding authoritative sources of user identities may take some detective work, but it is well worth the effort. If an existing trusted source is isolated and used for identity information as the basis for issuing user IDs, the business processes within the applications that rely on identity begin on sound footing. You can be reasonably sure that the real people behind the data exist and that the information can be relied upon.

Ad hoc (help desk calls) and manual administrative processes dependent on a system administrator are not particularly good methods for larger organizations because of the resources required and the potential for inadvertent errors. They can become targets for internal scams as well. Granted, in some environments, face-to-face enrollment of a user by a systems administrator is the only way to verify the user's paper credentials to the identity management process.

The ideal situation is one in which an existing process is already capturing identity information and placing it into an application's database after appropriate vetting of the paper credentials. The most frequently occurring process that can be leveraged is within one of the HR applications holding payroll, performance, tax identification, or benefits information for employees. Employment hiring, transfer, and release processes already are doing some of the vetting of employees, and HR staff would be entering identifying information into their applications anyway. The HR process is one that can be used as an authoritative source of employee identification information and other employee attributes that help determine the IT services needed. Figure 7-4 illustrates a few of the potential authoritative sources for identity information in a marketing firm.

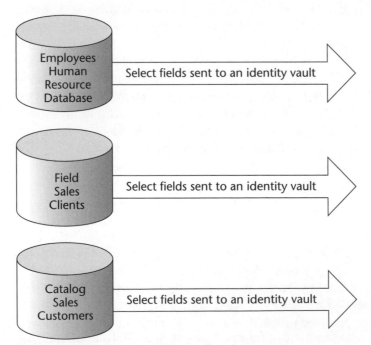

Figure 7-4   Some potential authoritative sources.

Using Unique Population Information

Nonemployee categories of end users that share systems require analysis to determine their characteristics. Each group of users sharing similar characteristics and resource needs becomes a logical collection of user information identified and dealt with as a unique population. An organization that has a sales force that visits every client of the organization may be keeping customer contact information in a custom software application database. Information collected by a sales agent one-on-one in the client's office and entered into the database would be an excellent resource for identity information for the client who uses the organization's Web applications for monitoring order status and/or performing routine reorders. These customers may be two populations or merge into one if the characteristics and resource needs are nearly identical.

Nonprofit organizations may already have automated client lists, a donor database, and grant recipients managed within some computer application. The identifying information for these groups based on the resources they need and the similarities they share would be extracted from those authoritative sources and used in the identity management process for access controls.

Government entities have innumerable databases already containing identity information for citizens — property tax rolls, voter registration, driver's licenses and identity cards, and income tax filings. Granted from a vetting process some of the government data makes better authoritative sources than others. There are also limited services and processes that would be provided to each of these distinct populations served by government entities.

Every user population served by an organization's IT systems may not easily link to an on-hand authoritative source. Some reasons may include that there are so few end users in that group, the vetting is taking place elsewhere out of your control, or the application's use is so geographically spread out that digital authoritative sources are inappropriate or simply not readily available. This circumstance can still be dealt with in an overall identity management and identity provisioning environment, but each comes with some cautions.

Exploring the Risks of Self-Enrollment Identities

Considering the demand for self-enrollment into an identity system, the first consideration is the potential negative consequences of no vetting of any kind. The risks are present and numerous, when from the very beginning of the process, all you really know is that you have a potential end user who is trying to establish a relationship with your online applications. The identifying information could be totally contrived or belong to someone other than the enroller. Self-enrollment may fit with your organization's risk for a small set of applications. However, caution is the watchword for allowing Web self-enrollment identities to be used for access to protected information without some business process verification or vetting. Transferring of weak vetting of identities to protected processes is simply not good practice. The risks are enormous.

Distributed administration is allowing a third party to enroll someone's user identification information into your identity management systems. Here the risk revolves mostly around how much you trust the third party to vet new end users' credentials and to internally control the key to the enrollment process while keeping the information accurate to your standards.

Weaknesses at any point will seriously erode the trust that can be placed in the third-party enrollments. The application sets that can be reached by third-party-enrolled users should be limited. Evaluation of the risks in trusting others to enroll end users should cause considerable cautionary evaluation to take place before using this approach. Verification or secondary vetting should be the norm for any further access to protected systems for third-party enrollees.

One method that can be used is holding the access rights in escrow until the end user's authenticity is verified. A second method to reduce the risk is to use a mailing process to the known address of the enrollee; this can be used in some lower-risk situations where you already have some reliable data on the enrollee.

Understanding Identity Vaults

An identity vault is best described as a directory isolated within a security policy domain installed solely to be the central point for collection and distribution of end-user identity information. The vault utilizes the two important features surrounding meta-directory functionality: the capability to aggregate information to provide one view from multiple sources of information and to combine under the control of programming or business logic to move bits of the information to other storage points. The other storage points can include other directories, databases, or access control lists. Figure 7-5 illustrates an identity vault in its security policy domain.

In ideal circumstances, users and applications never make authentication calls directly to the vault. Administrative access to the vault host, directory, and facilitating software applications are limited to a very few highly vetted and trusted individuals. The vault is isolated in every way possible on a separate host that is in a restricted visibility zone, on its own highly managed switch port, and further isolated by firewall rules that severely regulates which IP hosts can contact it, what protocols can be passed to and from it, and the port numbers used. These are just a few of the necessary security policy items to consider.

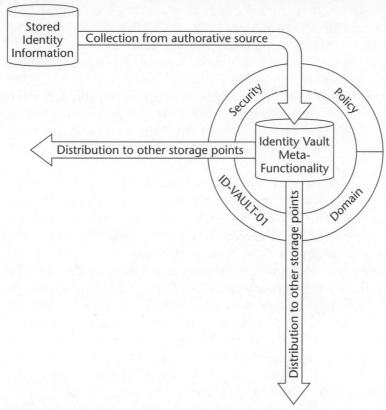

Figure 7-5   Identity vault and security policy domain.

Every OS security feature on the host system that improves security without hindering the collection and distribution of data should be deployed. No other unnecessary or unrelated applications or directories should be present on the computer hosting the identity vault. The security features that surround the identity vaults should be the digital equivalent of Fort Knox. "Spare no workable security features" is the design mantra for the identity vault design and implementation.

One identity vault should be deployed for each unique population served. If a company has employees and customers accessing applications, at least two identity vaults would be used — one for employees and one for customers. Each identity vault would receive near real-time changes from its own associated authoritative source of identity information. The HR application would be the source for employee changes over the employee life cycle with a marketing database of customers for the customer authoritative source.

The software tools used to extract the information from authoritative sources are referred to by different names by the various vendors' products that provide the meta-functionality around directories. This book simply calls them source monitors. The source monitor is a program that is running on the same host as the monitored database (the HR application, for example). The program logic controlling the source monitor is watching for changes in some fields of the database such as job description or last name. When changes of interest occur, the information is passed by the source monitor through more program logic that filters and/or translates the changed data into a format that is needed by the identity vault. The vault stores the new information for further use and distribution to the other storage for control points within the systems.

The movement of the information from the identity vault is called *identity provisioning*, which is discussed in more detail later in this chapter. Automatic deprovisioning of end users at the end of the user life cycle is an important feature. To disable access accounts immediately when an employee leaves the organization or on changes in job duties reduces risk factors.

The source monitor's inverse process is an application receptor that is set up to receive and use the information sent from the identity vault and to place it into another directory, access control list, or database. The receptor application is called various names by different software vendors also. It runs typically on the same host as the target application, and its logic can interface with the target to change passwords or to write data to specific fields. The receptor's role is to place the appropriate data into a target storage point to be used by the target in some manner such as internal-program-level access control.

Understanding Service Directories

For the Web application environment, the most important destination for identity information derived from the authoritative source and moved through the identity vault is the service directory. Service directories become the information source for authentication, authorization, and access control information for each user ID provided to the actual gatekeepers. They are also the storage location where any user self-service changes can be made.

End users are not given access to change every field in the directory. They are limited to only select data fields that do not change overall authorization mapping, such as cell phone number or home e-mail address. The service directory associated with each population is the central point for authentication (see Figure 7-6); as such, it is treated as a unique security policy domain in the same fashion as the identity vault but with a much different profile. For example, the service directories communicate with different hosts and should be limited to only necessary hosts.

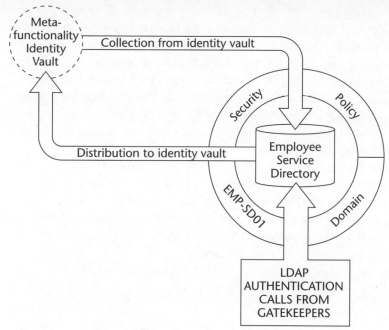

Figure 7-6   A service directory handles authentication.

The analysis to establish the security policy domain boundaries surrounding the service directories has to include limiting and controlling every possible aspect that affects the security profile. Each network and computing environment will be rife with opportunities and challenges to enhance security within all of the security policy domains. Each organization's environmental factors are unique and require detailed analysis to create the best design for their situation.

Understanding Identity Provisioning

Identity provisioning enhances IT operating environments first by cutting down on the need for routine manual administration. Identity provisioning is using the collection and distribution features associated with service directories coupled with business logic to supply other applications with the information. Innovative uses include automatic creation of e-mail accounts for new hires, building the voice mail profile for new hires, and populating an online intranet telephone book of company employees. Identity provisioning includes moving password changes to the other storage points to reduce sign-on complexity for employees using multiple services and application.

The provisioning engine is powered by directory meta-functionality and the capability to collect and distribute the small packages of identity information to the right places. Software vendors who currently make available product suites in the provisioning marketplace also supply the source monitor and receptor software for many popular directories, applications, and databases. Partly because LDAP is one of the standards used in the directory space and the vendors want to satisfy customer demand for interfaces to legacy applications, they offer development kits to custom-build program interfaces to many existing application environments.

Provisioning is achieved by using the identity vault as the information hub. All data collected goes to the appropriate vault, and all distributions of identity information originate there for each population. It increases the accuracy of the information because one source is used and only one record supplies the information for each unique end-user identity. Figure 7-7 shows an identity vault as the provisioning hub for two services.

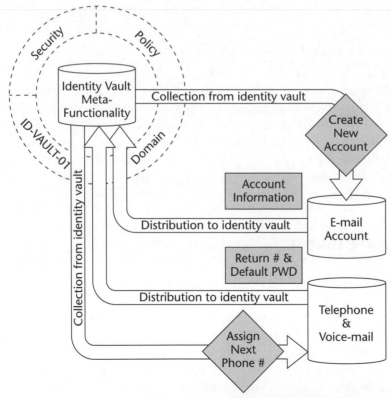

Figure 7-7   Provisioning improves the correctness of information.

Leveraging provisioning features by using the vault to move identity information into the existing security structures of applications and databases increases efficiency and accuracy and reduces administration time. Where end-user self-administered password changes can be done without compromising security, the quantity and frequency of help desk calls can be reduced. A single-sign-on (SSO) user ID and password may not work across all applications, making the implementation a reduced-sign-on capability.

Provisioning features should be exploited where it is technically possible, and where the security is not reduced by its use. Very old legacy systems and applications with a small population may not always be worth the effort to bring them into the provisioning structure. Some one-off situations are inevitable in complex legacy environments. The design goal is to have as few as possible.

Part of the security policy domain definition should also enforce the password policy for length, complexity, and frequency of changes. Having a single point to apply the policy rules removes a good degree of the complexity inherent in standardizing access controls.

Summary

Begin your designing for implementing the five critical elements — identity management, authoritative sources, identity vaults, service directories, and identity provisioning — with the security policy domain definitions that will surround them. Whenever they're available, use population-specific authoritative sources over distributed administration or manual methods of data entry into the directories.

To keep security protection elements under your organization's control, use distributed administration of the identity management process only when there are business drivers for doing so that cannot be ignored. Never put a high degree of trust into self-enrollment processes without some means of verifying that you are dealing with information from the real person and that the real person wants to deal with your applications.

Establish the relationships between the identities in the authoritative sources. Migrate from the authoritative source only the minimum required identifying information to the identity vault. Use the identity vault as the focal point to manage the usernames throughout the end-user life cycle. Leverage the provisioning capability based on that life cycle to as many points as may be practical in your IT environment. Finally, point all the authentication calls at a separate service directory, never at the identity vault itself. Surround the service directories with well-developed security policy domain definitions.

Engineering Privacy Protection into Systems and Applications

How much privacy is enough? How high and how strong a wall should organizations build around their protected information, resources, and IT assets?

There is a variable range of tolerance on the privacy issue, with some thinking that not all information in the public domain should be there. Others are willing to share private information with impunity, believing the risks are few and acceptable, to get what they want in information exchanges and in commercial transactions. From the perspective of modern regulated organizations, access protections must extend both for maintaining the integrity of the information they publish into the public domain and for restricting protected information access to a select identified group on a need-to-know basis.

To accomplish this, it's necessary to examine every point of communication flow, every interface, and every opportunity for applying protective measures. It is work requiring attention to the technology in use and the details within that technology.

Basing Designs on Asset Values

The build-out of your security strategy begins with recognizing that the data in the three classifications — public, protected, and restricted — have different values to the organization and deserve protection appropriate to their values. The sorting of the data becomes linked to the overall strategy of the security architecture design.

The objective is to create a starting point for the security design that leads to dissecting the data interfaces so that highly specific policy domain definitions can be uniquely applied. If all classes of data are transmitted and shared with end users on the same network segment, then that segment is only one security policy domain by default. Having one security domain that has a wide range of source and destination addresses with multiple protocols and port numbers becomes problematic in that such a design limits the capability to apply finite control at each level, creating a weak protective link for every item in the policy domain.

Protecting Open Public Information

Few protections for access to public information are required beyond those involving its accuracy and integrity. Restricting access only involves restricting who can post new information and ensuring the data is not hacked or modified in any way from internal or external wrongdoers. One strategy is to place all public information behind firewalls to the Internet, on its own firewall port, and in a totally isolated network segment that is never physically connected in any way to the back-office networks and computer systems (see Figure 8-1).

To make this strategy work, you have to place the public databases used to generate dynamic content as read-only copies in that isolated segment and accept the fact that there will be an information delay for posting of new time-sensitive information to the secluded cluster hosts. The trade-off of seconds, minutes, or even hours to post data may be well worth it if hack attempts can be kept away from the rest of the systems you are working to protect.

The protections for the integrity shown in Figure 8-1 include routing of the information seekers by URL to the first ISP firewall, then through a second firewall with three ports. The first port would connect to the first firewall. Another port on the second firewall leads to the Web appliance that appears to be the entire Web infrastructure for the serviced URLs. To a potential hacker, the appliance looks like the Web servers. The third network port would be used exclusively to manage access to the Web hosts behind the appliance(s) through a VPN concentrator, which would be the data path for Web content publishers to post changes and new information to the hosts within the public-information Web cluster. This approach creates a virtual island for the public information, gives a target separate from back-office systems data paths to potential hackers, and allows for the application of a highly customized security policy domain for the open information.

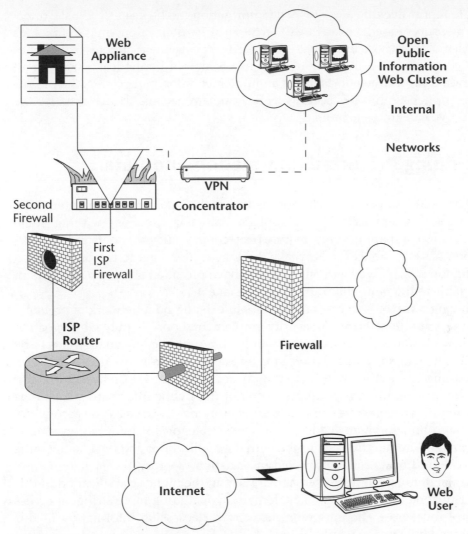

Figure 8-1 Isolate public information from private.

Adding control features such as two-factor authentication for system administrators and content contributors to access the hosts in the cluster contributes to protecting the integrity of the data. Alternatively, system administrators could be required to use a physical presence on the cluster network to gain administrative access. Then again, the firewall and software selected to separate the zones could be individual firewalls from different manufacturers instead of different ports controlled by separate rules based on the same physical firewall.

Even with a public-information island design like this, it makes sense to include intrusion detection within the Web cluster network to learn from it and to report hacking attempts. The information can be used to adjust protective measures to reduce the threat. As the security policy domain is defined for the island, the advice to evaluate all possible enhancement options also applies here. Protecting the integrity of open assets should be the least costly of all your data protection efforts. From an implementation perspective, the protections applied within this security policy domain become the baseline for the other two categories to build upon.

Shielding Protected Information and Data

The protected information category is where the challenges to maintain adequate security and access controls substantially increase. For one thing, some information and applications require protection, while other data in the information base is public. Hackers take the easy route to get to the protected information if you give them one — if you have provided an easy path through the pubic to the nonpublic data, they will take it.

Having a mixed security policy domain existing on a network is probably the most frequent error in security implementations. If public-information hosts can become the weak security link, all nonpublic information has to be treated at an equal level for protection and access control measures as the protected information it shares network address space or host drives with. The security profile must include protection of the public information that is as confounding to someone trying to gain unauthorized access as you are willing to design and implement for the protected category of information. Public information frequently must reside with the applications and data on the same network and hosts as the protected information category. If this is your case, the open data has to be treated as if it were in the higher classification in this security zone and security policy domain by including more stringent access control measures. The minimum measure for accessing information in this combined data group would be to:

- Require an identity.
- Check out that identity.
- Issue a username and strong password combination.
- Require authentication and control access via directory services.
- Provide auditing and intrusion detection measures.

The best practice is, of course, to segregate public and protected data and to enforce stringent security policy domain definitions. Figure 8-2 shows an example.

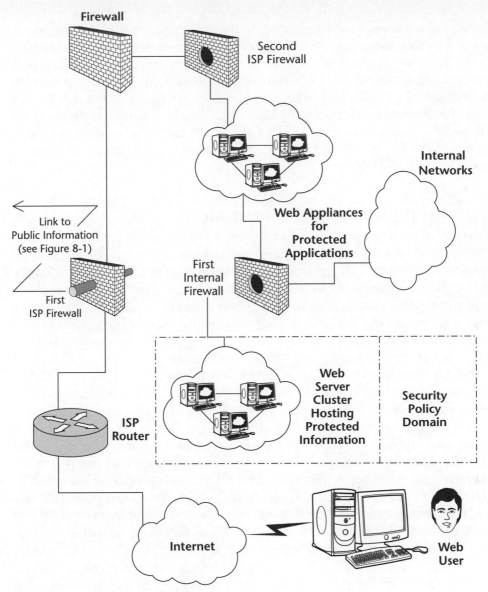

Figure 8-2   Isolate protected information.

There are other measures to apply within the security policy domain surrounding the protected information and application Web hosts. The front-end Web appliance can be used as the first place to authenticate users against the access control directory, before permitting access to the applications and data itself. The appliance becomes a proxy for accessing the Web servers and applications. It makes sense to apply all the protection designed into your public-information domain to include requiring internal users to use a two-factor authenticated VPN to access the hosts to update or change information.

When applications in the protected space are used to collect information from external users, consider setting up batchlike processes to move recently collected information on a tightly controlled periodic schedule to more protected hosts on the internal network. If a hacker attempt is successful at compromising a database in a Web services cluster, only a small amount of the new data could be lost. Scrubbing these hosts every 15 minutes and using an automated process to move the information to hosts with a higher protection profile would not be too aggressive an approach to take. Use of some intrusion detection devices and software is even more important for host systems in this zone and security domain.

Defending Restricted Information

When your organization's business requirements mandate that restricted information be available for access on the Web, bear in mind that the classification for restricted data implies use of the highest protection levels. The design requires security measures as good as security can get, includes as many access control features as your organization can afford, and achieves protections to the outer limits of the technology tools currently available. That's a tall order for design quality by any measure.

Access controls applied to open and protected information become the baseline for restricted-information security policy domain definitions. A two-factor token card is also required for each user seeking access. This means in addition to a directory service, you need an additional server (see Figure 8-3) that provides a second level of authentication for validating the changing numerical string of data from the end user's token card. The directory and the AAA (authentication, authorization, and accounting) server work in conjunction to authenticate identified users who correctly provide the strong password and the correct time generated random numerical string from the token card. The protocol used by the AAA servers is called RADIUS (Remote Authentication Dial-In User Service). Each username profile is stored in the server's central database, and the RADIUS protocol provides the needed communications interface between the server and the actual gatekeeper device to authenticate users.

A hacker's favorite method of attack is to get control of the operating system on a poorly protected server and to use that foothold to access other nearby hosts. Physical network isolation of restricted data affords the opportunity to tighten up the access controls and protection of the data to the maximum extent possible without hindering the freer exchange of information classified at lower levels.

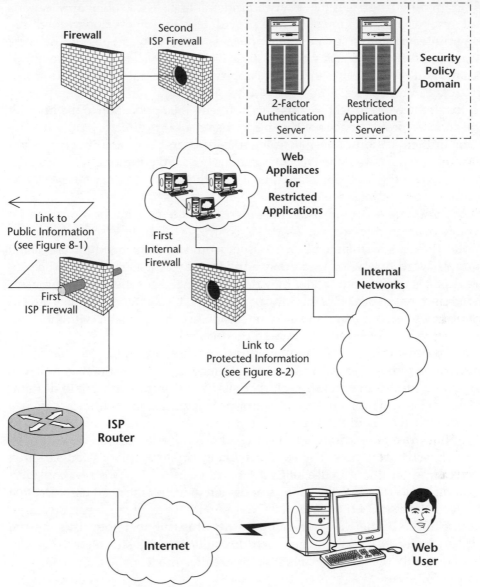

Figure 8-3 Add two-factor authentication for access to restricted information resources.

Securing Legacy Applications

Organizations that have been using computers for a number of years, even decades, often have a huge investment in hardware and software written in programming languages that many consider extinct. These older applications and systems are often impelled into providing continuing value through the use of intermediate software to allow access to the applications on the Web. Wrapping sufficient security around these types of applications becomes problematic and often requires innovative approaches to maintain adequate access controls.

One of the ways to achieve this is to front-end the application to the Internet with a Web proxy appliance capable of using LDAP directory calls for by-name authentication of various categories of users. Use of VPN encryption between the proxy and the Web applications host and additional VPN encryption between the Web application host and the back-end data hosts help to secure the communication channels.

Existing access control lists embedded in the legacy applications can be exploited as an added layer of access controls when the Web intermediate applications are written to allow it. Users would be challenged for username and password first at the Web proxy appliance, and then later within the program pages of the application, they'd be challenged for the embedded username and password. It is not always possible to abandon a legacy access control method, but there is usually no reason not to build on it with the security offered by a Web proxy appliance product.

When older applications and operating systems offer little to enhance the security or access profiles, a remaining strategy is to isolate them as much as possible with routing and firewall controls to and from appropriate destinations. In this situation constant monitoring, logging, and audit of access is a necessary last layer of defense.

Architecture teams are often most challenged by the legacy applications' limited security models. The cost of making rip-and-replace changes often keeps the applications in use long past a normal life cycle. Two new considerations should enter into the value proposition to justify the need to make such changes: the risk of litigation and the risk of failing any of the regulatory compliance audits, either of which can be costly. It is true that both risks may be hard to quantify in dollars, but such difficulty is not justification to ignore them in the fix-or-replace analysis by the architecture team.

Correcting Current Application Development Efforts

There is no future in building tomorrow's adverse audit findings today. If your organization is currently developing new applications requiring access controls that will be made available to the Web and diverse groups of users within your organization, there is likely no better time to include those controls.

Directory-enabled access controls at the application level are the minimum needed for critical applications. The emerging control target is the capability to apply access controls over single data fields within the application's database storage.

Regrettably, there are vendors who still think that applying access controls at the directory group level is a sufficient access control model for applications in today's enterprises. A closer understanding and blending of principles between the accounting profession and the computer professionals is needed for successful applications. The separation of duties, responsibilities, and powers between individuals involved in processing financial transactions and accounting for them must be exactly reflected in the application's development requirements documentation. For example, the cash controls for the processing of accounts payable typically have one person processing the vouchers and another approving or signing the actual checks. Allowing the processor access to the check-approval application violates the cash controls by providing an avenue for the processor to pay fraudulent vouchers.

There is no doubt that many vendors involved in financial reporting software development will find it necessary to improve the internal security controls in their products to meet current regulatory requirements. Whether pressuring a vendor to improve embedded access controls or adding requirements to in-house applications development projects, it is time think of the security for access control as a utility service provided by a full implementation of an identity management system. That strategy has merit for a number or reasons, including the following:

- It simplifies current and future application development to use the same access control methodology.
- Access control administration can be automated (at times), centralized (when appropriate), and distributed (when needed).
- Auditing of access controls can be focused and simplified.
- Stronger security domain definitions can be applied.

Securing New Applications

The functional requirements for new applications at the planning and development stages can include strong access controls from the start. When designing access controls and security for new applications, you must consider security from end to end of the business process; from the original keyboard entries into the application right to the printed report on its way to the mailroom.

Table 8-1 provides a design starting point, building on the OSI Seven-Layer Network model by adding a layer for physical access security as the first point of concern for end-to-end security designs. It also adds three other layers to consider: data file storage, data fields within a file, and operating systems. Take each application through an evaluation based on Table 8-1 by answering Yes or No for each of the 11 layers.

Table 8-1   Access Security Checklist

SECURITY LAYER	COMPONENT	CAN SECURITY MEASURES BE APPLIED?	WHAT IS THE SECURITY PROTECTION BASED ON?	CAN LDAPV3 DIRECTORY SERVICES BE USED TO CONTROL ACCESS?
1. Physical Security	Physical Access			
2. Physical Media	Transport Media			
3. Data Link	Logical Order			
4. Network	Node-to-Node Delivery			
5. Transport	Quality of Data Delivery			
6. Session	Organization of Data			
7. Presentation	Syntax of Data Transfer			
8. Application	Work Done With Data			
9. Data Store	Data Storage (Digital Files)			
10. Data Field	Specific Data Field in Stored File			
11. Operating System	Host Services			

Note: 2 to 8 are from the OSI Seven-Layer Model.

As you sketch in the answers and information for your unique environment, realize that some layers will have subsets to consider, particularly where a single host system is running multiple application processes. Another example is a

Web application that interfaces with many other applications in the background to work. The checklist may be best applied to each of the applications. It's intended as a guide to a consistent, organized approach to analyzing for the security design treatment of every new application and for the review of existing applications.

The security profile achievable from the checklist will vary by platform, operating system, and application software. The checklist requires the analyst to evaluate every level to determine if there is the possibility of control at that layer, if available controls are being used, and whether existing controls can integrate with the LDAP directories used as the foundation for identity management and provisioning. The core question answered from the checklist is whether everything that can be done to restrict the access to selected individuals in your environment is being done.

For those applications that can be integrated for management of access controls with an LDAP directory, the matrix in Table 8-2 can be used to determine how deep a layer access can be controlled. The goal for adequate security controls and for auditing/reporting is to be able to control access by username to any one field of data (within a database), such as a single dollar entry in a financial report.

You can use Table 8-2 to rate every application that can be controlled within the context of directory services in an identity management system; put an R for required control at each level and an A in the box for achieved if the design and implementation can deliver that level of control.

Table 8-2 Control Level Matrix Applied by LDAP Directory Checklist

LEVELS	ACCESS CONTROLS APPLIED BY:		
	GROUP MEMBER	END USER BY NAME	TWO-FACTOR (TOKEN)
Network			
Host			
Application			
Data File			
Data Field			

Seeking Management Support and Funding

Your management's perception of the threat posed by the hacker who may make his way into your data may have a lot to do with how much your executives are willing to budget for access controls and data protection from design through implementation and system operations. Every day the news media provides hard-hitting reports about breaches in security. Even if you do not review the IT trade literature that constantly adds to the reports and analysis of what went wrong behind the headlines, the trends in the reports are scary to anyone responsible for valuable data.

Profiling Hackers

There are few things your executives should know about the Internet hacker threat. The hacker could be in any country where connecting to the Internet is possible. With the Internet's worldwide scope, it is very difficult for law enforcement to find and prosecute the perpetrators. New hackers join in the "game" every day, and it isn't possible to prevent them from connecting.

Hackers range in age from very young to very old. Some hack for sport, some for ego, and others for profit. The education levels of the hacker community range from high school dropouts to those with advanced degrees in programming or computer science. Their profiles include those who work alone, those who have formed loose member co-ops that share information about known system vulnerabilities, and others who are organized groups with the intent to harm or criminally profit from stolen information. There is the potential that some of these organized groups may be sponsored by or at the very least are tolerated by foreign governments. As alarming as that may be, the most fearful element making up the would-be hacker profile is that he or she may be working in the office cubicle next to yours.

Building a Case for Security

As you build the case for sufficient funding of security controls within your organization, scan for current media reports of other companies that have failed to provide adequate controls and use them as references. Often the articles will report the consequences and hint at what the cost to the victimized company might be. When you know that some of your applications or systems share the same vulnerabilities, say so — that may take courage, but it the professional course of action.

Vendors who've implemented systems for current and former clients, it could be argued, have a responsibility to tell clients that the applications and systems previously implemented fail to meet currently needed access controls and security profiles. If done with true concern for the client and some finesse, tightening the security and improving the access controls can be a tremendous source of new business for the vendors capable of making the necessary improvements and enhancements.

In-house IT professionals should be acutely aware of system and application vulnerabilities within their areas of responsibility and should be working to remove the no-cost and low-cost weaknesses out of the systems while asking for the funding for those requiring cash infusions to correct.

Seeking a Benchmark

Organizations differ considerably on the types of information that constitute intellectual property and those collections of information that provide competitive advantage in the marketplace. The value of that information also varies. The lengths to which organizations will go to protect against the loss of valuable data have a direct impact on their willingness to provide funding for data protection.

All companies that hold personally identifying, medical, and personal financial information belonging to their clients face similar risks. Researching the competitive landscape or seeking information from industry consulting firms may enable you to quantify what others in your industry are spending to protect privacy and financial data, and to provide a benchmark. Unfortunately, it may not be possible to discover what the firms who failed to succeed in protecting this type of information spent. The numbers from failed organization may be in the consultant's totals. In any case, what matters most to you are your own cost projections for getting it right in your organization's unique system and environment.

The cost data for how much IT spending will be necessary to provide adequate security controls to comply with regulatory requirements is just beginning to be known for each industry type. The spending figures will be collected by consulting groups and reported over the next few years. A few audit cycles will be needed to determine the value returned and validate successes from that spending.

Summary

If the design and operation of security controls and data protection measures were likened to a game of chess, the player's objective is complete success, measured by never losing a single game piece and never being stalemated or checkmated. As you design and build your security controls, consider taking advantage of every possible opportunity for increasing the security measures your systems can provide. Use the checklists in this chapter as a tool to examine your existing or planned environment to ensure that every level where security can be applied is fully evaluated.

Take steps to ensure that management fully understands the challenges and threats facing the systems. Then assist management in translating the requirements for creating those protection measures into dollar estimates in the budgeting process. Losing the security game is not an option.

The Value of Data Inventory and Data Labeling

To protect information on your systems from unauthorized access, you need to know some things about that information. First, you have to know what the data is. Next, you need to know where it is. Is there only one instance of it or is it scattered to dozens of locations? Who should be allowed to access, create, modify, or destroy the file?

Organizations rarely hesitate to put in place a system to inventory and manage widgets of all manner, equipment, desks, tools, hardware, and consumables of all kinds. Companies often track hard goods from the point of purchase to the point of disposal. The chains of custody are traced and recorded at every point of exchange. Digital data files and the information contained in them are not always treated with that same level of concern regarding custody and control.

It could be argued that the overall risk of compromise, loss, or destruction of digital data is greater than the risk of losing physical things if for no other reason than that someone half a world away with a personal computer on the distant end of a pair of 24-gauge wires can steal, alter, or destroy your unprotected data. The intellectual property contained in your data systems could be far more valuable than all of the physical assets your organization owns. Certainly, unauthorized compromise of customer financial data could generate liability exceeding the value of the company itself, even leading to the devaluation of company stock or complete financial collapse.

Data classification, regardless of the system you use, implies that you know what it is, where it is, its classification, its retention cycle, how it was acquired, who is responsible for it, and why you still need it. Ideally, you'd know all of this about every shred of data your organization has, or could get the information by querying a database in your organization, and every file, database, and document is labeled externally and digitally. Odds are your organization has only some data identified in such a way that these answers are immediately available. Once you have all of the information about the data in your systems, establishing the controls and access authorizations is an easy next step. Without this information, finite access controls become impossible to determine. The system security designers, application developers, and data administrators all need to know who can be permitted access and which groups should be denied any access to each piece of data.

Information assets have value to the organization, and it's a good idea to have some idea what that value is. What's a fair way to quantify and compare the values placed on various assets, including digital ones?

Comparing Value Protection Ratios

One way to discover whether digital information assets are highly valued within an organization is to calculate a value protection ratio for each category of assets and compare them.

The formula for value protection ratio (VPR) is the annual cost to protect (ACP) divided by present book value (PBV):

```
ACP ÷ PBV = VPR
```

Compare the value relationship placed on physical assets to that of digital information assets by counting the number of people assigned and resources allocated to control physical inventory versus the resources and people accountable for the control of the digital assets. Here's an example:

A gasket company has physical assets worth $2,500,000 that are overseen by three full-time employees who, with benefits, cost the company $240,000 per year. The company also uses a physical asset inventory computer system, program, and database that cost $10,000 per year to operate. The total annual cost of overseeing the physical assets is $250,000 ($240,000 plus $10,000). Dividing that cost by the book value of the assets ($2,500,000) yields a value protection ratio of 0.1.

The value of the proprietary program and formulas stored in the computer systems for blending the mixtures the company uses to make its gaskets has a present value of $10,000,000. The computer systems controls and two employees assigned to maintain the security of the computer systems cost the company $150,000 per year. The value protection ratio for the digital assets is the annual cost to protect the asset ($150,000) by the assets' value ($10,000,000): 0.015.

The relative value expressed by the company management between the two asset groups (physical and digital) is found by comparing the ratios. In this example, dividing the physical asset value protection ratio by the digital asset value protection ratio (0.1 / 0.015 = 6.67) shows that the management places a much higher value on its physical assets than on its digital data assets — more than six times higher.

There is no set rule on how much spending is enough; however, most people would agree that the gasket company example has its priorities out of balance. Loss of a few thousand dollars' worth of equipment would not harm that organization very much. Loss of the proprietary formulas to industrial espionage could very well lead to the company's demise.

The value protection ratio provides a way to compare resources allocated to protect various asset categories in an equalized manner. In situations where digital assets also carry the risk of litigation from the loss of personally identifying information or customers' personal financial information, an estimate of the cost of that risk can be to the assets' value. Alternatively, two ratios can be calculated: one on actual value of the digital assets and one for the risk-of-litigation component. In larger organizations it's helpful to enlist the assistance of the finance and accounting departments to make these comparisons.

Without top management recognizing that digital assets provide value to the organization, getting agreement to apply the resources necessary to fully inventory and maintain a process supporting digital data inventory may be difficult. When regulatory requirements cannot be met without a data inventory, the cost of doing so may not be a factor.

Understanding Data Inventory

Getting a data inventory for a company that is not already engaged in the practice is hard but necessary work. It is not possible to protect or apply access controls to digital data that is just out there somewhere on the company networks and file servers. With cut-and-pastes, copy commands, and desktop software, it's easy to proliferate digital information on hundreds if not thousands of desktop and notebook computers. Authorized and unauthorized share points on servers create the potential for a protected data file to find its way to an unprotected host.

For access controls to be successful, you must be able to apply controls by username to any one piece of digital data. This fine division of access control is unachievable without a complete inventory of the data requiring controls and protective measures.

Removing the risks of data loss or inappropriate alteration to meet Sarbanes-Oxley or other externally imposed compliance criteria requires thinking out of the box by which many organizations are controlled. For example, if a catalog sales company allows access by telephone sales staff to every one of its customers' credit card data in the database, the risk of compromise and misuse by internal staff increases. If all internal staff members can access every record, it isn't unrealistic to think that a successful external hacker can easily steal every record.

Access controls' success can be defined as having a complete inventory of all data and applying controls that are capable of supporting a one-user-to-one-data-element relationship. Controlling access in that manner meets any test of adequate controls regardless of which external or internal compliance audit is taking place. Controls can't get any better than that unless you're looking for a technique in which two or more users must combine in some way to access data. (Some militaries, for example, require two officers several feet apart, to turn separate keys at the same time to launch a missile from a silo, and only after each has verified the launch order.)

Getting a handle on the data through an exhaustive inventory, moving the data to digital containers where controls can be applied, and keeping the data managed under tight controls is the only way compliance audit requirements can be met and maintained.

Polices covering access to and the creation, modification, and destruction of data are required. They must map to the organization's digital data inventory requirements and policies.

Examining the Basic Data Inventory Model

Managing data inventory is best done at a companywide level. Without software tools to automate the process, though, it may be necessary to distribute the responsibility for the data inventory process to various levels in the organization. A standardized data inventory model should be used across the whole organization.

A database application is probably the best way to manage the information and facilitate rapid lookups of the information. If you're building an in-house application to collect and manage the data, you could customize a schema and use an LDAP directory to store the information. Spreadsheets could be used for smaller amounts of data, although that is not the recommended method. In the long run, the larger the amount of data going into the inventory, the more valuable it is to be able to search and retrieve by each of the fields in any company's given data inventory model.

Following is a list of recommended data inventory control fields and a brief description of each:

- **Data Description and Tags** — Field to include a very brief description of what is contained in the file such as Articles of Incorporation and By-laws. This field also includes the tags used to help find and retrieve the information. Tagging is particularly important for documents that will be retrieved by using a search form and Web browser. (Tagging is discussed in more detail later in this chapter.) The tags used in the inventory should be the same tags that will be used to facilitate use with browser search engines.

- **Data Classification** — The classification scheme used by the organization determines this field. Keep it simple and use the terms *public*, *protected*, and *restricted*.

- **Type of Dataset** — Record the broader category in its relationship to the organization. Is the information financial or educational? Does it deal with manufacturing, facilities, or HR benefits? Use whatever category applies.

- **Filename** — This is the actual data filename as it appears in the operating system. Most operating systems support longer filenames. It should be an exact name match to what OS level drive access would reveal.

- **File Type** — Filename extensions such as PDF and JPG often help describe the file type. This field should include version numbers when needed. A brief description is sometimes helpful, as is pixel or resolution information for digital pictures.

- **Department Responsible** — Record the name of the department and work section responsible for the management of the data.

- **Content Owner** (Individual, Group, or Job Function) — Name an individual when appropriate; otherwise, use job function or workgroup.

- **Created By** — List the internal or external entity that created the data.

- **Author (Content Creator)** — Name the copyright owner or individual who created the content.

- **Creation Date** — This is the date the information was created or was entered into digital storage by this organization.

- **Last Edit Date** — This is the date of the most recent authorized edit or modification to the data.

- **Review Date** — This is the date the information should be reviewed for current relevance.

- **Scheduled Action Date** — This is the next date for action on this data file, particularly when it should be sent to archives or destroyed.

- **Associated Application** — The computer application(s) that either created or acted on the information contained in the file would be listed here.

- **Business Process Supported** — This field is the name of the business processes — catalog sales, credit card processing, or financial reporting, for example — that are supported by this file.

- **Storage Host Name** — This is the name of the computer, data mart, or server host where the file is stored.

- **Encryption Definitions and Requirements** — Protected and restricted files typically need to be stored and communicated using one of the many encryption technologies. This field holds the information regarding the encryption technology and hashing of the file in storage or when in transit across the network.

- **Access Control Definitions** — Record the access control levels required for access to the data. This information helps define whether the file is accessed by named individuals, groups, job function, or open to all. The user-data association level of access is also defined here: read-only, modify, create, and destroy.

- **Access Controlled By** — Defines how access is achieved. This field tells what methods are used to control access and at what level the controls are applied, such as by operating systems controls, an LDAP directory API from the application, or access control lists within the application itself, or one of these combined with a token card. Whatever the methods are, they're listed here.

You may find that including additional fields is valuable or necessary in your organization. Collecting the information and maintaining additions, changes, and deletions to the data inventory facilitates the architectural design and maintenance of the access controls. Use the list to create the entries in the LDAP directories that will provide the hub for the identity management and identity provisioning process, which ultimately controls who can access any data. Mapping the relationship between the data and the user's access is impossible without an inventory that expresses the required security relationships.

Labeling (Tagging) Data

Labels (descriptive tags) provide a way to find the information you want. Web servers and search engines use the labels to allow searching for text-based information. These same tags provide value in larger companies on the company intranet portal to find needed information. The tagging method is naturally a part of the document creation process that fits very nicely into the data inventory model.

A standard called Extensible Markup Language (XML) is designed to be used across the Web to find the tagged information you are seeking.

The tags can be very valuable, particularly for companies interested in pushing marketing information out to the Web. Some Web site designers have elevated the tagging for Web searches to nearly an art form. You've probably noticed that some sites are always presented (sometimes inappropriately) in search engines. That's a result of tagging. Each company needs a policy that specifies the strategy and standard for data labeling and XML tags.

Having a complete data inventory is the only way an organization can be certain that every piece of information that requires protection has the appropriate access controls applied.

Summary

Imagine for a moment that you inherited a large box full of beautiful rings, necklaces, bracelets, earrings, broaches, and watches, and some of the jewelry looks like it might be diamonds, rubies, and other precious gems. The lawyer who brought you the box said some of these items are just costume, others are known to be valuable, and some pieces may be priceless beyond imagination. After you signed the receipt for the probate court record, the lawyer quickly drove away. Your organization's uninventoried and unlabeled data assets present the same challenge as the box of jewelry. What needs to go into the home safe, what can be given away, and what needs to go into the safe deposit box at the bank?

The inventory, data classification, and labeling provides the basis for how the data will be treated, managed, and controlled within your systems for storage, access, disposition, and release over the life cycle of the data. Building quality access controls and leaving some of what should have been restricted material out of the sphere of the systems' controls is not going to achieve regulatory compliance and may lead to very undesirable consequences for your company. The data inventory takes a lot of work, but it is a necessary prerequisite for achieving adequate access control over valuable digital assets.

Putting It All Together in the Web Applications Environment

Applications made available via a Web browser on the Internet, company intranet, or partner extranet currently dominate the applications development efforts in most organizations. The straightforwardness of requiring only a Web browser on the desktop or notebook to access complex applications makes it extremely easy for the staff responsible for supporting the end users' computers. It is that simplicity that explains much of the popularity of Web-based applications. The built-in VPN (virtual private network) capability of TLS 1.0/ SSL 3.0 in Web browser software also facilitates the security model because SSL is handling it automatically. The future of Internet commerce depends on the continued viability of the TLS/SSL standards.

NOTE TLS/SSL (Transport Layer Security/Secure Sockets Layer) protocols are designed to provide privacy and data integrity between two communication points over the Internet. They're generally used for security with a client's Web browser and a Web server at some Web applications portal. (See IETF Network Working Group RFCs beginning with 2246 for more information on TLS 1.0)

Web-based applications reliant on SSL/TLS are an ingrained part of the current Internet landscape. The nearly universal availability of these programs is a windfall to the marketing efforts of any company or organization, and as a result, more and more applications are being Web-enabled. This software often collects personally identifying and financial information, and provides in-house users a way to exchange sensitive information across the Web.

An organization's Web-based (and other) applications frequently use a plethora of different methods to control access and have tens, even hundreds, of repositories of access control lists, directories, and embedded code containing identity information. This situation brings with it a complexity of design, an administrative burden to manage the lists, and inefficiencies in the operation and maintenance of the applications and systems. Managing multiple methods and lists also makes it difficult to quickly modify integrated software applications when changes in business processes or new business opportunities require it.

Creating those applications with a common design approach and building into the application development process a standard access control security model makes application security easier, standardizes access controls, assists with the identity management life cycle, and facilitates archetypal audit processes. This chapter presents a common design approach using DEALS (directory-enabled application-level security) as the model for Web access. Although focused on the Web environment, the identity management and identity provision process could apply to any modern computing environment where access controls are important.

Using DEALS

Software that facilitates the use of a DEALS model is available from many vendors and under many trademarked names. This chapter does not focus on any of the vendors providing directories, identity management, and identity provisioning, or auditing capability in the access controls setting, but it tackles the concepts that, if they fit your unique needs and environment, you should consider when planning and designing the authorization, authentication, and access controls portion of your organization's system security architecture.

Finely tuned access controls coupled with restrictive security policy domains are mandatory for adequate security controls across computer systems. The negative reports currently headlining in the consumer and trade media teach that security considerations must take the driver's seat in application development instead of being the last check box considered before bringing a program on line. Current software's security features may not be as good as they will someday be, but they are sufficient to enable a knowledgeable architecture team focusing on one security policy domain at a time to design and implement a maximum level of security and access controls.

LOOKING AT LEGACY APPLICATIONS

The benefits afforded new applications by standardizing on authorization, authentication, and access controls are clear. But what about existing (legacy) applications? Should they be modified to work within the design presented here? Before you can answer that question, you need to consider the following:

◆ Are the existing control methods adequate to meet internal access control standards as well as those imposed by external regulatory bodies?

◆ How many access control lists does it use? Would consolidation of the methods provide some efficiency, even if only in the administration of the lists?

◆ Can your existing control methods provide a satisfactory foundation for future applications, or will you have to use a new method and access list every time a new application is brought on line?

Beyond these considerations, follow your organization's business case methodology for a design that implements the concepts presented here.

For your organization to achieve optimal access control designs, directory services and identity management must be treated in the context of security domain definitions with a focus on the population served. This means that any discussion of directory services should focus on how to use directory services to serve each unique population.

Every security aspect possible within the technology and products used must be set up in a way that carries the security domain definitions across as many layers as possible. Applying fine-grained controls in a manageable context across many layers is facilitated by the use of directories. When directory features are applied to control access down to the application level and within applications, the result is DEALS. DEALS means the systematic use of population-specific directories to control access to applications and, when needed, to specific data fields within an application. The scope of directory-enabled security begins at a point outside the organization's firewall and ends at the control of a single data field in a database.

Foiling OS Attacks with Web Proxy Appliances

As you know, Web servers that can be accessed directly via an IP address from the Internet are at risk from hacking attempts. Fronting all Web applications, regardless of data classification, with one or more Web proxy appliance enhances the security profile. The appliance is set up to be the only device directly accessed from the Internet. It connects with the user's Web browser and acts as a proxy to access through the internal zone firewalls to the servers that actually run the Web-based applications.

Your choice of appliance should include a feature that makes it capable of imposing an authentication routine for access. The appliance acting as a bidirectional proxy should be capable of collecting username and password information over an SSL link to the end user's Web browser and then verifying the username and password combination with the appropriate service directory before granting any further session access for that specific user by name. It must integrate well with an LDAP service directory, and it also must support SSL/TLS connections or another type of encrypted tunnel to the internal hosts it is protecting from direct access. Sometimes in legacy systems the VPN tunnel security extends only as far as a content switch. The content switch can then connect to legacy host applications that may not be capable of VPN tunnel communications.

The proxy appliance should also be capable of a two-factor authentication call to an access control server when the protection level of the data requires a token card to grant access to more sensitive applications. Access to restricted information and hosts should always require two-factor token card access.

Choosing and Using Authoritative Sources

It used to be that a systems administrator or clerk had to enter the information manually for every user on any given system or for access to particular applications. When the user's status changed (leaving the company or transferring to another department, for example), the removal of the user' information often did not happen, leaving systems at risk. There are plenty of stories in the trade press about discharged employees logging on to systems long after leaving a company and causing harm to systems, customers, or the company itself.

The best way to handle identity and access control data is to capture identity information from an existing authoritative source. The authoritative sources vary depending on the type of organization and the populations of clients they serve. The authoritative data sources for identity information fall into three primary categories: existing, distributed administrative entry, and self-enrollment.

Linking to an Existing Identity Data Source

The example of using the company's employee database to collect identity information for employee access may apply to organizations of all types. The purveyor of the identity vault (meta-directory) software should provide always-on monitoring software (source monitor) that looks for changes in the underlying source database and forwards the specific changes that are sought as inputs to the identity vault.

The concept is that when changes are made in the authoritative source (such as a new employee being hired), the identity information that provides the basic information regarding access rights is forwarded to the identity vault. The vault's meta-functionality and logic then uses that data to provide information and access rights to an application receptor that is always listening in on other directories, access control lists, or the innate access controls of specific applications.

When an employee is released from active status in the employee database, he is deprovisioned of all access and removed from other directories, access control lists, and software controls by the workings of the source monitor and application receptors. For this process to work, sufficient data fields must be in the database and shared with the identity vault directory. For example, if a phone line is going to be issued and turned active, it may be necessary to extract the exact work location of the new hire to match with the available phone line. Provisioning other services such as operation system access for files and printing or automatically provisioning an e-mail account may require input from the employee database regarding the department and workgroup to which the new hire is assigned.

The schema design of the identity vault must include data objects, attributes, and properties to accommodate the transfer of information. Although the main reason companies create and employ identity management and identity provisioning is to improve the quality and reliability of the access control process, the payback from reduced administrative activities and expense is no less valued and may be significant enough over time to help justify the expenditure to create the system.

As you increase the number and type of end users in the identity management and provisioning process, security sectors and security domain definitions (discussed in Chapter 3) begin to hit the designer's decision tree. Even though LDAP-compliant directories can handle millions, perhaps billions, of identity objects, putting all of your end users in one directory — particularly when their access to applications and needs differ — significantly limits your design options. (You would use one directory only when you have to serve a single population of end users with little difference in their access rights and privileges.)

Putting all of organization's differing user populations in one directory also reduces the security domain definitions to one, which severely limits the additional security features that can be designed into access controls at other layers in the design. Limiting traffic flow across the network to specific hosts by IP address is an example of what cannot be done well when every host, regardless of security classification, must access the same service directory for authentication and access control information. There would also be limited capability to build out the security sectors and segregation of hosts based on data classification and potential risk. It may be easier to use only one directory, but it is definitely not more secure.

Each specific population granted access to similar applications should be afforded a one-to-one-to-one relationship between authoritative source, identity vault, and service directory. When this relationship is established, the security zones and security domain definitions can match the access controls with the application hosts that population needs. By design of the security zones and security domain definitions, populations are unaware of and cannot see other populations' applications.

Allowing Distributed Administrative Entry as a Identity Data Source

In some cases, a direct link to an existing data source may not be possible. Some categories of end users may need to gain access rights on a rapid timetable or the organization may find benefit in allowing some other trusted person or entity to enter usernames and identity information for access to protected information.

Distributed administrative entry allows a person within your company or outside of your organization, other than the end user, to manually enter identity information into a directory. It should be handled only through a trusted agent who is authenticated to your systems with a two-factor authentication method. State government health departments, for example, could allow county-level health officials to enter identity information for local health workers who need access to state resources in an emergency situation. A company's road-warrior salesperson could be permitted to enter information for new customers needing access to online catalog sales. The trusted agent would have to authenticate with her token card to perform these functions.

Avoiding Self-Enrollment as an Identity Data Source

Some applications are made available to any user on the Internet through self-enrollment via Web interfaces. An end user enters all of his identity information from a Web browser anywhere on the World Wide Web. This information can be moved from its original storage point on the Web server, entered into the appropriate identity vault, and passed to a service directory for future authentication. It is OK to do this, but it's important to realize that you are taking a risk that the person using self-enrollment could be someone other than who he is purporting to be. Many of the free e-mail services available to anyone over the Internet are examples of self-enrollment processes.

Without some other business process to verify identity or to perform reliable background vetting to prove the user information was keyed in or authorized by the person whose information is entered, self-enrollment should be limited to accessing only open or public information. The self-enrollment process can still add value in that the directory information can be linked with a content-controlling database that allows customization of the Web experience in the same way you can customize a login on many Web pages.

Web sites that currently do end-user self-enrollment and verify identity through the use of personal financial information such as a credit card have no real way of knowing that John Doe is entering his own information for legitimate purposes. All the site operators can know for sure is that the information is likely being entered by someone who is in possession of the credit card itself or who has knowledge of the information contained on the card.

The business process relationship in conjunction with the applications needed by the category of end users is the parameter that determines a population's security and access needs. In some cases, it may be appropriate to use meta-functionality to extract identity information from more than one data source into an identity vault for further distribution to a service directory. When two companies merge, for example, each of the original company's human resources databases might become sources for a single identity vault.

Unlocking Identity Vaults

Each population with similar access rights is provisioned from its own identity vault (meta-functionality). The identity and provisioning information is provided from the authoritative source through the source monitor software module discussed in Chapter 7. What is then done with the information is determined by the logic programmed and associated with the meta-functionality surrounding each identity vault. The logical exchanges of information to and from the identity vault directory unlock the power of meta-data exchanges to accomplish the provisioning work in identity management and identity provisioning systems.

Leveraging the identity vault to provide user ID, password, or PIN information directly to the access control scheme embedded in commercial off-the-shelf (COTS) software and database applications such as Oracle databases can be done with ready-made intermediary applications called application receptors. These are provided by the identity management software vendors and run on the data host systems. Their purpose is to take the information from the identity vault, format it to match the security schema needed in the application, and then place the formatted information in the appropriate control list within the COTS application. This capability to interface into the application security of existing software applications with ready-made software modules or with custom development tools is how identity management and provisioning software provides real value in meeting Sarbanes-Oxley control requirements. Without this feature, a person would have to make these entries, or other methods would have to be created to move this information to embedded access controls, keep the information up-to-date, and set up procedures to deprovision access as needed when staff changes occur.

The challenge present in building the access control relationship between the end user and the data falls to those responsible for creating the design of the directory schema that will be used in the identity vault and, equally important, the schema for the service directories. A directory design that begins with a defined standard schema must be extended to include data within the directory, associated with each user, that will indicate to the applications the access rights afforded to the authenticated end user. There is a temptation for directory designers to use group affiliations within the directory to control access, which in turn makes it difficult to restrict access in a fine-grained fashion. It is fair to say that there is some art, as well as science, involved in directory design that requires balancing the use of individual rights, group rights, and schema extents without violating the security domain definitions.

The process logic used with the identity vault can be used to reformat information with the use of XML exchanges. For example, the exchange logic may need to reformat the abbreviation "St." for street used in one directory's schema to be fully spelled out as "Street" in another directory or access control list.

For the organization's employees, the file and print services operating systems directory can be also be provisioned from the identity vault. The usernames and passwords can be distributed from the identity vault to other services such as e-mail to reduce the number of passwords needed by internal users.

The identity vaults are to serve only one purpose: moving accurate information to the repositories that need it. The authentication calls are always directed to the service directories.

Serving Up Applications with Service Directories

Service directories are busy hubs, receiving all of the LDAP calls for authentication and access control. They receive their authoritative information from the identity vault, which in turn received the information from the authoritative identity source.

Service directories become the identity and access control information point of reference used by every gatekeeping device on your network except for those imbedded in an application. Application-embedded security may require that an interface from the Web application be established with the end user's Web browser through the proxy appliance, challenging the user to enter another password or a PIN. In some COTS software, the application may already include the data-field-level challenge to make changes or read certain data fields. When authentication is taking place on the appliance, the LDAP authentication calls are directed to the service directory for that population. When a Web application needs the user to authenticate a password or a PIN, the service directory is referenced and compared to the user's keyed-in entry.

If biometric measures are used to speed up the authentication process at the user's computer, the information needed to verify the biometric measures is stored in the service directory.

Service directories store the access controls for everything in the controlled environment that can make direct calls to LDAP directories. Every gatekeeper juncture in the environment should be using the same service directory for any given user population.

Exploring How It Works

Figure 10-1 shows the data flow relationships between the access control components.

Starting with the employee database shown in the Figure 10-1, a source monitor watches for changes in the database, such as a new hire. The one-way real-time synchronization logic forwards the information on the new hire to the identity vault. The vault processes the information to synchronize that new identity information to the e-mail directory, a Linux application server, and Active Directory for file and print services. The employee identity information, along with department, work group, work location, and job code, are forwarded to the employee service directory.

In this scenario, the employee can log on to an intranet Web application for the first time while still in the personnel office and enter a password that meets the company password policy. The identity vault then distributes that password to the service directory and other directories where one is needed. When the employee reaches her new work location, all services and applications for which she is authorized are available as a result of the logic linking the repositories.

Equally important is that if the employee leaves the company, monitoring notices the status change in the employee database, the change is transferred to the identity vault, and the employee's access rights are terminated.

Figure 10-2 illustrates the operations that take place when the customers are limited to Web applications. In the diagram, the customers, through a Web application in this example, are granted an account access on the company's e-mail server.

There is no limit to the number of times or the layers within the flow of applications that the service directories can be accessed. There is also no limit to the number of other repositories with which the identity vault can synchronize. It should be clear from the discussion and diagrams that the needs for staff to manually administer the various repositories that may be present in your organization IT systems is reduced and is a significant benefit of setting up identity management and provisioning to control all access rights. Perhaps less obvious is the advantage of having the information accurate in all repositories. Having one method to control access across all of the entire IT systems and applications within an organization and one point of control for each population is the most important benefit.

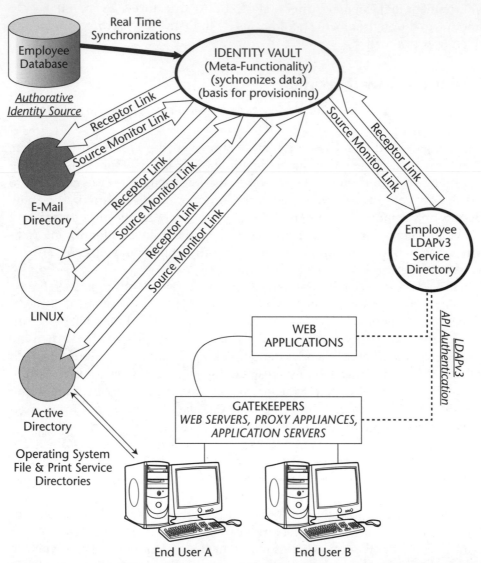

Figure 10-1 The identity provisioning data paths for employee end users and authentication calls for file and print services and employee Web pages.

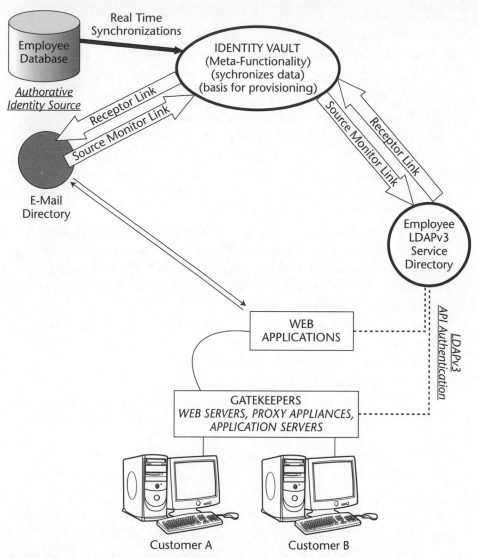

Figure 10-2 The identity provisioning data paths for customers with controlled access to Web pages and complementary e-mail services.

Looking at an Access Control Sequence

The following end-user session illustrates all of the connections that have been discussed:

1. An end user already identified in the system launches a Web browser and enters the URL for your application.

2. A session is established with the end user from the Web appliance

3. The appliance presents a page with a greeting and a link with the word "ENTER" to click.

4. An SSL session is established between the browser and the appliance, and a new screen requesting a user ID and password is displayed to the user's browser.

5. The user responds with the correct username and password. The appliance makes an LDAP call to the service directory and verifies the username-password combination.

6. The user's browser is then presented with a new screen containing application choices served up by the appliance. The choices are taken by proxy from the actual Web applications server. The traffic link between the appliance and Web server is also protected by SSL encryption.

7. The end user chooses an application that requires two-factor authentication. Her token card random access numerical string is requested and checked against the authentication server.

8. If the numerical string entered by the end user is correct, access to the application is granted through the passing of the application page back to the user's browser, from the application Web server via the appliance acting as proxy for the user.

9. The end user pages through some of the application to which she has normal read-only access.

10. She needs to change one field of data and is challenged within the application logic to provide a PIN to validate her having the authority to make the change. She provides the correct PIN and the change is written to the database. (The PIN was provided earlier to the database application's embedded security controls from the identity vault.)

11. Having successfully made the change, the user logs out of the application and all sessions end.

This access control sequence example shows how security access controls can be layered into the process beyond Web server access and application-level control right to a specific field of data — and all controlled with information provided from the identity vault's meta-functionality.

Examining Other Capabilities

Commercially available identity management and identity provisioning solutions include the capability to distribute some identity information contained in the service directory to the end users via a Web interface. This feature makes it possible for an end user to update a home phone number in the directory, change a password, or reissue a lost password. To maintain security, passwords are usually e-mailed to the employee. This is an acceptable method, particularly when you are using e-mail software products that maintain encryption in storage and in transit by default.

The identity software available will typically include in the Web interface programs the capability to apply policies to the changes. For example, users who use the interface to change a password can be required to create a complex (strong) password.

The following section lists 12 important considerations in the product selections and in the implementation of any design.

Understanding Key Design Considerations

There are 12 important considerations for any identity management, directory, and identity provisioning solution to include for identity, authentication, and access control to applications requiring any level of controlled access requirements.

1. Set up URLs requiring authentication and access control to be fronted on an Internet appliance capable of providing SSL sessions based on access controls from LDAP service directories and/or authenticate to an AAA server when needed.

2. Choose an Internet appliance capable of alternative use as a SSL VPN server.

3. Choose an Internet appliance that is capable of SSL communication to content switches to accommodate legacy applications with secure communications.

4. Populate each service directory with identity information from an authoritative source via meta-functionality from an available authoritative source for each population served.

5. The ID vault or meta-functionality directory should be treated as a secure vault and not accessed directly by users or by applications. Use only service directories to provide application authentication. Limit the direct access to a very restricted list of administrators. Use the logic

programming associated with the meta-functionality to populate and depopulate other directories.

6. Use meta-functionality to populate, provision, and deprovision the operating system directory used for file and print services for internal employee users.

7. Enable end users to change passwords and post noncontrol changes to the service directory via a secure Web application.

8. Use the ID vaults as the basis for all further enterprise provisioning and deprovisioning when administration can be reduced.

9. The service directory schema designs must be population-specific, and one schema should be designed and used for all applications made available to that population.

10. Leverage the identity vault meta-functionality to provision and deprovision passwords for Web applications, OS, and legacy applications wherever possible.

11. Allow delegated and remote administration capability for certain populations' service directories only when necessary to accommodate business processes.

12. Design service directories to contain only the minimum necessary data elements to achieve successful identification, authentication, and access control.

Moving to a service directory-centric model for access controls requires that the Web application developers in your organization become familiar with the LDAP API and use it for authentication. The developers must also work closely with the security analysts to determine when simple usernames and passwords will be sufficient controls and when two-factor token card access controls should be used. The identity vault should also be used to synchronize identities into the token card authorization servers to maintain the single point of control over user identities.

When multiple populations are present in your IT environment, the relationships established from authoritative source to identity vault and from identity vault to service directory become a pattern that is reiterated for each population. Organization size and the diversity of business conducted are probably the main determining factors in setting the number of populations. Large companies, state governments, federal government, and international companies have multiple populations that applications must serve. It is important to maintain a relationship in the design between the populations and the applications they will access.

Summary

This chapter's puts together the concepts presented earlier, particularly those presented in Chapter 7, to show how they converge to use identity information to achieve authentication of end users and apply fined-grained access controls to meet regulatory requirements. The value of every component described here and its contribution to increasing the security levels and strength of access controls is complemented when used with each of the other components. None of the functionality of these components should be left out of your design. The specific products required to implement a design like this are available in the marketplace, along with the expertise to provide the integration should you need assistance.

CHAPTER 1

Why Federated Identity Schemes Fail

All of the specification and standards — including Security Assertion Markup Language (SAML) standards, the Liberty Alliance specifications, and the Web Services Federation (WS-Federation) specifications, Microsoft's .NET, and Passport — are a part of the ongoing conversation in IT circles about federated identity systems, which present potentially interesting and individually valuable features to simplify the sharing of identity information and digital identity credentials over the Internet and on private networks.

Understanding Federated Identity Schemes

The idea of sharing identity information and credentials in the current distributed environment — where many companies, perhaps tens of thousands, hold identity information about millions of their customers — is a good one, particularly when each company is holding identity information about the same consumer, client, or receiver of services. A distributed model is a risk for the consumers because their identity and personal financial information are entrusted to as many organizations as they deal with online, by mail, or over the phone.

For the companies, a large amount of IT and other support resources are used to store, manage, and protect the customer identity information. That's why sharing identity information and digital credentials over the Internet to transact business with someone else's client appeals to many firms; it's an opportunity to leverage other companies' relationships with customers. It also allows the partner company's investment to have leverage in all of the costs of maintaining that customer.

Affording Convenience to Customers

To accept a customer's identity and credentials from another company, the organization granting access and applications to the customer (end user) must place trust in the inherent reliability of that identity and electronic credentials. From the user perspective, federated identity schemes are appealing because the user does not have to enter the data every time she does business with a partner company.

Companies that implement federated identity schemes often do so with partner companies on a business-to-business level rather than with all consumers. Part of the reason is that although there are standards involved, the technology is not totally plug-and-play. There is often some effort required to program your applications to the applications of the sister company so that for the user's experience appears seamless to the customer. When you look at the potential for identity federation across all companies potentially doing business with the same consumers, the customization of even simple applications would require significant programming effort.

Risks Are Complex

Although federated identity puts forward admirable goals, the risks in all such trust relationships remain problematic. The merits of federated identity are easily understood and appear to present value in reduced administration, convenience, and the potential for context-aware transactions with a shared customer. For example, a customer could within a few minutes order a new CD player from one company, a music CD from another, and extra speakers from another, all with one instance of identity from the first transaction. The customer finds the process easier, and the second two companies get the benefit of the sale with less effort. Business-to-business transactions are conducted in a similar fashion, with employees of partner companies being granted trusted user status to your systems. In the practical implementation, however, federal identity systems are left wanting for reliable high levels of trust that have little to do with the technology.

The implicit trust in federated schemes is no different from a person saying, "A friend of a friend is a friend," which is the concept upon which federated identity is based. Anyone who has ever been to a summer sports camp and trusted an acquaintance of a friend only to be stolen from or defrauded knows from experience that trust is earned, not casually granted. Aside from the technology issues of having to do some customization of the Web environment and having the programming in place to provide the interoperability, there are flaws in the basic premise of reliance on credentials passed from another organization. All of the risks you normally face when trusting your own identity vetting processes are amplified when you are asked to place confidence in the processes of other organizations whose practices and access controls may be far inferior to your own.

Acknowledging Benefits

Federated identity exchanges of electronic credentials do serve a useful purpose in reducing the requirements on the end user to enroll in different systems; users might otherwise be asked to provide the same information time and time again to every entity where a transaction is needed. Federated exchanges are desirable simply because the process of using them is convenient for both the user and the providers of online services. The exchange of tokens when a user moves from one site to another can be used to present a Web page experience most suitable to the end user. There is minimal risk in the use of federated identity to provide customized end-user experiences for Web sites containing open or public information. In some limited-risk circumstances where your potential for loss is small or where transactions can easily be reversed if done feloniously or erroneously, it may be advantageous to allow access to protected information from credentials passed from a foreign federated site on behalf of an end user. In its current forms, I recommend extreme caution in the use of federated credentials whenever restricted information is involved. The risks of loss and litigation may be too great for their use anytime personally identifying, personal financial information or HIPAA-restricted health information is involved.

Caution should be exercised as well when anyone using federated identity credentials is going to have an impact on the organization's operational or financial processes or financial reports. At its worst, when safeguards fail, federated identity could be likened to opening the door to your home (vault, wallet, trade secrets) to a group of people who are all wearing costumes and masks. Its best use may be to share public information in a context-sensitive customized Web experience to users from business partner sites.

Exploring the Five Stars of Federated Identity

There are thee key players in federated identity models, plus a concept and an idea, which, for discussion purposes, I'll call the five stars of federated identity:

- Identified user (or entity)
- Identify and authentication provider
- Service provider
- Transfer of trust
- Circle of trust

Even without critical comment, at least some of the weaknesses in federated identity should become apparent by examining its workings.

Looking at the Identified User

In federated schemes, an end user or entity is enrolled or self-enrolls with one of the federation's member organizations. A username is applied, along with an authentication method such as a password associated with the end-user name. In subsequent sessions, the end user provides the name and authentication to conduct transactions with the organization. While logged on with a member of the federated group, the user is permitted to access other organizations' Web portals without resupplying the identity information.

If the user is bogus and has hacked his way into the first company's systems, he is now into yours with no difficulty. If, for example, fraudulent credit card information is presented to the first company, your company would be party to the misdeed as well and would end up spending time and energy later to correct the problem for the person whose card and identity were used.

Looking at the Identity and Authentication Provider

Theoretically, the first organization an end user enrolls with becomes the identity and authentication token provider to the other members of the federated group on behalf of the user. The first site (token provider) could also be a service portal that does not conduct any other transactions other than asserting the identity and access credentials into the access process on other portals.

Again, your organization not only accepts the identity and the credential; you also accept the risk of hacking because of weaknesses in another organization's site.

Looking at the Service Provider

The service provider role could be on the Web site of the organization with which the user enrolled, but most frequently the term refers to subsequent Web sites with which the user might transact business after successfully logging on at the original portal. A service provider, then, is any portal that provides services to an end user based on the exchange of identity and access credentials information passed from another organization member of the group.

A hack into any of the companies in a federation, which could number in the hundreds, can ripple across every member. This makes it hacking into a federation group a very attractive target for wrongdoers.

Looking at Transfer of Trust

The concept at work in federated identity is that if someone else trusts a login to be John Doe, my systems will trust that it is John Doe and treat him accordingly by allowing access based on this transfer of trust.

With federation transfers of the end user, all of the service providers must trust the user's credentials completely. There is no opportunity to reauthenticate the user, provide a challenge question, or ask for a password to verify identity, because there's no direct knowledge of the customer. If your company uses federated identity, you have, by default, accepted the weaknesses in the systems run by every member of your federated group.

Looking at the Circle of Trust

Federated identity revolves around the idea that every organization in the federation has sufficient reason from its enrollment process to place enough trust in the identity of the user that the other members should trust it as well. Furthermore, the other organizations' processes are sufficient for my organization to place trust in the identity of users that they enrolled.

This might be a more acceptable risk if there were similar security protections and audits conducted on every federation member's security defenses and identity verification processes. Such an agreement begins to add costs, though, canceling some of the savings that might be expected from the use of federation in the first place.

Seeing the Fundamental Flaws

The elementary question of value with use of federated identity is who can be trusted immediately and over the long haul to provide authentication to your critical systems and processes? And can you trust a credential passed to your systems that you and your organization had no part in verifying or issuing? There are so many points of potential process failures, outright fraud, and erroneously implied access rights — and no solid relationship between the end user and the data — that federated identity schemes should not be used for systems subject to external audit criteria for controls compliance. The security risks are simply too great.

Exploring Options

The major players that could benefit from the use of reliable identity information in a federated environment include individuals, financial institutions, government, commercial and nonprofit organizations, and credit reporting agencies. If federated identity could be universally trusted, it would be a benefit for the advance of Internet commerce. How can we develop that trust?

Creating a National Standard

One way to get past limiting the use of federated identities for customized content and better management of the user experience between clients and customers of the circle of trust would be for the collective state and federal governments to become the only providers of identity and authentication for federated identity services on the Web.

It's a suggestion that garners the wrath of those most concerned about privacy and those who fear the creation of a "police state." In reality, the paper credentials supporting your identity in the United States are issued by county, state, and federal government agencies. Birth certificates, for example, are usually done at the county level, driver's license and state-sponsored identity cards are typically done at the state level, and Social Security numbers are handled by the federal government, which also issues "green cards" for foreigners staying in the United States.

Given that government already dominates the issuance of paper credentials and identifying documents, it may not be that big a stretch for the state and federal governments to place that information into a single-source service on the Internet.

Moving Forward

Two fairly recent federal initiatives may well be the harbinger of things to come. First, the Real ID Act (Public Law 109-13 of 2005) sets standards for the states in the issuance of driver's licenses, the predominant method of identity verification in use today. The law creates standards for the issuance process; it seeks uniformity across all states and certainly points toward the potential for a national identity card. States have the next three years to move into compliance.

Second, the President has issued a Smart ID Card mandate for federal agencies to use the same or similar smart-card technology to access systems and physical spaces. The PIV (personal identity verification) card standard is being developed with the help of the National Institute of Standards and Technology (NIST).

The only missing steps for a national ID system are to mandate that the states use PIV for driver's licenses and to put the key identity information into one database on the Web; the result would be national identity cards and a nationalized federated identity scheme.

Examining Third-Party Certification of Standards of Practice

If the idea of the government becoming the sole broker of federated identity credentials scares you, as well it might, the next best possibility to extend the value of federated identity models might be to create a voluntary third-party compliance certification audit of all the members of the federation with which you intend to build shared trust relationships.

The members of the federation would establish standards of practice for the processing, use, and sharing of federated identities, including vetting of identities, penetration tests of the identity repositories, and speed and reliability of the identity deprovisioning process. Third-party certification would essentially establish standards of practice for all member organizations. Those standards would be designed to counter or reduce all the risks of using federated identity. The certification process also would audit the initial build-out of each member's implementation of federated identity hosts and require a follow up and periodic audits of operations to ensure ongoing compliance.

Federated identity does not fit well into the fine-grained control models necessary to meet externally imposed regulatory requirements, as discussed earlier in this book. Along with organizations needing to have some control over the identity management process for the entire end-user life cycle, the security architecture and access control designs must thread and weave the cloth that connects what you know about the end user and the data access that user needs to create, read, or change information, while at the same time preventing others from doing so.

Without tackling the bigger issues of who might be relied upon globally to maintain identity stores, pass uniform credentials, and keep the information accurate and up to date, we can say that federated identity processes will continue to fill a niche but are unlikely to become universally trusted enough to be used everywhere authentication is required.

Summary

If hackers and fraudsters did not seem to be overcoming so many companies' security defenses, perhaps the use of federated identity would have caught on more than it has. The technology that facilitates federated identity use is not the weak link. The flaws are in the processes other organizations may use to verify user identities, in limitations in their access controls systems, or in their overall security measures. These weaknesses and risks are amplified for your company as a member organization each time a new company is added to the federation.

There may be places within your organization to use the passing of credentials from one internal Web portal to another for your own users, or a niche use where you would participate with others. In this case, taking the time to learn more about the standards used would be of value. If your management finds the risks acceptable and that its use would add value despite the weaknesses, you may need to implement some use of federated identity. If so, proceed with caution and tighten up every aspect of your security and access controls so that your organization will be passing only valid users and credentials to others.

A Pathway to Universal Two-Factor Authentication

In the physical world, you are nearly universally granted access to enter into financial transactions with a simple credential issued by your state: a driver's license or state-issued identity card. When you travel internationally, you are granted entry into other countries and reentry to your own with a credential called a passport issued by the federal government. By visiting a travel office with a valid state driver's license, paying a modest fee, and sitting for a picture, you can be issued an internationally recognized driver's license for United Nations member countries.

All of these extremely powerful paper credentials are vetted simply by providing a valid certificate of birth and some proof of residency at a secretary of state office or motor vehicle bureau in the state of issue. If only it were that simple and straightforward for digital credentials. Imagine for a minute having a secure digital credential that you could use to access everything online: your personal computer at home, the workstation at work, the online government services, the application you need at work or while on the road, access to the company's file server while vacationing in the islands. You get the idea — the digital equivalent to the nearly universally accepted driver's license. It'd be a one-size-fits-all approach to your digital identity, accepted at every digital access point where you need to do business of any kind. Wouldn't that be a major improvement over the highly distributed maze of access controls in use now?

Heading toward a Single Identity Credential

The technology to accomplish a single-credential access in a secure fashion already exists. It is just a matter of assembling an appropriate infrastructure to accommodate it. So what would that magic key to the kingdom be?

Finding the Magic Key

As discussed earlier in this book, the user interface tiers begin with a username (digital identity; your digital alter ego) followed by methods for authentication (verification that it is really you) — first a password, then a secret PIN can further enhance the assurance you are who you purport to be, and finally a two-factor token card tied to your user ID, verified by yet another PIN and an accurate match of the floating number keyed in from the card and the AAA (authentication, authorization, and accounting) server's calculation for that card's unique time-derived floating number. The magic key is the addition of the two-factor token card to the mix.

Of the technologies available today, the floating-number token card is the best option for maximizing end-user authentication. In this chapter, you'll explore some of the challenges, work that needs to be done, and opportunities for leveraging this relatively inexpensive technology.

Looking for a Vision

Some financial firms have already recognized the added security value provided by two-factor token cards and are issuing them to their clients who choose to transact business over the Internet. A great fear would be a future where every company with a significant stake in having a reliable authentication method issues its clients a separate token card. This could easily get out of hand and require end users to carry around five pounds of token cards to conduct personal business transactions.

What is needed right now is a vision to get a grip on leveraging the benefit provided by token cards with the strategy and infrastructure such that each person would need to use one, maybe two token cards at most to authenticate all high-value online transactions anywhere on the company network or across the entire Internet.

The rest of this chapter presupposes that two token cards are sufficient: one for your role in your work or business and another for your personal transactions. (The personal one could easily suffice for both in many working environments.) The chapter also discusses a possible future where access control systems across the partner networks and the Web are tied to tightly coupled AAA servers for access control to sensitive systems and data. You'll get a peak into a vision of the future where two models for global access control services prevail: first, a distributed environment in which organizations opt into a two-factor authentication association when individual members are backed by identity management and provisioning systems that inspire confidence in administration of the end-user identity life cycle, and second, an environment to accommodate secure Internet commerce with a general trusted identity credential authenticated from government-provided identity data.

Examining the Challenges in a Global Access Controls Strategy

You could easily argue that there is a general failure of access control quality within applications made available over the Internet. The recurring news reports of tens of thousands of instances of personally identifying or financial data being compromised certainly verifies that serious problems exist with keeping data secure. There are no doubt other incidents going undetected, as well as instances where breaches to a system security and loss of information occurs and is not reported. There is also a category of networks, systems, and applications that lack adequate controls and have yet to surface as interesting enough to draw the attention of hackers intent on doing harm to organizations and their clients.

The problem of providing adequate access controls across-the-board is further complicated by the fact that system security, access, and control measures vary significantly from industry to industry and from one organization to the next. There's far too much variation in the philosophy of what should be protected information and what data should be held as confidential and thereby deserving of protection measures. Adding to the mix is that the access control lists, service directories, and data stores for any one individual within an organization and certainly within the public, nonprofit, and for-profit sectors often number in the tens and hundreds, if not in the thousands.

Seeking Common Goals

As an IT professional, you are correctly focused on solving the access controls issues for which you are accountable. The access controls challenges need to be met in the immediate and near term in the existing highly distributed environment. It would be helpful if the level of cooperation would increase and everyone with concerns and a stake in the future of all types of online transactions would set their sights on the same future, or at least a similar one.

That future should begin with the same uncompromising overriding goal: adequate access control measures. By that I mean a future where privacy (data protection) boundaries are respected, where systems are able to enforce them, and where digital credentials can be trusted. The rest of this chapter is devoted to discussion of one avenue to get to that ideal. It is not the only path, but at least you can dream the possible dream, and maybe others will come along to join the discussion.

When examined individually, very few existing technologies have the potential to reach that ideal future. However, when certain existing technologies are brought together and joined with some longstanding legal principles on a grand scale, the potential exists to reach for and hold that future in the near three- to five-year term.

Seeking Cooperation

As with other notable technology achievements, the technology may be the easy part of making this happen. Often, useful ideas are lost to the trash heap of time due to lack of sufficient cooperation among the stakeholders. If anything thwarts a global access control scheme, it will be a the lack of cooperation among the parties that could benefit from getting on the train and going with universal two-factor authentication, which may work better for everyone if the integrity of access to online transactions can be maintained.

The questions to ask are when will all the negative press turn consumers entirely off on the whole idea of online commerce and what can be done to ensure that will not happen. The "one little thing" phenomena described in Malcolm Gladwell's book *The Tipping Point: How Little Things Can Make a Big Difference* suggests that the demise of online commerce could be caused by a seemingly small change. Fortunately, the phenomena described in that book can work both ways — a small group of early adopters can cause acceptance of change on a massive scale. The move to universal two-factor token card authentication could easily become the next big thing to have and use.

Understanding the Consumers' Part

Cooperation and participation at the consumer level will only be facilitated and hastened by some understanding and trust in the underlying technology. If governments and the private sector make no other offers of alternative methodologies for access control to sensitive data for important online transactions, however, then consumers must take the terms or pass on the convenience afforded by those transactions.

Consumers should not expect the organizations they deal with to bear the burdens of providing convenient access and of taking the litigation risks, because access controls are not strong enough. Consumers have a high interest in the use of reliable online authentication to protect their personal and financial information. The convenience trade-off of having to carry and use a token card should be viewed as a small load to bear to enhance security sufficiently to protect the privacy of identity, financial, or medical information.

The token card concept, once sufficient infrastructure is in place, could also be used to verify identity and authenticate users over the telephone with human or automated voice interactive systems. The token card's time-randomized number can be entered as easily over a touch-tone phone as it can be on a computer keyboard.

You can imagine the prospect of a two-factor token card to raise the level of security on debit and credit cards. For example, perhaps transactions up to $500 could work in the conventional fashion, with just the secret PIN used, and any amount over that would require authentication with the PIN and the random string from the token card. Even ordering by telephone could be facilitated with an authentication entry using touch-tone phones to enter the number string from the token card.

With a proper deployment strategy, a token card could substantially reduce the risk of doing online transaction by preventing misuse of identity data even if it were stolen or compromised. If token cards were required for all high-value transactions, the compromised identity data without the token string would be useless. Certainly, consumer would appreciate that benefit.

Understanding the Government's Part

If you examine some of the recently passed and pending legislation at the federal and state levels and attempt to predict the trend, you begin to see a struggle between privacy advocates who want little or no government mandates involving identity and those who want to find a way to simplify identity methods that can be still be trusted, on- and offline. Legislation to protect the use of or limit use of personally identity information such as Social Security numbers is currently on the agenda.

The prediction is that legislators would eventually also recognize that three other elements of identity deserve protection equal to SSN from predators and wrongdoers. Those elements are date of birth, driver's license number, and credit and financial account numbers. The challenge for governments, both state and federal, is how they can participate in a global access control scheme that universally works, is derived from true identity information and yet discloses none of it, and appreciably retains some elements of control by the individual citizen concerned.

It is easily expected that the state and federal governments would continue to play their roles as regulators of the commercial processes in use. You expect the law to lag behind events and to codify what is already reality. Rarely do government initiatives lead the way with technical change.

On the issue of brokering identity credentials in the paper world, government has been the traditional point of entry for a person's identity. Privacy advocates' concerns being the exception; it would be a small stretch for the states to play a role in providing some reliability to digital credentials for citizens.

Needing Government to Contribute

Without meaningful government participation, the IT community and business are faced with choosing less desirable alternatives to collecting, brokering, and digitally credentialing identity information.

The government's contribution would be simple enough to do but not without cost or controversy. The states would first have to blend voter registration files with driver's license and identity card files and use identity management software to publish this information to a state citizen directory. Every resident known to the state and of driving or voting age would be in the directory. When citizens come in contact with the state for services, they would be asked if they want to participate in online global identity. If a resident agrees, a data field would be turned on in the service directory, linking to a state-run AAA server active. The citizen could then be issued a token card right at the driver's license bureau, or one could be certified mailed to her home address. A PIN could be picked while in the office or mailed separately from the card.

Finding Everyone

This plan would put 50 states' and the few territories' AAA servers and service directories on the Internet with the names and token card seed record association available only for those citizens who opted into the global authentication system. Having the states keep the information current in the service directories would be very important. Using meta-functionality to remove people who are deceased and applying address changes and the like would be critical to the long-term success of the access system.

Not every citizen will be present in the respective states' systems, so the federal government would have to provide service directories and AAA servers for citizens overseas via U.S. consulates and existing processes for tracking Americans born and living abroad. The standard domain naming of the service directories and AAA servers would be a part of the infrastructure and could play a role in authentication by requiring input by the end user who wants access to a given domain.

There are a number of identity data sources available within the federal government that could be exploited to facilitate the advancement and use of universal two-factor authentication — SSNs, tax records, military records, and passport data are some prominent possibilities. A universal token card authentication infrastructure would certainly provide benefits at the federal level and could even help prevent Medicare and Medicaid fraud.

Understanding the Private and Nonprofit Sectors' Part

The challenges for organizations in the private and nonprofit sector include how to afford to participate and how to modify business practices and build IT systems that can reliably participate in global access controls — with adequate access controls and meeting all current externally imposed regulatory criteria from Sarbanes-Oxley, HIPAA, and Gramm-Leach-Bliley Act. Universal use of two-factor authentication brings the standard for authentication to a higher level for most organizations. It also sets as high a standard as can reasonably be supported in the current environment. If tightly coupled relationships with business partners' AAA servers are established and external users are entered into your service directory, controls are more resilient to inappropriate access.

Organizations would likely have to participate in two systems: one that issues token cards to their own employees and cooperates in a tightly coupled group of AAA servers with business partners, and one with access controls specifically designed for participation in a global identity and authentication model, with the government or some disinterested third party brokering the identity information and providing AAA servers.

Understanding the Technology Vendors' Part

The statement regarding cooperation is particularly relevant here. Part of the reason there are countless instances of directories and access control lists playing a role within firms and across the Internet is the lack of cooperation among operating system and software vendors. Software producers handle directories and access controls typically in a proprietary fashion, with none being very willing to cooperate to the point where some competing vendors' authentication and access controls are trusted to work seamlessly with their own operating system or applications. Application developers would be well served by demanding that authentication, authorization, and finite access controls become like a power utility, something that you plug your networks and applications into, that is trusted, and that nearly always works.

Understanding the Standards Bodies' Part

There is one piece of this puzzle that is missing for making the possibility of global access controls based on two-factor authentication a universal reality in the near-term future. That piece could become the work of a standards body like so many other things have in relation to expanding or improving uses of the Internet. Interested parties with a stake in the result need to come together and find the common ground to create a new standard within the technology.

The biggest potential problem with the universal use of two-factor authentication is data transmission speed, or, actually, the lack thereof. The rolling numbers on the token card are time-dependant, and any impeded transmission of traffic to and from the AAA server holding the seed record for that individual token card could make authentication calls fail frequently. The other uncontrollable element is how rapidly end users enter the number string; taking too long also contributes to a failed authentication.

The improvement needed is an Internet protocol designed specifically to be recognized as authentication traffic and treated with the highest possible speed of service by all vendors' routing and switching equipment. The small data payload in the packet would obviously need to be encrypted and decrypted in a uniform manner. That detail could become a part of the standard for the proposed High-Speed Authentication Protocol (HSAP). In an ideal situation, the private encryption key of the pair would be dependant on and unique to the specific token card.

The universal quality of service across networks and the Internet is by far the most important part of the standard. A to-and-from guaranteed speed of 80 to 160 milliseconds for authentication packets may be all that is necessary to make this work reliably in the real world. The HSAP packets would be relatively small, and with bandwidth generally increasing and becoming less expensive, it isn't likely that this new protocol would become too much for the Internet, company WANs, or internal networks to handle as priority traffic in a quality-of-service fashion.

Understanding the Token Card Manufacturers' Part

Strong advocates of two-factor token cards still see some room for improvements in them. First, the shelf life of the cards needs to be extended with, for example, the capability to recharge the battery so fewer replacement cards are needed. And wouldn't it be great to have token cards that, when plugged into a computer's port, function as a private key in online encryption while still providing an independent, nonrelated random-number string for authentication?

Lowering the costs of procurement and implementation of the cards themselves would certainly encourage increased adoption of the technology. Card purveyors are quick to point out that use of the cards over password schemes can result in fewer help desk calls and lower cost for support.

Providing a standard, easy-to-configure software communication feature to tightly couple the cooperating AAA servers to authenticate users within the organizations who agree to participate with one another in a trust model also would be beneficial.

Exploring a Future with Global Access Controls

There are two places to look for insight on the subject of access controls, and both of them lie outside the immediate realm of information technology. One is biology, discussed next. The other is borrowed from the legal profession regarding the definition of access rights and roles discussed later in this chapter. A lesson can be learned from the interactions and diversity of controls in the human body. With so many substances in the blood flowing in your arteries and veins, you must wonder how everything works like it should without interfering with the body's other activities. The chemical interactions and the results of proteins, hormones, and peptides at work within human bodies are amazing.

Going with Biology

The scope of the three chemical signaling systems is defined as autocrine, paracrine, and endocrine. If you liken the human bloodstream to the data flow on the Internet and the chemical signaling of the endocrine system to data access controls, you begin to appreciate both the complexity and accuracy of the relationships in biology. The bloodstream carries a substance (hormone) from a gland to a waiting receptor on a cell to do its job of causing a certain reaction to take place. The receptor on the cell ignores the other substances and reacts only to the one type targeted to it.

Autocrine is basically the secretion of a substance that stimulates the secretory cell itself; paracrine describes a process in which a substance is released and reacted to within a group of nearby cells, and endocrine refers to a process in which substances are released into blood and body fluids and reacted to by receptors in different parts of the body. So an IT adaptation of the biological reality is to have three tiers of two-factor authentication models.

Authentication signaling systems could follow the model from nature. There is a need, for example, to be able to lock down a single computer or portable computing device with the use of a token card. The autocentric (within the machine) model would not boot the computer and/or provide a log on without the presence of an associated plug-in token card or the correct random number string from one.

Checking Out the Paracentric Approach

Ratcheting up a notch, environment changes provide the use of that same token card for authentication to networks and hosts in a trust relationship. That relationship would be intracompany and also include established relationships with business partner organizations on extranets or the Internet. This paracentric approach involves having your AAA services participate with those with whom you have a close working relationship. What is needed to accommodate that would not follow the current model for federation but would create a hierarchy much like DNS services, where a trust relationship defines those AAA servers of which you have become a member service. If a token-card user is not present on your AAA server, then the higher-level service would be queried, which in turn would either seek validation from every AAA server, with only the one containing the correct user ID and seed record responding, or use a directory to look up the identity of the AAA server associated with that user. The control data traffic would either be passing through the high-level service or sent directly to your AAA server; which would, in turn, authenticate the user ID.

The actual grant of access would be allowed from your local AAA server only after it received the correct response from the external AAA server, maintaining the point of control under your management and providing the single auditing node as well. A directory service would then further define allowed access for guest users authenticated in this manner, or extra privileged access for those users specifically defined in your directory.

Leveraging the value of LDAP directory services in the paracentric model requires that active access accounts for all users first be defined in one of the service directories. It wouldn't be necessary for users external to your organization to have large amounts of identity information in your service directory — only the minimum needed to establish the access rights for that individual user. It would also be possible to use pseudonyms for them in your service directory because you are counting on the end users being able to supply the correct random-number strings from the token cards; in some circumstances, such as when a nonprofit is collecting small charitable contributions, you may not need to know the true identity of the end user to accommodate the transaction.

Checking Out the Endocentric Approach

In the endocentric model it doesn't matter what service portal you are on anywhere on the Internet and there is no need to set up preestablished relationships. When you request a service that requires identity, the portal participating in the global access model looks first for your username presence in one of the state or federal service directories. The process is hastened if you provide the domain — Florida, for example. The Florida directory supplies to the Web application only the identity elements necessary to complete the transaction and only after you key in the correct secret PIN and random string from the token card.

The random string is the key (hormone) that allows the receptor (the application) to work only when given the right random number. The difference in the endocentric model is that there is no previously established or continuing relationship between the hosts and no routine exchange of data. The exchange of information is taking place on a per-transaction basis and only when the proper token string is correctly entered. The application's business processes are entirely dependant on the information provided from the global service. Figure 12-1 shows the communication paths for the different models.

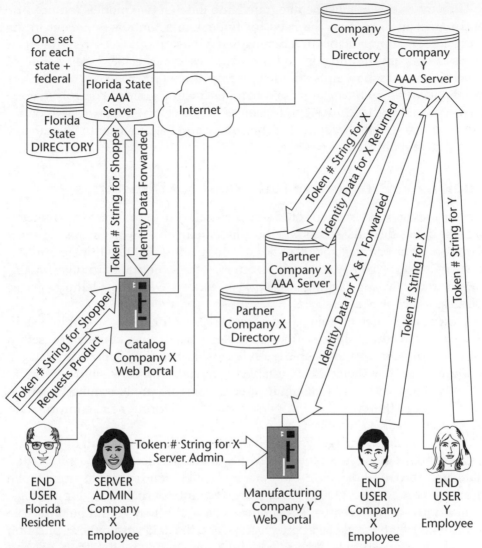

Figure 12-1 Autocentric, paracentric, and endocentric authentication models.

As discussed in earlier chapters, the role of service directories is substantial because they also stipulate the access rights granted once proper authentication is completed. Currently it is necessary to use meta-functionality to move information into specific applications' own security structures to get to finite access controls to a particular database entry in an identity management process. Directories are used to house identity information and participate in authentication by storing passwords and PINs. Service directories also play an important role in determining what an end user can access to once he is authenticated.

Directory services must be integrated into the first two models (autocentric and paracentric) because the need for finite access controls is greater in the working environment of an organization whose employees require open access to certain information and limited access to other data. Separation of duties such as cash receipts and disbursements and controls over who enters what and when on financial reports requires the fine-grained controls that are best achieved with well-designed schemas in a directory-driven access control model coupled with the identity management and the provisioning features of meta-functionality.

Looking at Prospective New Roles for Directories

Another layer of abstraction could be beneficial by using a directory to categorize the data side of the access equation. Essentially this involves moving away from the proprietary elements of access controls internal to software applications by using a data information directory, with some standard data classification and category tagging, to work in concert with the identity service directory to control access.

The idea is to extend role-based access controls for the data within a standard access relationship to defined data elements. Conventionally you set up end-user directories and establish a relationship between the person and the resource. The new thought is to establish a relationship between the information and the access roles to facilitate access where no predetermined relationship between the data and the person exists by storing access information about the data in a directory. .

Two advantages emerge. First, you do not have to know ahead of time that a given individual would benefit from or want to gain access to the application data, and second, if database and data application vendors could agree to the model, access controls would be standardized and external to the applications, data storage, and databases. The proposed data-directory would hold the role definitions of who could be granted access, and the data within the application would merely need to be associated with a role. In this model, then, relating the service directory with its defined roles to the data directory with its defined data would allow anyone in a given role to access data defined for that role, and do so across all data stores regardless of who provided the underlying application or database software.

Examining a Standard Approach and Terms for Data Access Rights

For the future of access controls, from a legalistic perspective to rights of access, it would be helpful to develop common terms and achieve an industrywide agreement of the standard rights associated with those terms. This would also facilitate global access authentication and the granting of access rights based on relationships to the data owner or on standardized end-user roles.

If access rights are defined in a uniform manner and based on a standard, access controls become easier to create and apply both within applications and across the various gatekeepers to the data. Each of the rights across applications could be uniformly applied, and the subrights would be switches to be individually granted or denied by the data's gatekeeper. All of the roles discussed in the following sections are considered from the perspective of the data owner.

Understanding Standard Data-Related Access Rights

The first set of standard rights to consider is for the *data creator*. The data creator can impose certain fundamental rights in her creation

This concept is analogous to U.S. copyright law. Once data is fixed in permanent form, the rights are granted to the creator of the data or information. Copyright distinguishes between original creations for oneself and work for hire, and we also must use that approach. The fundamental rights of the data creator role allow for the collection or original creation of the data. The creator of the information can edit at will, allow the work to be distributed to others, allow or deny the display of the data, and destroy the original work that he created.

The following sections discuss how the outlining of these access role definitions could be standardized and used in the granting of data-related access rights.

Exploring First-Person Access Roles and Rights

As mentioned, the fundamental first-person rights of the data creator would include the ability to do the following with data or information:

- Create
- Edit
- Distribute (with or without rights to further distribute)
- Demolish
- Own

A *data owner* has the same fundamental rights as a data creator, although she may not have been the original creator of a work done for hire or may have acquired the ownership by outright purchase or contractual agreement. The data creator is the default data owner if she has not distributed ownership rights.

Exploring Second-Person Access Roles and Rights

A first-person creator-owner can grant subrights (based on his basic rights) to his work to a second person or entity. The first access right of a second person is to access for the purpose of consuming or reading the data. Each of these rights can be expressed in terms of the following subordinate rights:

- **Data consumer** — Read-only
- **Data holder** — Read and store one instance
- **Data editor** — Read, store, modify/change
- **Re-creator** — Re-create for further distribution if granted that subright

Exploring Third-Person Access Roles

Third-party rights relate to powers of attorney in the paper world. This set of rights of access or powers exercised over access rights are held by interested or disinterested third parties that are granted fundamental rights or have by assignment the power to grant rights and subrights to other parties on behalf of the data creator or owner, so they are best described as roles. Third-person roles and their limited powers include the following:

- **Data executor** — Provides for disposal or distribution of data on departure, incapacity, or death of the data owner.
- **Data guardian** — Is permitted to make decisions (grant access) and provide user rights on behalf of the data owner.
- **Data trustee** — Is responsible for protecting the data when it is not being accessed or actively used in any way.
- **Data custodian** — Maintains the data for safekeeping and provides the data to satisfy authorized request for it.
- **Data escrow agent** — Is a disinterested third party that maintains the information or data in inventory until certain conditions are met by one or more of the other defined parties.
- **Data administrator** — Facilitates the technical distribution of access rights via fundamental rights or roles to others.

The third-person roles are entrusted with the data to take or moderate actions in its regard. The terms can apply to devices as well as to people. Gatekeeper devices, such as a Web proxy appliance that authenticates an end user against a service directory whose schema for that user allows her to make changes on a financial statement, are filling the role of data guardian when working in concert with the service directory.

Figure 12-2 shows that these roles and rights would be difficult to do with just inheritance features and must be doled out with the aid of a directory where the identity is known and treated for access rights in a predetermined way after authentication. If you are not the data creator or owner and you have access to or custody of the data, you are considered for this discussion an agent. Agents can receive rights from other agents, but only if the granting agent has those rights.

Exploring Subordinate Roles

Subordinate rights are those that are received through grants from others. Subordinate roles include the following:

- **Rights grantor** — One who can grant or has granted rights or subrights to a grantee

- **Rights grantee** — One who has received rights or subrights from a grantor, usually a from a data owner

- **Rights arbitrator** — A person or device that resolves disputed access rights

- **Beneficiary** — A person or entity that received fundamental access rights on the departure, incapacity, or death of the data owner

- **Rights dependant** — An entity or person whose access rights are controlled by others

- **Entity** — An organization, not one person, that holds data as if an owner or creator

- **Rights immigrant** — One whose access rights are granted temporarily or are limited in some way

- **Rights personal representative** — A person, entity, or device permitted to grant access rights to others for a specific purpose

- **Rights proprietor** — An operator of an access control system or access gateway

- **Rights proxy** — A person, entity, or device permitted to grant access rights to others on a temporary basis

- **Rights alien** — A person, device, or entity granted access rights without any appreciable identity information known about that person, device, or entity

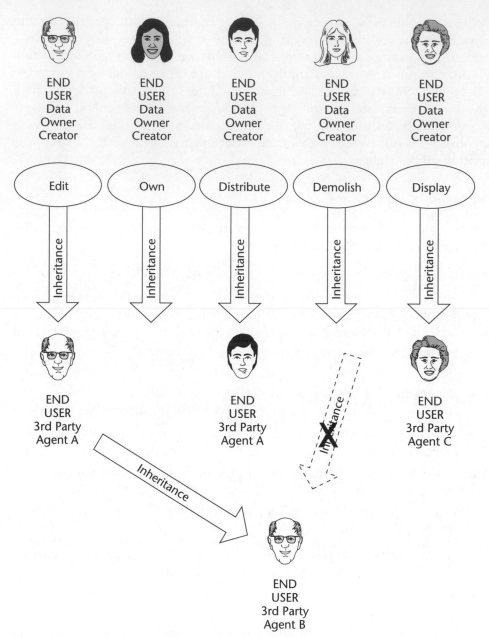

Figure 12-2   A user cannot inherit rights not granted to his agent.

By borrowing the basis for these terms from the legal profession and standardizing on the discussion of them, there's hope that the design of access controls reflects the terminology and capabilities over time. Ideally, off-the-shelf products for identity management, identity provisioning, and access control would express their features and capabilities in concert with the standard terminology. By using rights and roles that follow general principles from legal terminology, the applications' technology would mirror what is needed in the real world for controls in a uniform way. The audit function would also be facilitated by this standardization.

Looking at Interim Steps

Integrating two-factor token cards coupled with a population-specific service directory model into your access controls makes perfect sense even if the ideal presented in this chapter to reach a standardized and global access control model is never achieved. The minor inconvenience of users having to carry (and keep track of) token cards is far outweighed by the value of tighter controls on critical data, applications, and processes.

The strength of the matchup between username, PIN, random-number string, and AAA server seed record is hard to improve upon in the existing IT environment. Adopting this technology early into a well-designed overall access control architecture will keep your data safer and fix responsibility for auditable access. It also would facilitate an eventual move to a global access model should that alternative become more widely accepted.

Recognizing Responsibilities

The success of any access controls system is first dependant on having well-articulated requirements reflecting the needs of your business processes woven into the implementation of the technology. The technology tools necessary to lock down application data are available today from an array of vendors, but the responsibility for getting the design right for your organization cannot be fully outsourced. Someone or a coordinating group must be able to express your organization's business processes, understand the implications of the regulatory requirements on those processes, and be able to map out the necessary control points that comply with the letter and spirit of the regulations.

Product and vendor choices and implementation steps must be made to fit the map. Choosing products first will prove troublesome because you are likely to be stymied by current limitations in the individual products.

All of the components discussed in this book are essential for achieving and maintaining a successful authentication, authorization, and access control architecture. There are no shortcuts, and nothing should be left out of the mix. Each part provides some of the functionality needed to complete a system of adequate controls. Your minimum shopping list will include products that provide the following:

Service directories	Two-factor token cards
Meta-directories	Web proxy appliances
Identity provisioning	Content switches
Identity management	Firewalls
Legacy integration software	AAA servers

The list includes powerful products with extensive features to apply controls over the various access layers. Companies and nonprofit organizations that have made the news with startling revelations about their data and client identity information being compromised often have all of these products in place, and their defenses have been breached anyway. There are many individual reasons or excuses for the failure and many places to point to for blame in these regrettable incidents, but in every case, the chief reason was lack of a quality controls architecture design. Such a design must be based on solid requirements that are met by the products' implementation. It is real work — hard, detailed work — requiring a group of technically competent people all working meticulously from the same design diagrams and documents. There is no way that picking a few products and placing them in your environment with their best features enabled and turned on will lead to adequate controls and protection for your data, let alone meet the regulatory requirements.

Using Third-Party Security Review

The value of a second look by another pair of eyes has long been recognized as valuable in catching errors, mistakes, and omissions before they become costly. It's a method that can catch any errors in your architecture design, project specification, or project bid specifications. The worst time to find those errors is when playing the role of armchair quarterback after the hacks and compromises have cost your organization a huge amount of money or capital value.

Third-party plan review is sometimes done with plans for commercial buildings. Astute owners or project managers who have been hurt by erroneous building plans and specification before will often take plans for new projects to an architectural and engineering firm that had nothing to do with the design, and pay for a review of the plans for any obvious and glaring errors or omissions. Mistakes are not always found before the project goes out to bid or build, but when they are, you will save substantial amounts of money over the fee for that second opinion.

A third-party security review process would go a long way with information technology procurements and in-house projects, particularly when security and access controls are a part of the project. Unlike vendors, disinterested third-party reviewers face no repercussions and have no financial gain in pointing out problems mid-project.

If you are in a fiduciary position in your organization, you may want to give consideration to submitting your IT controls projects to a trusted third party for project or plan review. Whether you're working with in-house or contracted IT staff, that second pair of eyes finding the weaknesses before the hackers do is well worth the time and cost.

The information technology industry as a whole would benefit from creating a certification program both for vendors wanting to provide security plan review services and for the security specialists who staff them.

There is much at stake in keeping systems safeguarded for online transactions and an incredible amount of detailed work necessary to accomplish it. Knowledgeable specialists in many subspecialties are required. A security plan review is another way to leverage the security expertise available for access control quality and make it available to more organizations.

Summary

Following the steps outlined in this book to create a controls architecture will get you if not there, closer, and if not closer, at least headed in the right direction. There are a lot of things to think about and document along the way, beginning with your organization's business processes, detailing all of the regulatory requirements that have an impact on those business processes, and mapping the needed control points to support your unique business needs in ways that comply with the regulations. The rest is nuts and bolts to achieve enforcement of the points of control.

Most organizations need outside assistance from product-centered experts. Seek their assistance, but only after your requirements are solidly defined. Adequate documentation is a must for clear, quality client-to-vendor and vendor-to-client communication. The documentation described in the early chapters facilitates that communication.

WWW Resources for Authentication, Authorization, and Access Control News and Information

The following Web sites are sources for news, articles, white papers, and research for finding out more about many of the information technology topics in this book. You'll find some free content and some paid content. The sites are listed alphabetically, and nearly all of them have a topical search capability. These are not the only IT info sites out there, but they give you places to start. To find current information about technology topics of interest to you, visit these sites and use their search capabilities or drill down through the sites' menus. Try researching all of the sites with the same key terms associated with your topics of interest to find the most current new releases and to gain insights on the topic from different contributors.

ADTmag.com — www.adtmag.com (*Application Development Trends* online)

Bitpipe — www.bitpipe.com (Technology white papers, IT product literature, webcasts, and case studies for IT professionals)

Burton Group — www.burtongroup.com (Focuses on network infrastructure technologies relating to security, identity management, telecom transport technologies, and application platforms)

CIO.com — `www.cio.com` (*CIO* online; information for CIOs and IT executives)

Computerworld — `www.computerworld.com` (*Computerworld* online; technology news and newsletters. Links on the bottom of the page take you to other IDG publications.)

eWEEK.com — `www.eweek.com` (*eWEEK* online; breaking news and special reports on technology topics of interest to the enterprise; links to other Ziff Davis publications)

FCW.com — `www.fcw.com` (*Federal Computer Week* online; technology news of interest to federal and other government entities)

Forrester Research — `www.forrester.com` (Independent technology and market research)

Gartner — `www.gartner.com` (Provides research and analysis about the global IT industry)

GCN — `www.gcn.com` (*Government Computer News* online; general computer topics of interest to government readers; hot topics, white papers, and products)

Government Security — `www.govtsecurity.com` (*Government Security* online; security news topics focused on government)

Government Technology — `www.govtech.net` (*Government Technology* online; technology articles focused on state and local governments)

GovExec.com — `www.govexec.com` (*Government Executive* online; not all IT, but often has articles relevant to IT and IT security)

InfoWorld — `www.infoworld.com` (*InfoWorld* online; technology industry articles and content)

InformationWeek — `www.informationweek.com` (*Information Week* online; source for articles and information on technology and the businesses providing the technology)

InternetWeek — `www.internetwk.com` (Daily business and tech news for IT professionals)

InternetWorld.com — `www.internetworld.com` (Tech news, blogs, info, and more)

ITPapers — `www.itpapers.com` (Library of technical IT white papers, webcasts, and case studies.)

Network World — `www.networkworld.com` (IT research, news, and more.)

New.com — `www.news.com.com` (Tech news)

NewsForge — `www.newsforge.com` (News for Linux and open source)

NOREX — `www.norexonline.com` (Consortium of IT professionals)

Red Herring `www.redherring.com` (Covers innovation, technology, and more)

strategy + business — `www.strategy-business.com` (*strategy + business* online)

TechRepublic — `www.techrepublic.com` (IT discussions, Q&A, blogs, white papers, and more)

TechWeb Network — `www.techweb.com` (Original content and directory to IT information on the Web)

vnunet.com — `www.vnunet.com` (VNU news, blogs, tech info)

ZDNet — `www.zdnet.com` (Blogs, white papers, news, tech info)

Important Access Control and Security Terms

The following is a list of key access control and security terms that are core to the discussion of compliance. Take the time to become familiar with their meaning in this context and use them appropriately in documentation and discussion.

Administration

Automated user enrollment — Use of any automated process to move user identity information over the network from a data source to a directory where it is needed.

Digital certificate creation, administration, and revocation — A package of services done by a certificate authority to issue digital key pairs (one public and one private) to an end user or system and to manage that certificate over a defined life cycle.

Distributed enrollment — An enrollment process conducted by persons at one or more remote locations acting as agents for enrolling end users.

Password reset — Creating a new password to replace an existing one, and canceling the old one; done by the end user, help desk personnel, or an administrator.

Password synchronization — Using automated processes to move the same password and sometimes the same username from one repository to another.

Self-enrollment — An online process in which the end user is permitted to enter his own identity information.

Access control

Data confidentiality — Limiting data access to those with a need to know and denying access to all others.

Data integrity — Maintaining the reliability and accuracy of published and nonpublished information.

Directory-enabled access controls — Also known as directory-enabled application-level security (DEALS); equates to access to digital resources that is controlled by entries in a service directory.

Extranet access — Access to internal Web-enabled applications for employees and business partners.

Finite access control — Capability to control end-user access for one username to specific resources, potentially to one data field in a database.

Internet portal access — Access to applications over the Internet.

Privacy protection — The act of building physical and/or digital barriers around an individual's personal information to prevent unauthorized access. Private information includes the following:

> **Personally identifying information** — Identity information of sufficient quantity and accuracy that the individual can be separately identified from the larger population.

> **Personal financial information** — An individual's credit card numbers, bank account numbers, pay stubs, investment account information, tax returns, or any financial account information.

> **Personal medical information** — All private medical information, particularly medical information regulated by HIPAA.

Web access control — Controls limiting access to Web servers and Web applications.

Workflow — A process where work product is transferred and tracked as it is passed from one person to the next for approvals or additional content, and each transfer is recorded.

Application access — Access to an application via direct connection, Web services, or a terminal.

Database access — Access to one or more data entries in a database.

Data field access — Access to one or more selected fields in a database.

File access — Access to the contents of a digital file.

Folder/subdirectory access — Access to storage space on a temporary or permanent digital media, hard drive, or disk.

Host access — Direct access to an application, service, or operating system.

Network access — Access to network connected resources.

OS access — Access to host operating system as an end user or administrator.

Authorization

By-name authorization — Specifically connecting authorized access from an individual username to a data target.

Group-membership access — Assignment to a group sharing similar access rights.

Role definition — Authorizing access based on a job or work performed; applied to one person or to a group sharing the same work.

Role-based access control — Controlling access based only on the role definition.

Target data or resource — Information, data, or a device to which an end user or other device requires access.

Authentication

Nonrepudiation — Reducing an end user's ability to deny she was the one who authorized an action or sent a message.

Reduced sign-on — Using the same username/password combination to access every resource over multiple logon events.

Service directories — Directories used to provide identity information and authorization data to a gatekeeper device or application.

Single sign-on — Using the same username/password combination to access every resource from a single logon event.

Token card — A device providing a two-factor authentication method: having the card and knowing the username/PIN combination associated with the card. Possession of the card is verified by comparing a time-sensitive number keyed in from reading the digital window on the card and comparing that number with the number an authorization server believes the number should be in that time frame. If username/PIN and token card number are all verified, access is granted.

Two-factor authentication — Authentication is dependant on two factors: something the user has, such as a swipe card, token, or retina (for a retina scan), and second factor might be information the user knows, such as a PIN or a password.

Username, password, PIN — Common entries for authentication assumed entered by an identified end user.

Identity

Authoritative source — A source, usually digital (database), for end-user identity information where the identity entry process is trusted and the information is believed to be accurate.

Directory services — A digital directory set up to provide identity information services to a gatekeeper device.

Identity provisioning — A process exemplified by the use of meta-functionality to move identity information from one directory or storage point to another; provisioning can automate the initiation, maintain identity information, and handle the removal of user access accounts for digital resources.

User identification — Paper or digital credentials presented to verify an identity.

Vetting — A process of verifying the authenticity of an individual identity.

Assessment

Data classification — A determination as to the sensitivity of data that includes categories such as those defined as:

Open — Data and information rightfully found in the public domain.

Protected — Privacy information, personal medical information, trade secrets, intellectual property, and public financial reports are all examples of information that needs protection.

Restricted — Highly valued protected information that, if inappropriately released or compromised, could cause significant harm to the data owner or custodian.

Financial exposure — Risk potential expressed in terms of a quantifiable financial loss.

Hacking — Unauthorized access or attempts to access digital resources.

Identity theft — Stealing and/or using someone else's personally identifiable or personal financial information to cause harm to the actual owner of the identity information.

Litigation exposure — Risk expressed in terms of a valid possibility that could require mounting a criminal or civil defense.

Regulatory compliance — Meeting all (not just some) of the objectives defined in laws and regulations governing the operation of your organization.

Risk levels — The result of an analysis of various risk categorized in stair-step fashion where risk is ranked, ordered, and assigned a value.

Audit

Archiving — Storing logged access information for long periods of time for future reference or for use when required to meet an external regulation or internal policy requirement.

Auditing — Using persons or intelligent tools to analyze logged information for items that should cause concern or require an action or reaction.

Logging — Recording access and use information for later analysis.

Recording — Saving access and use information in case it may require analysis.

Critical Success Factors for Controls Design

You've read the book and now you are ready to roll your sleeves up and get to the important details of the design. Designing and implementing access controls to conform to the internal needs of the company for efficient access and to meet all the externally imposed regulatory requirements is hard, detailed work. If it were easy, there would be no news media reports of external hacks and insider jobs leading to the loss of tens of thousands of customer identities and hundreds of thousand of credit card numbers, or of insider fraud costing publicly traded companies millions of dollars.

You have likely heard this before, but it is a fundamental truth: The bad guys have to be right only once, and your systems are compromised. The real worst-case scenario is that the systems may already have been compromised and you just haven't found out about it yet.

The controls and security measures discussed in this book are ones you would want to achieve for your organization's information technology systems even if there were no regulations such as Sarbanes-Oxley, HIPAA, or Gramm-Leech-Bliley. The fact is that these regulations do exist; your conformance to them will be audited annually. Regardless, having your access controls fail is not a viable option for your company or your career.

Keeping the protected data in your systems solely for those with authorized access is in some ways like trying to keep all the heat in your house in winter — if there is one little hole, one door not sealed, one window left open, the heat is gone and you can't get it back. One leak in your system and your data is gone and you can't get it back. Reaching for that 100 percent success for your access controls requires recognition and understanding of those factors that will combine to make your system's access controls more secure. The listing that follows consists of the minimum critical success factors for achieving the controls architecture outlined in this book. Don't forget to add some of your own to meet any of your organization's special requirements.

- Implementation of an identity vault and service directory model improves the security profile of past, present, and future applications.

- The design of the identity management systems rationalizes the number of directories to a manageable minimum and provides a set of population-specific service directories based on security and access control requirements for that population.

- Unnecessary differences and variations found in the organization's directories are eliminated.

- Differences in the directories' schemas for any specific population of users are based on relationships to authoritative sources of identifying data and to security criteria.

- Identity vaults (also known as meta-trees) are only used as advanced data synchronization hubs or nuclei. End-user authentication and access control is never done to and from or by any direct access to the vault.

- End users authenticate with a call to a service directory, or to a service directory and to a two-factor token authentication server when required to do so by any one of the gatekeeper devices.

- Implementation of identity management and provisioning leads to the identification of redundant identity data sources and unnecessary administration costs and eliminates them both.

- A service directory model provides a clear framework and method to tie directory information and access control rights to well-defined authentication and access controls for all current applications fronted on Web servers and facilitates future application development trends toward context-sensitive standards such as JSR 168.

- OS file and print directories (also known as platform directories) using existing end-user identity directories that are reliant on complex organizational relationship structures, such as operating system (OS) directories where an OU (organizational unit) is some string of data, have multiple tiers of OUs eliminated to the extent possible. The objective is for the multiple tiers of `division=OU`, `department=OU`, `workgroup=OU` within OS directories stacked on top of each other to become less important, perhaps totally unnecessary after the implementation. Ideally, OU directory structures contain only nominally necessary directory entry information with the fewest possible number of objects, most of which would rarely, if ever, change.

- Multiple operational service LDAPv.3 directories (working directories) provide the security context in a strictly controlled security environment, within distinct sets of parameters defined by the security policy domain.

- Directory objects for identity populations are derived from and linked to appropriate authoritative data sources.

- End-user identity information for access controls should be placed in a flat directory structure.

- Directory schemas should be designed with only minor and necessary differences in schema structure between the various populations.

- Each directory schema should be designed in ways best suited to the unique group of end users and the corresponding applications as required by defined security needs. A working directory is designed to provide controlled access to services and applications most frequently used by specific and by-name identified populations with similar access needs such as:

    Employees, trusted agents

    Business venture partners

    Web information seekers at large

    Customers

    Contracted suppliers of goods and services

    WWW information-only seekers

- Each service directory exposes only the minimum identity data required by a directory information data consumer or gatekeeper device.

- Each service directory is designed, performance tuned, and sized for its specific purpose.

- Identity vaults and their associated service directories are protected from unauthorized access by design and implementation that includes at least the best security practice recommendations of the directory vendor and, at a minimum, the best security practices recommended by the operating system vendor.

- The business's application development community is fully trained in the programming principles necessary for full leverage of the new security model presented by the identity vault and related service directory structure.

- The organization's core directory services support staff is fully trained in the use of the directory data synchronization tools, particularly as they relate to the OS access synchronization features. The training specifically takes into account how future applications should be designed and integrated for access control and security into the directory environment.

- Staff training should be conducted on topics that include DEALS (directory-enabled application-level security), XML tagging, JSR 168, portlets, and how the current Java servlet environment integrates applications into this managed identity environment.

- Identity vault and service directories tie future development more closely to a standard, LDAPv3 API than to directory and product vendors' proprietary methods.

- Identity vault implementation provides for integration of other access controls such as token card authentication and possible future integration of client-side (end user) digital certificates.

- The implementation's maximum use of provisioning features provides measurable administrative savings in staff time for directory and identity administration.

- The identity vault provides measurable improvements in security from such things as the implementation of automated "unauthorization" (deprovisioning) from minor changes in the referenced authoritative source.

- End users can perform Web-based self-service password administration within defined parameters and password enforcement policy.

- The objective of having only one meta-directory and one service directory per unique user population is achieved.

- The entire directory infrastructure includes backup, failover, and disaster recovery features.

- Access controls facilitated within the directory structures and schema are of sufficient design to meet all externally imposed regulatory requirements such as SOX, HIPAA, and Gramm-Leech-Bliley.

Sample Policy Statements for Compulsory Access and Security Controls

If your organization has already developed a body of security policies that recognizes the need for meeting security objectives, perhaps all that your documents need is a thorough review and updating to ensure they are reflective of the necessity to meet the recently imposed external regulatory requirements. If your organization has not developed security-related policies or the policies are in need of improvement, the information in this appendix should help move your security and access control policy development along a bit faster. The examples here cannot match every situation and every need an organization may have, but they will give you a head start in creating policies totally tailored to your organization's specific requirements.

Please take the time to review Chapter 3 to see where policies fit into an overall plan to develop and enforce the IT architecture. Policies are, by definition, high-level statements. Historically, some organizations tend to develop policies that are vertical and include things that are better left to the more detailed standards, procedures, and guidelines. A well-written policy is one that would never have to be countered by management discretion or operational needs. Not that policies should be weak, but they should be fundamental operational truths, high level enough to govern every circumstance encountered over the life cycle of the policy.

Technology policies define expected and required actions and responses from employees, processes, systems, and applications and are therefore relevant to a large audience inside and outside the IT organization. Those elements of policy that apply to employees may need input and approval from your human resources department or someone in management. These policies also benefit from wide-ranging exposure and easy access by that broad audience, so be sure to publish them on an intranet Web site or include them in new-hire packets. The ultimate, of course, is to be able to conduct mandatory training sessions that everyone is required to attend to learn about matters of policy.

The examples in this appendix are each preceded by a discussion of the reasons for and the importance of that topic in the security matrix. (See Chapter 5 for details of the security matrix.) After reading this book, you should see the security matrix topics as the umbrella covering the incredible amount of subtopics and detail that make up the matrix. Polices are simply one of the subtopics in every wedge of the matrix.

Technology policies are most important to all the decision makers in the IT organization. Polices become the managers' reference manual for making decisions when unique and challenging circumstances that have never been encountered before arise.

Each of the example policies focuses on security topics and principles. IT policies governing other aspects of your IT operations and management should never be written to counter any of the policy statements in the security policies. The other policies should draw from and indeed complement security policies in every way possible. The whole of IT policy should speak with one voice that is consistent in both detail and principle. Keep in mind that the policy statements presented here are to demonstrate policies, the focus is on the general topics in this book, and the statements are not meant to be all-inclusive of what should be in your organization's security policies covering the same topic. The statements are good guides for the writing of your own.

Administration

A security administration policy governs all aspects of the processes, manual or automated, that involve issuing, applying, or tendering of something and also involves record keeping supporting the administrative processes. As you look across the breadth of activity involved in the administration of your IT systems, you will find many things that need to be done. Failure to do the administrative actions or doing them incorrectly can lead to very negative outcomes instead of being able to consistently achieve security objectives. The human administration actions may well be the weakest point in all security defenses. This potential for human error would certainly be compounded without well-understood and -executed policy for security administration.

Why You Need an Administration Policy

The word *administration* often makes you think of someone behind a desk acting on a huge in-basket and taking action on each item in turn. With security administration, there are many players involved, both inside and outside of your IT organization. Automated processes are usually involved as well, and they must be designed within the confines of the policy for administration. Administrative processes are involved at many junctions in IT systems, from changing firewall rules to issuing a username for a new systems administrator. Clearly it is important to have the processes consistently applied when any changes are made across the IT systems.

What to Include in an Administration Policy

The following are suggested topics to include in an administration policy:

- System and application access controls
- Network management practices affecting security
- Security aspects of application development and maintenance
- Process to maintain security when using event recovery procedures
- Audit and monitoring
- Awareness and training
- Classifying information assets (open, protected, restricted) and resources
- Physical security procedures

Topic areas that focus on administration of access controls include the following:

- Self-enrollment
- Distributed enrollment
- Automated user enrollment
- Password resets
- Password synchronization
- Digital certificate creation, administration, and revocation

Sample Administrative Policy Statements

End-user self-enrollment: The end user is permitted to enter her own identity information only when accessing open or public information on our company Web sites. The identity information so entered is not to be relied upon for access to any financial transactions and will only be used to provide the end user with a customized Web page when entering our portal for information seeking purposes.

Distributed enrollment and administration of end-user identities: Level-two system administrators within the company may enter end-user identities into service directories and access control lists as prescribed by the user entry standard. Sales territory managers may enter customer identity information into customer sales identity directories only. All distributed enrollment will require the use of an approved two-factor authentication.

Access Control

An access control policy determines how access will be granted, controlled, and managed within your IT systems and resources. It should also include physical access as it relates to limiting access to areas housing the digital assets. Access control polices must be written to govern aspects of access control and maintain the controls to comply with internal needs for control measures as well as those imposed from government regulation.

Why You Need an Access Control Policy

Everyone involved in the organization's business processes has an interest in maintaining quality access controls. In today's regulatory and litigation-prone business climate, maintaining adequate access controls helps ensure the viability of the company. Employees also have a vested interest in keeping their own personally identifying and financial information in company digital records secure from unauthorized access. The possibilities for how access controls are handled could vary considerably, and policy helps narrow the options for implentation to the few that need to be done so they can be done well.

What to Include in an Access Control Policy

The following are suggested topics to include in an access control policy:

- Controls relationship to data classification
- Classification of users
- Linking authorization to access controls
- Mandatory access controls
- Access control methodology

Topic areas that focus on access control include the following:

- Data confidentiality
- Data integrity
- Privacy protection
- Personally identifying information
- Personal financial
- Personal medical information
- Workflow
- Web access control
- Extranet access
- Internet portal access
- Directory-enabled access controls
- Finite access control
- OS access
- Network access
- Host access
- Application access
- Folder/subdirectory access
- File access
- Database access
- Data field access

Sample Access Control Policy Statements

Data access will be restricted to those with a need to know, denying access to the data by all others. The business units will determine need to know for all employees.

All possible control measures will be applied for maintaining the reliability and accuracy of published and nonpublished information without conflicting with read-only rights.

Personal medical information will be managed for control of access in conformance with HIPAA regulations.

Directory-enabled access controls will be used for all applications capable of integration with our service directory architecture either through standard LDAP API or custom coding.

Finite access controls restricting access to by-name access rights will be used for all financial databases, spreadsheets, and reports.

Authorization

Most simply stated, the process of authorization is about determining who will get access to what and for what reason. Authorization policy should direct such decisions. Once an end user is authenticated, the results of the authorization policy as applied to any given user or group of users determines how that end user will be dealt with by the access controls. From the perspective of protected and restricted data or resource classifications, authorization policy determines which end user will be granted access and what authentication methods will be required to grant access in various circumstances. Authorization is the link between an identity verified by authentication and the defined access to resources.

Why You Need an Authorization Policy

The best-implemented access control methods and systems will prove useless in the long run if the relationship between the business units in the company and the IT department do not have a working relationship to determine how the end users in the various populations logging on for services are handled. The authorization policy sets the stage for that interaction between IT operations and business needs for exercising controls over the entire system end-user life cycle.

What to Include in an Authorization Policy

The following are suggested topics to include in an authorization policy:

- Access rights and privileges
- Confidentiality agreement
- User life cycle events
- Request or approval by responsible business unit
- By-name authorizations
- Group and role authorizations
- Read, write, edit, and distribute rights
- Unique user identity
- Annual reevaluations of rights granted

Topic areas that focus on authorization include the following:

- Role definition
- Role-based access control

- Group membership access
- By-name authorization
- Target data or resource

Sample Authorization Policy Statements

Role-based authorization will not be permitted for protected or restricted application or data.

Role-based access control will be permitted for access to open nonclassified information and applications. This does not apply to the data generated by such applications; follow the data classification and storage policy for data storage and archiving.

Target data or resource must be classified and tagged before it is made available for authorized access.

Authentication

An authentication policy determines how you will gain confidence in the purported identity of end users or devices before granting them access to resources. Achieving that adequate confidence is not entirely without risks. The authentication policy must focus on ways to reduce security risks in your organization's environment. The policy statement will also define which access points require authentication and the strength of the authentication needed at that node.

Why You Need an Authentication Policy

The traditional method of using a simple username and password combination can take only minutes to break with the right tools and weak access defenses. Web-connected systems are vulnerable to hacking around the clock and from around the world. Internal risks of compromise are ever present even outside of office hours because of facilitations for employee Web and VPN access. Having a clear policy requiring authentication methods appropriate to the value of the data and risk presented helps to counter the risks. Identifying every access point and applying an authentication requirement strengthens overall security defenses.

What to Include in an Authentication Policy

The following are suggested topics to include in an authentication policy:

- Entry points requiring authentication
- Approved authentication methods
- Authentication method matched to risk
- Technical methods of authentication

Topic areas that focus on authentication include the following:

- Service directories
- Nonrepudiation
- Single sign-on
- Reduced sign-on
- Token card
- Two-factor authentication
- Username, password, PIN

Sample Authentication Policy Statements

Service directories will be used for all Web applications authentication.

Use of the same username/password combination to access all restricted applications will be permitted.

Two-factor authentication will be used for system access and access to all restricted resources.

Identity

Identity deals with who or what device is seeking services from the IT systems. The device or end user your systems need to identify could be down the hall, across town, or a half a world away. Identity management policy addresses how the identities will be verified, classified, stored, used, administered and managed in the organization IT systems. Once an identity is entered into the system, the policy of identity management is really about handling the end user's pseudonym or digital alter ego, referred to as the username in most systems. The policy lays the groundwork for dealing with the username over a life cycle with your company's systems.

Why You Need an Identify Management Policy

It is nearly laughable when you read in an IT trade journal about employees who were "let go" and find they have access to critical company IT resources a half a year later. Failure to recognize the importance of having rock-solid vetting of identity in the first place and then appropriate policy that is enforced over the user life cycle can lead to very negative consequences. There is enough difficulty in managing appropriately valid user accounts without adding to the risks from transfers, promotions, and departures from the company. A policy that addresses handling of user identities over the entire life cycle contributes substantially to the reduction of risk from unmanaged or mismanaged identities floating around in your systems, Web portals, and networks.

What to Include in an Identity Policy

The following are suggested topics to include in an identity policy:

- Positive Identification
- Verification of identity
- Documentation
- Anonymous end users
- Identified end users
- Privileged end users
- External end users
- Administrators
- Directory and identity system

Topic areas that focus on identity include the following:

- Directory services
- Vetting
- User identification
- Identity provisioning
- Authoritative source

Sample Identity Policy Statements

Digital directory services will store all identity and access control information for employees, administrators, and customers.

An insured and bonded outside service will be used for vetting the authenticity of and backgrounds of all employees granted access to computer resources.

Authoritative sources will be used to acquire customer identity information whenever it is available.

Assessment

Assessment of the threat factors resulting in risks to your systems helps determine how you will react to the threat and what defensive measures you will need to take. Decisions such as how strong your controls need to be are influenced by the results of your risk assessment actions. A policy is needed so that risk assessments are done in a consistent manner, particularly by assigning a magnitude to the assessment. The threats and risks facing any organization change over time, so periodic assessments are required.

Why You Need an Assessment Policy

Poor assessments result in poor protections — although you could argue that there's no such thing as too much protection of IT assets. A thorough evaluation of the threats facing your IT systems and ranking them will help determine criteria for access controls, obtaining resources to counter risk, prioritizing operations, and reactions to security incidents.

What to Include in an Assessment Policy

The following are suggested topics to include in an assessment policy:

- Identification of risk vulnerabilities
- Documentation of risk factors
- Assessment method
- Risk ranking methods
- Risk evaluation cycle

Topic areas that focus on assessment include the following:

- Risk levels
- Data classification

- Regulatory compliance
- Financial exposure
- Litigation exposure
- Hacking
- Identity theft

Sample Assessment Policy Statements

Risk will be classified into one of five risk pools.

All data owned or held in trust by the company will be classified at the time it is created or when it is received into one of three security classifications: open or public, protected, and restricted.

The company and IT systems will be assessed for regulatory compliance.

Financial risks will be calculated and ranked in dollar-value terms.

Litigation risks will be calculated in terms of a probability of cost as determine by the legal department head.

Audit

Under Sarbanes-Oxley Section 404, the annual external auditing of company financial records requires the inclusion of an assessment of the adequacy of internal controls impacting public financial reporting. Included in that assessment is a requirement for company management to report on the effectiveness of internal controls and for the auditors to comment on the report. With so much of today's business entirely dependant on computers and IT systems to gather financial information and prepare financial reports, the need for evaluation of the IT controls is evident. It would be hard to assess the adequacy of IT control impacting financial statements without having traditional IT logging and access audits taking place and some serious analysis of the information collected for audit. Audit policy will determine how these IT audits are accomplished.

Why You Need an Audit Policy

Everything tested through auditing presents an opportunity for making improvements in the way things are done. So, in a sense, audits are opportunities to learn how well you are doing. Audits help you discover if your systems are being targeted and by whom. They disclose whether there are internal end users attempting to gain unauthorized access. The analysis of the audit information may tell you that your systems have already been hacked or that someone is poised to do exactly that. Set aside the negative connotations you might have about audits, and recognize them as a tool to help you maintain control over access to your systems.

What to Include in an Audit Policy

The following are suggested topics to include in an audit policy:

- Event logging
- Log archiving
- Log review cycle
- Penetration testing
- Analysis of access, unauthorized attempts, administrative access, and security alerts

Topic areas that focus on auditing include the following:

- Auditing
- Logging
- Recording
- Archiving

Sample Audit Policy Statements

Auditing access logs will include the use of human analysis and the use of intelligent tools to analyze logged information for access anomalies affecting security.

Access to every device hosting protected or restricted information will be logged for later analysis.

Access logs showing no anomalies with be retained for 18 months after initial recording.

Logs containing detected security breaches will be archived for a period of three years.

Documentation Examples

For those readers not familiar with the architecture documentation process outlined in Chapter 3, this appendix provides examples of the development of an architecture idea or vision as it is processed through the required set of text-based architecture documents.

Guiding Principles

A guiding principle is an idea that governs an organization at the highest levels of management. Guiding principles influence decision making and how alternatives will be chosen should they need to be presented to top management.

Here's an example of a statement of principle:

Customer and employee privacy will be respected and protected.

Guiding principles give rise to and support for statements of policy.

Policies

Policies are high-level statements that govern the daily operations of a company and its IT organization. They bring form and shape to the architecture and establish and control the boundaries necessary to achieve certain objectives. With each statement of policy, it should be possible to look back to a guiding principle.

Here's a policy statement example:

The design, implementation, and operation of all information technology systems and the business processes they support shall be done in a manner that respects the maintenance of privacy of personally identifying information, personal medical information, and personal financial information for customers and employees alike.

Employee measures: Adequate controls will be implemented across all systems to ensure that only employees and designated human resources office staff are permitted access to employee personal privacy information. The HR director only may grant managers access to employee privacy information upon authorization. Systems design will not permit access by system administrators; encryption in storage and passwords will be required for employee and HR access.

Customer measures: Adequate controls will be implemented across all systems to ensure that only customers and their designated sales representative are permitted access to customer personal privacy information and nonaggregated purchasing records. Systems design will not permit access by system administrators; encryption in storage and passwords will be required for customer and sales representative access. Sales representative will be limited for access by directory entries to only to their current and (90-day) former customers. All customer Web transactions will require encryption and two-factor authentication to protect the data in transit.

Policies give rise to and support for technology standards.

Standards

Standards are midlevel to detailed-level statements that help to define restrictions or limits and refine the usefulness of the applications and systems. Standards differ from policies in that they outline the details of the technologies used and describe the specific use of identified technologies, developmental models, deployment techniques, methods, and rules.

Here's an example of a standards statement:

Access controls will be applied to all applications and databases containing privacy information for customer and employees. Systems and application controls shall be designed so that any one customer or employee can only access his or her own information; all other cross-customer access shall be denied. Systems shall accommodate privileged access for designated HR staff for employee data and to sales representative only for their own assigned customer data. This privileged access shall be accomplished with a by-name access control in the appropriate service directory and the use of a two-factor token card to invoke the privileged access. While on disk storage, any privacy data will be encrypted with a wallet database token and not with in-table encryption keys. Only the customer's user name will be allowed in clear text in indexes and for search purposes.

Standards often require a procedure to aid in the implementation.

Procedures

Procedures flow from policy and/or standards. A procedure is a way to accomplish some task, a method, or steps that need to be taken to accomplish something.

Here's an example of a procedures statement:

The procedure for granting privileged access for HR or sales representatives requires that a signed request form is received from the HR directory/territory sales manager to grant access to directory-associated records. When the form is received by IT and placed on the work schedule by the IT supervisor, that same day a new issue or verification of issue of a token card is performed. The seed record in the token card is linked to the service directory entry for that employee, the schema entries are made for the appropriate group memberships, and schema extent codes are added. IT staff will not do testing of privileged access rights.

Best Practices

Best practices suggest a routine and acceptable way to accomplish some task. In-house staff either develops them or some external resource is used and adapted to the organization's unique needs.

Here's an example of a best practice:

Each application using directory-enabled access to provision privileged access to privacy information will be assigned a DN (distinguished name) in the directory and will be afforded group memberships as needed to accommodate access.

Guidelines

Guidelines are not directive in nature. They are more instructive and do leave some discretion to the guideline user to follow them or find or use other methods to achieve the task at hand.

Here's an example of a guideline:

Always determine the sales territory or region number and enter it first in the directory when adding privileged access. That way, the directory hierarchy is maintained and will not have to be corrected when territory-dependant entries are made.

Go with the Flow

These examples all flow from the one beginning guiding principle regarding protection of privacy information and demonstrate how the idea or concept flows through the entire documentation process.

Another interesting thing that you may have noticed is that this appendix is showing only one small IT concept; the examples were all abbreviated and not formatted in a document context in any way. Yet the example statements alone (without the explanations) fill a page and a half of this book. When you consider all of the concepts that go into systems architecture — or just the access controls portion — and multiply by what is here, you begin to get an idea of all of the documentation it takes to create and support the architecture.

Sample Job Description for Directory Engineer/ Schema Architect

If you do not already have directory designers on staff, the following partial job description may help you in your hiring process. When the focus for security of access controls is dependant on a directory hub model and service directories, having the right staff to work the issues in important. A lot of detail work must be done to establish and maintain an identity management and provisioning system for medium to larger organizations. A directory designer would be an important, perhaps critical, staff member to design, build, and manage your identity management system and access controls.

The directory engineer/schema architect will work in cooperation with the company's executive team and under the supervision of the IT director and will be responsible for the successful design and implementation of service directories and for creating all aspects of the synchronization functionality for other directories and other access control data repositories.

This person will be accountable for resolving the user schema, group, and role differences among the directories that will merge into various population-specific service directories. Responsibilities will also include designing and writing scripts and templates that facilitate the synchronization/provisioning elements from authoritative sources and in and out of service directories and access control repositories.

The directory engineer will conduct training for applications development staff on the use of directory-enabled application security and will, on an ongoing basis, continue working on the development and implementation of directories and supporting processes and maintain the entire identity management/identity provisioning/access control system.

Index

Index